353.0313   Montauk Symposium..
M767w   The White House

THE WHITE HOUSE:
ORGANIZATION AND OPERATIONS

THE
WHITE HOUSE:
ORGANIZATION
AND OPERATIONS

Proceedings of the 1970 Montauk
Symposium on the Office
of the President of the United States

Sponsored by:
CENTER FOR THE STUDY OF THE PRESIDENCY
Proceedings: Volume I, Number 1, 1971

R. GORDON HOXIE
Editor

Contributors:

John T. Carlton
William J. Casey
Anna M. Chennault
Charles L. Clapp
Kenneth W. Colegrove
Murray Comarow
Thomas G. Corcoran
Thomas W. Evans
Gordon Gray
L. Richard Guylay
James C. Hagerty
Francis H. Horn
R. Gordon Hoxie
Dorothy H. Hughes
Dwight A. Ink, Jr.
Herbert G. Klein
Louis W. Koenig
Peter I. Lisagor

John H. Martin
James P. McFarland
Joseph P. B. McMurray
Edward W. Mill
Leonard P. Moore
Robert D. Murphy
Richard F. Pedersen
George E. Reedy, Jr.
Arthur T. Roth
Robert B. Semple, Jr.
Robert H. Sharbaugh
Robert E. Simon, Jr.
Helmut Sonnenfeldt
Walter N. Thayer
John J. Theobald
Lee C. White
Stephen J. Wright

v

Preface

On April 3, 4, 5, 1970, near the easternmost tip of Long Island, at Montauk, New York, a now historic Symposium on the Office of the President of the United States was convened. There, at Gurney's Inn, a handsome setting long familiar to the President of the United States, one hundred business, professional, educational, and labor leaders from throughout the United States, gathered together with senior White House Staff members of every administration from the Hoover through the Nixon period.

These White House Staff had witnessed, had participated, in the growth of the modern Presidency. It is a far cry from the Hoover period with two White House secretaries forty years ago, to the Office of the President today with several hundred members of the most powerful lay office in the world.

The most revolutionary of these changes have either just been enacted, as in the case of the Domestic Council and the Office of Management and Budget, or just proposed, as in the case of the consolidation of the executive departments.

What are the implications of these changes? Is this, as one of the Symposium participants, George Reedy, suggests in the very title of his new work which appeared for the first time that weekend, the *Twilight of the Presidency?* Has the Presidency, formerly the most sensitive of political offices, become so insulated and so institutionized as to lose touch with the people? Are these most recent changes and proposals the final steps in this loss of sensitivity? The keynote speaker, Herbert G. Klein, Director of Communication for the Executive Branch, a new position inaugurated with the Nixon Administration, believes not. He perceives in the Nixon White House reorganization, a gearing up for the 1970's to meet attainable goals of peace, security, and human dignity.

How has the press viewed the Presidency during the past four decades? What has been the effect of television? What is the significance of the new Domestic Council? The Office of Management and Budget? What are the prospects for further governmental revision? How are domestic and foreign policies formulated and implemented? What is the role of the task forces? What is the role of the Ash Council? What are the inner workings of the National Security Council? What is the future of the Department of State? Is the Cabinet in decline? Is the Presidency becoming over-institutionalized?

The foregoing are some of the questions discussed with complete candor in this closed conference. Because of the importance and timeliness of these concerns and the expressed interest of students of public affairs, permission has been secured from each of the participants to here publish for the first time the full text of the proceedings, including the biting incisive commentary of Peter I. Lisagor, President of the White House Correspondents Association, Robert B. Semple, Jr. White House Correspondent of the *New York Times*, and such veteran White House Press Secretaries as James C. Hagerty and George E. Reedy, Jr.

One senses a sweep of history in the observations and recollections of Robert D. Murphy, former Under Secretary of State for Political Affairs, who began his career in the Wilson Administration and today serves on the President's Foreign Intelligence Advisory Board along with his fellow participant, Gordon Gray, former Secretary of the Army, who had played a key role in national security organization in the Truman and Eisenhower administrations. This sweep of history is further illuminated in the reminscences of Lee C. White, Counselor to Presidents Kennedy and Johnson and of Thomas G. Corcoran, "Tommy the Cork," of the New Deal era. Mr. Corcoran's analysis of the balance of forces in this nation, contained in these proceedings, has been termed by senior political scientists present, as one of the most masterful discourses on this vital subject ever delivered.

The "view from Foggy Bottom" is ably presented by Ambassador Richard F. Pedersen, Counselor of the Department of State, and from the National Security Council by Senior Staff Member, Helmut Sonnenfeldt. The task forces are analyzed by Special Assistant to the President, Dr. Charles L. Clapp. The new Domestic Council and the reorganized Office of Management and Budget are presented with expertise by Walter N. Thayer, Dwight A. Ink, Jr. and Murray Comarow, all closely associated with the work of the Ash Council. The "detached view" of a distinguished scholar on the Presidency, Dr. Louis

W. Koenig, provides an additional perspective as do the comments and questions of such educators as Dr. Francis H. Horn, Dr. Joseph P. B. McMurray, Dr. John J. Theobald, Dr. Stephen J. Wright, Dr. Kenneth W. Colegrove, and Dr. Edward W. Mill.

Such distinguished attorneys and jurists as William J. Casey, Thomas W. Evans, and Leonard P. Moore provide searching inquiries in their presentations, as do business and labor leaders, jurists and educators with their questions. Lest the distaff side be forgotten, three, Anna M. Chennault, Dorothy H. Hughes, and Mildred Custin kept all the participants on their toes, proving the wisdom of their serving on the Center's Board. The Symposium Proceedings contain an historical vignette portraying statesmanlike qualities of labor leader participant, Joseph D. Keenan, Vice-President of the AF of L-CIO, and the discerning questions of such business leaders as John H. Martin, Vice-President of Litton Industries; James P. McFarland, Chairman of the Board, General Mills; and Robert H. Sharbaugh, President, Sun Oil Company. Among the military the questions of Colonel John T. Carlton, Executive Director of the Reserve Officers Association, seemed particularly pertinent.

One of the unique values in writing a preface to a symposium is the view from hindsight of the conditions and events related therein. Looking back nine months later, some of the things that were said, were pointed up, take on a remarkably statesmanlike view. To give but two examples: first, with amazing clairvoyance, Gordon Gray observed the future significance of Cambodian events. On April 4, 1970, when most observers gave the then brand new Lon Nol government scant chance beyond a few weeks for survival, Mr. Gray, far from accepting this as a portent of enlarged Communist take over, declared "that those events in Cambodia could have a reverse effect. Because, if the reason that Sihanouk was deposed was the presence of Hanoi and Viet Cong troops in the country, and if this new government should rally a determination to eliminate sanctuaries and make it stick, this could have a profound implication for the situation in Vietnam."

As if to confirm this hindsight, Marshall Green, Assistant

Secretary of State for Far Eastern Affairs, observed in an address before the Far East-American Council on January 19, 1971: ". . . The outstanding event in East Asia in 1970 was Cambodia."

The second example revealed itself on the evening of January 22, 1971 in President Nixon's State of the Union Address wherein he proposed the consolidation of seven of the present executive departments into four, a further recommendation of the Ash Council. In a very real sense, this Symposium was the harbinger both of the letter of these recommendations and their spirit. For as the *New York Times* observed editorially January 24, 1971, President Nixon's "plea for bringing the promise and performance of government closer together sets forth a credible common sense criterion." In the final analysis this was what this Symposium was all about.

To all of the participants who made this Symposium so meaningful, we of the Center for the Study of the Presidency, are most grateful as we are to the Earhart Foundation and others for financial support. Three of the Center's founders, Richard Salomon, Andrew O. Miller, and Henry O. Dormann, participated in the Symposium. Their co-founders, Edward L. Cournand and David A. Schulte, were much missed.

To my staff, headed by that remarkable Major General Robert E. Condon, ably assisted by John D. R. Jones, Lenore Langerman, Bernadette Casey, Elaine Aikenhead, and Barbara Wagner, go personal thanks. In these days supposedly characterized by built-in incentives, I should like to gratefully record the volunteer services of Anna L. Wagner, who typed in its entirety this final manuscript. I should further like to record the fact that this manuscript was read in its entirety both by Dr. Kenneth W. Colegrove, our erudite Senior Associate, and Miss Ellen Choffin, talented Editorial and Research Associate here at this Center. Any remaining errors of omission or commission are my own.

Finally, we toast that rare personality, the Keeper of the Inn, Nick Monte, and his associate, Rollie Waterman, who made Gurney's a happy memory for all of us.

R. Gordon Hoxie
New York City
January 25, 1971

Table of Contents

Chapter IV: "The White House and Foreign Policy: Formulation and Implementation"

THE WHITE HOUSE:
ORGANIZATION AND OPERATIONS

CHAPTER I

(Opening Session) The White House: Gearing Up for the 70's

THE PROGRAM

ARTHUR T. ROTH: Good evening and welcome to Gurney-ville! In spite of the torrential rains, the snows, the high winds, and the air controllers' strike, we are here for the Sympo-sium that is being put on by the Library of Presidential Papers with the cooperation of the Earhart Foundation. May I say that we are greatly indebted to all of you as participants. I want to thank each and every one of you for coming here and making this program the success I am sure it is going to be. All of you hold important positions in government, business, labor and education, and have traveled consid-erable distances to be here this evening.

The purpose of the Library of Presidential Papers is to con-duct studies on the Office of the President of the United States. To more correctly identify this purpose, we are proposing to the Board of Regents of the State of New York a change of our corporate name to Center for the Study of the Presidency. The Library (Center) sponsors symposia such as this one so that the leaders of our Nation may become better informed about how the most important office in the world functions. We be-lieve that if we are better informed, then we will take a more active role in helping to make America a better place in which to live.

I hope that in future years we may conduct symposia cover-ing topics such as: the role of the President in fiscal and mone-tary policies, the role of the President in initiating and guid-ing legislation through the Congress, and the role of the President in international affairs.

THE SETTING

R. GORDON HOXIE: We are delighted to have all of you here in the Admiralty Room of Gurney's Inn at Montauk. The miracle of seeing a hundred of you arrive from all parts of the country despite a postal strike, a middle-western bliz-zard, and an air traffic slowdown bespeaks of the resourceful-ness of the American people.

Our Chairman, Arthur T. Roth, is the man who came to a little country bank in Franklin Square, Long Island with less than $500,000 in deposits in 1934 and built it over the subsequent 35 years into one of the 18 largest commercial banks in the nation.

Libraries are both the interpreters and the transmitters of civilization. We, in our Library, have a particular purpose. We seek to build better understanding of the Executive Branch of our Federal Government. Likewise, out in Pekin, Illinois, there is a new library dedicated to the understanding of the Legislative Branch: The Everett McKinley Dirksen Memorial Library. Both the Dirksen Library and ours are built upon a private foundation in contrast with the federally subsidized presidential libraries under the National Archives. There is a place in these United States for this private sector as well as the public, and we are honored to work with both.

An institution of the character and purpose of our Library of Presidential Papers might more properly be termed, as Mr. Roth has suggested, a Center for the Study of the Presidency. As such it must work with persons not only in the Executive Branch of our Federal Government but also the Legislative and the Judicial. This symposium could not have been and would not have been possible without the cooperation of both those presently serving in all three branches and also those who have previously served therein. Most notably, we have here as participants persons from the Office of the President itself who have served in one or more of each Administration from President Hoover through President Nixon.

We are going to be together, hopefully, until after lunch on Sunday, and I anticipate there will be differing views regarding the most powerful lay office in the world. For example, at least one of our panelists is the author of a new book just off the press. I refer to George E. Reedy, Jr., former Presidential Press Secretary, author of *Twilight of the Presidency*. Whether it is, indeed, the twilight or rather the sunrise, we shall, in part, seek to determine this weekend. May I suggest that in either case, the angle of the sun is the same. Our final session will be devoted to a presentation of the new White House Organization—the first such major revision since the early days of F.D.R. In brief, we are here both reviewing history and witnessing it in the making.

Now it is my pleasure to introduce my fellow trustee of our Center, who, in turn, will introduce our keynote speaker. It seems to me that in our democratic processes it is so tremendously, vitally important that both the art of communication and the related business of building bridges of understanding be as strong as possible. The foundation for both is integrity and respect. Both of those are represented in the person of Mr. James C. Hagerty, an alumnus of Columbia College, who had served Governor Thomas E. Dewey in Albany and was selected by President Eisenhower to be his Press Secretary. For eight years, from 1953 to 1961, Mr. Hagerty so served with distinction, earning the respect of Republicans and Democrats alike and assuredly that of the working press at the White House. Today, Vice President for Corporate Relations of the American Broadcasting Company, he certainly knows his ABC's! Ladies and gentlemen, a friend and a student of the Presidency, and a member of the Board of Trustees of the Library of Presidential Papers, Mr. James C. Hagerty.

THE INTRODUCTION

JAMES C. HAGERTY: How do you briefly introduce an old and dear friend without yielding to the temptation to be overly effusive, which I am sure he won't like, or defensively laconic, which I am sure I won't like. I guess you try, according to the present Washington standards, to chart a rather middle course, neither raising nor lowering your voice except when necessary to tell it like it is. And, what Herb Klein is, he has always been: a wonderful human being and a highly competent professional who can handle whatever difficult assignment comes his way—be it in government service or in private enterprise.

He is Director of Communications of the Executive Branch of our Federal Government, a most significant new post. His is not an easy job. No major staff position in the Office of the President is, and I speak from personal experience. Those of us who have worked for a President know this.

You can discuss, even argue, with the President up to a

3

point. Then, figuratively, you salute and say, "Yes, sir," and do what he wishes. This happened to me not infrequently. Many times after he sought my personal opinion, in my field, and in my field only, President Eisenhower would say, "Do it this way." I would say, "If I go to that press conference and say what you want me to say, I would get hell." With that, he would smile, get up and walk around the desk, pat me on the back and say, "My boy, better you than me." I would go out and get hell. But you know something? That smile from the President and that pat on the back were worth all the hell I would get. And, so it is with Herbert Klein, who serves, or with anyone who serves, as a senior staff member to the President of the United States.

Our keynote speaker thrives on difficult jobs. More than anyone I know, he has the matchless facility of maintaining his perspective in the most trying, frustrating, and delicate situations. He never loses his temper—a claim I could never make—unless he wants to or seems to for a purpose. He takes his job seriously but not himself. He has never contracted that malady Potomac fever, which swells the heads and egos of some individuals who serve tours of duty in Washington. They lose sight of fact, of truth and of perspective. They forget they are not overlords of the public. It is a distinct pleasure to introduce one who has not succumbed to Potomac fever, one of the finest staff officers any President has ever had. Admired and respected, a true gentleman, he serves President Nixon with distinction, with dignity, with the highest degree of integrity. Ladies and gentlemen, I give you the honorable, and I do mean honorable, Herbert George Klein.

KEYNOTE ADDRESS: IS GOVERNMENT GOVERNABLE?

HERBERT G. KLEIN: Jim, thank you very much. It's been a great honor for me to be introduced by a colleague who I have long held in highest regard, one of our most senior and most highly respected former presidential press secretaries. It's been a pleasure for me to have this introduction by Jim Hagerty.

Dr. Hoxie, Mr. Roth, and distinguished ladies and gentlemen: It's a great honor to be here and have this opportunity to give your keynote address. It is a humbling experience seeing the scholars and professional leaders who are here from throughout the country. With regard to the news media, in addition to Mr. Hagerty, I am glad to see George Reedy, who has also served as press secretary in an outstanding fashion. It is also good to see Bob Semple and Peter Lisagor who have observed many Presidents in covering the news. Gordon Hoxie is to be congratulated for having invited you outstanding people from the world of scholarship, labor, business, and government.

First, this evening, I would like to try to lead off with some of my observations regarding the White House itself. Within this room are many who certainly have much deeper scholarship in terms of studying the Presidency, and many of you have had many more years of service within the White House. For example, Gordon Gray served with President Truman, and I believe each subsequent President thereafter. Thomas Corcoran served with Presidents Hoover and Roosevelt, as well as more recently with President Johnson. But, I am privileged to have this opportunity to throw out here some of the challenges it would be well to discuss while here at this conference in Montauk. I would like to say, also, that the Library of Presidential Papers, in sponsoring a symposium such as this, is taking a valuable forward step in the formation of a library which will be independent of those formed in behalf of each of the Presidents. The Library of Presidential Papers will provide a valuable service to students and others looking at the Office of the President itself. It seems to me that there is a need for an institution on a private foundation devoted to the study of the Presidency. In that worthy goal, I wish Dr. Hoxie, Mr. Roth and their colleagues much success.

Just two weeks ago, I was talking to the governor of a Western State about the nation's postal strike. He made a comment that startled me. "Now, I believe," the governor said, "the Government of the United States is to the point where perhaps we have to consider the fact that we're no longer governable." George Reedy's book raised this very question as to whether or not the President himself, today, in the complex situation in which we live, finds it governable within our system. Peter Lisagor, who is one of the most read persons in terms of the Presidency, has also raised the question as to whether or not modern government, such as it is today, finds us almost ungovernable.

In brief, many knowledgable people have been raising these questions. Mr. Peter Drucker has had much to say on this subject. In his books, such as *America's Next Twenty Years* and *The Landmarks of Tomorrow,* he sets our sights on the future. He says that too often most of us who are in positions of government, or who are working on governmental problems, still regard the era of Franklin Roosevelt as part of the current event. Similarly, there are those who view World War II and even World War I as part of the contemporary scene. Yet, in today's challenges, the challenges of the 70's he says, and I have to agree with him, it is far more important that we are looking to run government almost as if we are in the year 2000. As we enter a new decade, and enter a new era, if we are to solve the problems which face government itself in the years ahead, between now and the year 2000, we have got to begin looking at a new structure tailored to meet the demands of the time, tailored, as Drucker says, to the year 2000.

What could be a more significant occasion than *now,* within six years of the bicentennial of our nation's birth, for us to contemplate the goals worthy of our founding fathers and of our posterity.

The complexity and enormity of our problems are in many ways unprecedented. For example, the very population growth points up the magnitude of the problem for the President and for each of us. Yet, while size and complexity have increased, the basic principles don't strike this President in a much different way than they struck Presidents before.

For example, Andrew Jackson in 1832 said there are no necessary evils in government. Its evils exist only in its abuses. To Jackson, government should confine itself to equal protection, and, as heaven does its rain, government should shower its favor alike on the high and the low, the rich and the poor, with unqualified blessing for all. Grover Cleveland in his message of 1888 said a government for the people must depend for its success on the intelligence, the morality, the justice, and the interest of the people themselves. The people should support the government; the government should not support the people.

One of my favorite quotations for my own office comes from one of our nation's founding fathers, James Madison, who wrote that "A popular government without popular information or the means of acquiring it, is but a prologue to a farce or a tragedy or perhaps both."

Yes, these principles, those truths have not changed. But, as you talk about 200 years of the nation itself, it is this very population growth which has contributed to a major degree to the complications of government. In 1917, after we had European and African settlers in America for over 300 years, we finally reached the first 100 million mark in our national population. Just 50 years later in 1967, we passed the 200 million mark. And by the time we reach the year 2000, if our population grows at the present rate, we shall be up to 300 million people. The question is: How do we conquer that kind of complex problem? What should be the role of the President? What should be the role of the Federal Government in trying to guide that growth and where growth will go? It's a problem that involves environment as to how do people manage to find the means and the ability to solve the problem.

One of the studies we have underway, for example, is one which asks what will the Federal Government do to try to influence the dispersion of population? There are certain ways in which the Federal Government can make a contribution in population location. One of the key ways is in the location of new federal buildings. New federal installations can attract large numbers of employees and therefore have a great influence on the area that grows around it.

Should you look at the problem of the ghetto and locate these buildings in perhaps the heart of Watts or the heart of some of the problem areas of New York City, you may decide that you only make the problem more complex because by adding all these jobs to the congestion of that area, you add to the need for new highways and new facilities. You may be adding new areas of pollution of the air and water; thus, in an already complicated area, you may be making the problem more complex. Perhaps the new federal installation should be in a city of medium size, of about 250,000; or perhaps the answer is that it should be in a community of 10,000; or perhaps it could be in a brand new community and be the core to start building a new city in a desired area.

Once you decide a policy to go ahead in planning for the next 20 or 30 years on the location of federal buildings, you then have to face up to some other questions: What are the things that the Federal Government would do to make that work? Where do you locate your airports? What will you do in terms of highways? How will you divert those highways so that they serve those communities but don't further clutter up the land masses we have? How do you serve those communities so as to improve in a way that will service them yet not further pollute this environment? How do you help achieve a balanced population that will best serve all types of things during this development? These are the kinds of things which plague government today.

In his introductory remarks, Dr. Hoxie made reference to the postal and the air controllers' strike. Here is a new aspect of the problem facing the President. What do you do in terms of these public strikes? There are threats from others who say perhaps this is the way for federal employees to make further gains. It's complicated because they're violating the law when they go into this. Yet, the answer has to be a thorough look at the problem; the answer has to be to fulfill the constitutional responsibility of the President. On the one hand the mails must go through. On the other appropriate action must be taken within the court structure to penalize those who would violate the law. Such action must be made meaningful.

Recently on television from New York I heard one of the striking people who was interviewed say, "Why shouldn't we go out on strike against the Government even if it is breaking the law. The teachers already did it and nobody did anything to them." It's this kind of attitude that makes a study such as we're undertaking this weekend certainly appropriate and timely. I am glad to see that Dr. Hoxie has placed emphasis in planning this program on the relationship between issues, organization, and attitudes or outlook. The point which needs to be made, and I believe will clearly be made in this symposium, is that we must bring government up to speed. We must bring government into the era of the 70's. This need, this conference theme, has great opportunities and great complications, with implications for the future.

When we look at the role of the President himself and how he handles these things, I think most scholars would agree that a distinction must be made between policy formulation and policy execution. Perhaps the American public generally looks at the President of The United States as the man who's running all aspects of government. In point of fact, primarily the President, today, has to restrict himself to making the major policy decisions. He has to depend on the fact that he's gotten together a powerful team, a team he has great confidence in, to carry out and execute the orders once he has made them.

The qualities of leadership, organization, and esprit must be such that when the President has finally decided that this is the direction we will take, he may be confident that his policies are being executed. He must be able to devote his attention to the next problems and not have to worry about whether or not his decision is being executed. Even this fundamental principle is a complicated thing in today's government, if only because government has grown larger and larger each year. Seeking to reverse this trend this year, President Nixon, the first President in four decades to make such a reduction, has cut back the total number of federal employees by 50,000.

Still, we have this vast Government which has over 2 ½ million civilian employees. And, within this vast Government, there are very few positions which are open for changes even when you have changes in administration and party leadership. There is but little you can do to be assured that at all levels of the civil service there is wholehearted support for new views. Civil service serves a great purpose. It gives a great deal of continuity and security to a government itself, but it also provides a difficult factor for a President in that it locks in people who have been doing the same thing in the same way for many, many years. The result is great difficulty in actually moving programs through in the way that the President desires. We find that in trying to make changes in government today there is considerable resistance. With complete candor some civil servants say: We've been doing it this way for 15 years, and we believe that's the right way to do it, and, therefore, we do not believe that a new idea is a better idea.

A new leader must have tenacity to beat this problem. As a

part of his leadership the new President must seek out the best for all the top appointed posts in each of the various departments of Government. Only by such qualities of leadership can he make policies work in the complicated world in which we live today. Furthermore, the President, in terms of being a decision maker, has to be aware of the people he is leading; what their thoughts are; and where he can lead them and how. Then he has to resist the temptation to be a consensus president who would only follow what he thinks is the most popular direction. Instead he must carry the thing all the way through.

Reviewing the history of the Presidency in terms of these leadership qualities, we can learn much. In the nineteenth century, after the period of the founding fathers, perhaps three Presidents contributed most to the Presidential office, Jackson, Lincoln, and Cleveland. From the day of his first inaugural, Jackson brought the people to the Presidential office and the office to the people. Yet he came to be characterized, at least in the Whig press, as King Andrew the First. Lincoln never confused the popular position, even of his own Cabinet, with what he believed was right. And history found him right. Allan Nevins' great life of Cleveland was called a *Study in Courage*. Cleveland had the courage to make the right decisions, not the most popular. And history found him right.

The life of Lincoln, the life of Cleveland, reveals this courageous approach of presidents in decision making. The American people, while not agreeing with all the decisions President Nixon may make, believe he's a strong ruler, a man who knows the direction he wants to take and is attempting to lead the nation in that particular direction.

There is a gap, however, between what a President would like and what he can actually do. This is the gap that was expressed by President Kennedy. It exemplifies the kind of problems that a President faces as he goes into things today. After you've been in a job such as mine and others, one is concerned about the isolation of the President. How does the President get an input of ideas? Again, as you look back through history at previous Presidents, many of them have stated that the President is often the last one to get the word as to what is really going on in the nation and the world.

Thus, it is the responsibility of the staff to be certain that they're serving the President properly; that he knows what's going on; what's going on adversely as well as what's going on in a favorable way. I notice that Mr. Reedy in his book tackles this problem as one which is a very serious problem; one of having too many people who become conditioned to say "yes" and surround the President with that type of atmosphere; as such he lives in really a very unreal world, one which is not conducive to making the proper decisions based on all the facts that are available. This is not a peculiarity of our time. For example, you can go back to James Garfield who said: "The President is the last person in the world to know reactions of the people; what they want or what they think."

We're trying, in structuring this administration, to find a better way of establishing a two-way communication between the Government and its people, and to find what people are thinking. It's my opinion that government has the temptation too often to be bound by what people are thinking in Washington, D.C., and in New York City. Government, too, often fails to recognize that there are different feelings and different opinions that occur in Chicago or Los Angeles or Dallas or Boston or Waterloo, Iowa or Waterloo, New York, or wherever it may be.

Yet, if the President is to lead *all* the people, and if his Cabinet is to work with all the people in their regional offices and others, certainly it's vital that they develop the means and technique to establish this kind of rapport, this kind of understanding of the people who elected them, the people who gave them the mandate to serve and the people whom all of us in public service are charged with serving in every way possible.

We've tried to do this in some way that I think has helped to some degree. That is part of what my office is about. I find you learn by what people ask. I was at Yale last night, and I have this opportunity to be with you here tonight and again tomorrow. You learn by what kind of questions come forth. You learn from what is on the minds of the people with whom you've had the opportunity to have a discussion, such as in this Symposium.

This President received 71% more mail this year than any other American President has in American history, for any one year. We try to get a cross-section sampling of that mail so that not only do we see it, but the President sees it. The key is to have people who aren't going to back off and say we better just bring him in the favorable or else he won't feel good this morning. Instead, we seek to give him a true cross-section of what people are thinking, a good representation of the American thought processes and concerns.

During the 1968 campaign itself, President Nixon stressed two key points in this regard. He said first that he believed that a President today should be an active President. President Nixon is attempting to be an activist. He said also that the Government should be open so that whether or not people agree with what the President says on an issue they will have an understanding of why he said it. He believes that they should have an understanding of the background of what he was doing there.

One of the changes, which we've tried to make in the structure of government itself, in the effort to provide more information of this kind, is a change in the office which I am privileged enough to hold. The change is one in which we divided some of the responsibilities of the traditional press secretary and enlarged the scope of our government information policies. We have done this in a way in which we think makes more sense with government which has grown to the size which it has grown today.

The President's Press Secretary, Mr. Ronald Ziegler, serves in that office with great distinction, as, I'm sure, Mr. Reedy and Mr. Hagerty would agree with me. They've been through that firing line and know the difficulty of the job. Mr. Ziegler concentrates on the activities of the President on a daily basis, the activities which are so over-run and take hours and hours of time of the Press Secretary and, indeed, the President himself.

By contrast, in my own office, we work on policies as they are formed. We work on getting that information out to American editors, American broadcasters, and cities all across the country. As the title of my position connotes, we are attempting to do a better job of coordinating the various divisions of government in terms of an exchange of information; an exchange of values; with the entire Executive Branch of our Government we deal in fact and in quality. We deal in fact in getting out the information, whether it's information that is liked or whether it is information that may be regarded as embarrassing. The end product is better understanding, better quality, better service.

The tough task of how this works comes when you come to something that is embarrassing.. We have a grave responsibility to the American people, to be sure, to be willing to talk not only when things are going well but also to be willing to respond when things aren't going well at all. Communications is a vital thing today if the President is to serve as an effective leader. When the President loses the confidence of the people, he loses a good deal of the power he has to lead the American people. I think of two examples in the last four decades where this happened. In neither case can I say it was the fault of the President, but the fact is it happened in terms of the latter years of Herbert Hoover and the latter years of Lyndon Johnson. Having both lost the confidence of the people, rightfully or wrongfully, it made the processes of government, the leadership role of both men, far more difficult in all the things they were attempting to do.

To lead effectively, the President must work with the Congress. In like manner, to legislate well, the Congress must be fully conscious of the power of the Presidency and the power of the Executive Branch of the Government as it seeks to execute the policies and programs that the President deems vital for the country.

I believe, that if we look at the over-all problems of the Presidency itself, in this and in future symposiums, these are aspects we should be examining as we go along.

Finally, let me talk just briefly about the reorganization of the Government itself. Particularly in the final roundtable on Sunday morning, you will hear more of some of the reorganization which is underway. Certainly, we believe it is vital that a government today be reorganized in a way that will meet the challenges of the 70's. We're trying to reorganize it both in terms of the structure of the Executive Branch of our Government, and reorganize it in terms of the structure of some of the vital programs which will be sent to Congress for action, hopefully, within the next few months.

Looking back, the last major reorganization of the Executive Branch of Government was in 1939 by Franklin Roosevelt, at the time that the Bureau of the Budget was moved into the Office of the President. That was the time when the annual federal budget was 10 billion dollars; today it's 200 billion. It was a time when we had less than 1 million federal civilian employees, and today we have 2½ million employees of the United States Government. It was a time when the activities and programs which came forth were vital to that time period, but they are obsolete in many ways today in terms of meeting what has happened in science and other fields.

We have pending before the Congress the first key change in the executive structure since those early FDR days. This is one which would set up a Council on Domestic Affairs, which in many ways would be similar to the National Security Council which has served the last few Presidents very, very well. Through the National Security Council there is the process of staffing out the problems that threaten national security, whether they come from the Department of Defense, the Department of State or other agencies of Government involved in foreign affairs. It is the hope of the President, that by doing a better job of staffing, he can get more information from all sides to assist him in making the decisions he must with regard to domestic policy. This domestic council will be charged with staffing out programs, working with the departments of government on those programs, and carrying them through.

During that same period, since the aforementioned Roosevelt revision, the only other major change we have made is to add four cabinet posts to the Executive Branch of Government, plus a group of new agencies. We believe that to deal with the government departments today, looking at the complexities of the program, there is a need for this proposed domestic affairs council of cabinet officers, a world affairs council of cabinet officers, and a new environmental affairs council. By such means, you can have people sit down together in committees and work together between these departments of government.

Programs today find, too often, that they have funding in perhaps three different departments. And the implementation of them, regards employees from all of these various divisions. I sat down yesterday morning, for example, with representatives of HEW, the Justice Department and the new Vice Presidential Committee on Interpreting Racial Integration to see how we could get a team working together to go into regional centers across the country to explain the implementation of the President's new program of carrying out the court orders and following the development of an orderly process of developing our schools further and also carrying out the goal of integration all the way through. This is an example of the kind of complexity which involves government in that way.

The second part of the program, which was sent to the Congress, was one which sets up a Bureau of Management and Budget. Again, you'll hear more about that in detail, but I would just say, in brief, it puts more emphasis on evaluation as well as on measurement of the budget itself. It provides modern business practice which is needed for the management of the world's biggest corporation.

In terms of programs, we've tried to avoid doing the same thing over. Instead of putting a new patch with more dollars on it, we try to approach it with new ideas, young ideas, ideas which again recognize the idea of the change of time. The new welfare program is certainly the outstanding domestic program of last year. It rejects for today a program which perhaps worked well in the 30's and the 40's. Instead it seeks to get at the problem of welfare families, where generation after generation have lived on the welfare syndrome with no hope of really climbing out of the ghetto; no hope of really getting at the greater problems of finding jobs; of finding respectability from earning one's way. We hope to work in cities in that program, to start breaking up that syndrome. We'll start doing the job of building the kind of program which is necessary to meet today's problems.

I mentioned school desegregation, and certainly that's important. And in the field of education itself, the President's program challenges the schools to find a new way to evaluate what the progress of education is. We've been satisfied too long to say, too, that the solutions to all our problems in the schools are more rooms and better class ratios of teacher to pupils. The real challenge we must face is a better quality evaluation of the progress we're making in education and within each school. For example, we have been putting so much emphasis on colleges today, that it almost becomes a social sin not to go to a four year college. Yet, there's a real opportunity to provide better education and perhaps more adequate education for many of our young people through the development, to a better degree, of community two year colleges.

These are some things which government can do. These are things which we can do as a people, if we are willing to meet the problems with new ideas, ideas which I think provide the excitement and incentive which are necessary in these days which are ahead. One way to look at the challenge is this: in the years ahead you can pretty well predict that we'll increase the gross national product of the country by perhaps 50%. But, if we don't change our ways and meet the problems of the environment, the problems of education, the problems of understanding, the problems of inflation and others, we'll only be 50% happier. We'll only be 50% better off. Such percentages are no means of measuring happiness. We believe it's time to guide the Presidency, guide the Government itself in a way that we will meet that kind of challenge, not just by quantitative but by qualitative measurement.

Finally, this evening let me leave you with this thought. During the period of the last decade, we've seen a great economic growth; we've seen a growth in science; we've seen growth in medicine; we've seen many things which have been a big plus. Yet, we, perhaps, too often close our eyes to the fact that we've also seen a growth in social unrest, a growth in crime, a great growth in inflation, a great growth in other problems. I believe as we go into the 70's we can look with great pride at the fact that in 1961 John Kennedy said, "We'll make a national goal and go the moon." And, within a few years we sat in our living rooms and watched men walk across the surface of the moon as we viewed the television set. It's a thing you really couldn't believe when the goal was set. I've looked out from my home in La Jolla, California and seen men go out to live in a capsule beneath the sea for 30 days. Not too long from now women will have the opportunity to live beneath the sea in a similar manner. And for differing reasons, some men will thereby rejoice! In brief, we've seen great deeds in science, in medicine, and in technology.

And so I say to you, that, if man can perform such miracles, surely government is governable, and this instrument of the people can enrich our lives as it improves our environment. The Presidency can take the lead not only in solving problems of government, but it can also take the lead in setting the goals and priorities. I think the challenge we face today is to set the goals high. Let us look at this decade of the 70's as the period when we shall accomplish the kind of things in the social fields, in the international fields, which the 60's accomplished in science and technology.

By so setting those goals, we can accomplish these things which perhaps seem unreachable, unreachable at the moment. We need to set goals for peace for all mankind, for understanding of all mankind, for better education, for better job opportunities, for more thorough integration, for a more true look at what is really a sound economy. In every field to which you turn, whether it's culture or finance, or education, or the type of thing which makes money, or peace itself, we must set our goals high.

Government alone won't be able to accomplish it; to do it today requires a government which is willing to lead, a government which is willing to work with its people; a government which is willing to work with the local level, the state level, the regional level, the federal level. But also, it requires a people of compassion and courage who across the length and breadth of this land will do their part in their home communities. It will require a people, willing as you are at this Symposium this weekend, to look at the problems of government, as they meet the problems of today by doing what they can to serve. Certainly, it also requires people who, as regards these challenging programs, never forget that it's the duty of the American people, not only to support, but to be critical when they disagree with what is said by a public servant or the actions which are taken even in our highest elective office.

Neil Armstrong I think summed this up best when he talked to the Congress after he returned from the moon. He was relating to the Congress that just a few days before, he had a few days off, and he'd taken his two young sons to go to the top of the great continental divide to give them the opportunity to observe the deer and elk and other great wonders of nature.

Finally, he said regarding his sons: "They were looking at the wonders and looking for the deer and elk, and, in their enthusiasm for the view, they frequently stumbled on the rocky trail; when they looked at their footing, they did not see the elk. To those of you who have advocated looking high, we owe our sincere gratitude because you have granted us the opportunity to see some of the grandest view of our Creator. Those of you who have been our honest critics we also thank, for you have reminded us that we dare not to forget to watch the trail."

CHAPTER II

The White House
and the Media

GORDON HOXIE: Following last evening's illuminating keynote address by Herbert G. Klein, we have this morning the first of our four Roundtables. It is most appropriate that the man who introduced Mr. Klein last evening, Mr. Hagerty, should be the moderator for this Roundtable on "The White House and The News Media," and that Mr. Klein should be a participant. Both need no further introduction, nor, indeed, do their distinguished co-participants. However, I am asking Mr. Hagerty to please say a word about this unusual panel.

JAMES HAGERTY: I am delighted to serve as moderator on a non-controversial subject like "The White House and The News Media!" As Dr. Hoxie has indicated, all of you are acquainted with the names and the by-lines of this remarkable panel. On our extreme left, geographically but not ideologically, is Robert Semple, White House correspondent for the *New York Times;* next to him is Peter Lisagor, the Washington Bureau Chief of the *Chicago Daily News,* and the President-Elect of the White House Correspondents Association. The man with the bushy white hair is George Reedy, who served as Press Secretary to President Johnson; Mr. Reedy is an author of considerable note, of late; his book, *Twilight of the Presidency,* can be bought almost anyplace, including here. The last gentleman I introduced formally last night; where this morning I'll just say, Herb.

A moderator is supposed to just moderate, but I would like to set the tone and then ask these gentlemen to make their own particular remarks.

For one who has served as Press Secretary for eight years, the present dialogue between the news media and the White House is not exactly a new one. The emphasis may change on certain subjects, but the nature of this relationship is always potentially provocative. During working hours for eight years, I assumed I was the legitimate enemy of the news corps. After working hours, it was another story; they were friends of mine. But, in the Eisenhower Administration, as in all presidential administrations, it was up to the news media to be a hairshirt of the Government.

It is up to the news media to ask why and how. As long as those reports of why and how are honest and fair, and the great, great majority of the American press and their reports are honest and fair, they are providing an indispensable service. Like anyone else in any other profession, there are always self-seekers, and the professional members of the Washington Press corps know who they are, and they don't last too long.

At the present time there has been a considerable amount of controversy. I suppose it bubbled to the front with two speeches by the Vice President. Speaking for my industry, although I may be a minority voice in my industry, I think we overreacted like hell. This was nothing, again, new. One thing, however, that I personally have considerable questions on is the attempt to use the power of subpoena by the Attorney General to undermine the news sources of the newsmen.

If you start to destroy the confidence of news reporters by opening their notes and the traditional standards of confidence between a reporter and his sources to subpoena, then you are going to destroy the freedom of the press, indeed, the integrity of the press. You are going to destroy the information that you as the public get.

For myself, I stand in this whole news question with Benjamin Botts. Let me tell you about Benjamin Botts. He said: "In a government of responsibility like ours, where all the agents of the public must be responsible for their conduct, there can be but few secrets. The people of the United States have a right to know every public act. They ought to know the particulars of every public transaction in all their hearings and relationships so as to be able to distinguish whether and how far they are conducted with fidelity and abilities."

May I remind you that Benjamin Botts was one of five distinguished lawyers who defended Aaron Burr in the conspiracy trial in 1807. The Federal Government was prosecuting Burr on a charge of treason. Botts spoke in favor of the motion of counsel that the Court issue a subpoena *duces tecum* ordering President Jefferson to appear in court with certain papers required in the defense of Aaron Burr. All constitutional jurists tell us that Jefferson was correct in refusing to honor the subpoena.

I concede that there is a difference between a subpoena for a reporter's notes and a subpoena directed to the President of the United States. Even so, the essence of the eloquent plea by Benjamin Botts is good democratic principle to be followed by both newsmen and Presidents.

I am happy again to introduce Herbert G. Klein.

HERBERT G. KLEIN: Ladies and gentlemen, I know a little better now how Aaron Burr felt. I will keep my remarks brief. I had the opportunity to speak to you last night.

Philosophically, I agree with Jim Hagerty in supporting a press which is constantly vigilant in covering all forms of government. I agree 100% with that basic need. I think anyone who is responsible in the news field would have to agree to that. In our system basically we are set up in a way in which the press represents the public. They do so in such a way that the very questions they ask should represent the public itself. By doing so, they can constantly be on the alert for those who hide information and those who would mismanage the Government. Certainly in the bigger realm, the job of the press is to convey to the public what is happening within its government.

There has been no time in history when it has been more important that we get a very good job of reporting out of Washington. I mentioned last night that we have a very complex government with a very complex set of problems. The responsibility of the press corps during this period increases in direct proportion to the complexity. Just looking over some of the proposed programs, it is obvious that it takes a really outstanding group of Washington correspondents to clearly present the information as to what is contained in these proposals. It must be accomplished in a manner by which the public will have a full understanding and therefore have a full opportunity to make a judgment as to whether they oppose or favor these particular proposals.

During the last two decades, we have seen a new trend in all forms of journalism; that is, to do a greater amount of *interpretation*. In going toward more interpretation, you run into many problems as well as many opportunities. These problems stem mainly from the fact that more and more, when you go from just reporting exactly what happened in a quote, "he said," "they spoke" type of form, you have to rely on the judgment, the perceptiveness, and the research of the reporter himself in providing background material for those who read him or listen to him. This increases the need for reporters who are experts.

We have seen the trend where many in the news field now specialize in particular branches of government; for example, some of those who cover the Supreme Court and Justice Department are those who have also obtained law degrees. As a matter of fact, I think a few years back the *New York Times* sent a man back to law school to increase his ability to cover the Supreme Court. People such as Bob Semple and Pete Lisagor had long training and understanding of processes of government and understanding of political processes, in particular; as a result they have become experts in this type of field.

Analytical, interpretive journalism is essential in all that is now taking place. It would be a mistake if in any way this resulted in less interpretation either on the air, or less interpretation in terms of printed media. We have also seen in recent years an increase in editorials in television and radio broadcasting. Again, I believe this is a very good role for broadcasting provided it is properly labelled as editorial. This is the key to the matter: labelling things, particularly on the air, when in the course of reporting you make interpretative or editorial comments. Too often during the middle of a program things are inserted, and it is difficult for the average viewer to gather whether this is a statement of fact, or is it a statement of the reporter's own opinion.

It's easy with the trend toward more people listening to radio and watching television news to have misunderstanding of fact. If you look back yourself, I know that sometimes each of you have heard just a snatch of something on the radio and when you saw the story later what you thought was happening wasn't really the story at all, because your ears had played tricks on you at the time. This, again, gets to the point I am making; the need to properly label what type of things, factual or interpretive, are being done in this area.

Something of this nature is taking place now between the media and the Government, inspired, as Jim Hagerty says, by the Vice President's speech. This type of debate over the coverage by the news media has taken place for as many years as I have been in this field. I've also served on committees of the Associated Press on this matter. The only main difference I see today is that some things actually are happening as a result of the study. Everybody looked at earlier studies on this subject and thought about them, but very little ever happened.

In the situation we are now in, we can really have a result which is a really healthy one, both from the public standpoint and the press standpoint. The debate and the self analysis which have taken place in networks and in many newspapers does result in increasing quality and coverage. The several techniques of response, including rebuttal, background information, news analysis, and interpretation, and the public reaction to each of these, have been worthy of study.

Finally, may I say, I believe it best serves the relationship of all parties, government, press and public, now that the questions have been raised and looked at carefully, if all of us go to work and see if we can do a better job. It is my observation that this process is taking place.

PETER LISAGOR: I remember Jean Paul Sartre saying that the ultimate evil of mankind is to make abstract that which is concrete. We have been talking about generalities all morning and not getting very far. I would like to respond to a few things which have been said. One is a general proposition, and I think it ought to be remembered. The Administration wants as many cheerleaders as it can possibly muster. This has been true of every administration, I suppose, since the beginning of the Republic.

The effort, as George Reedy so aptly describes in his book, makes cheerleaders out of all of us all of the time—more intensively with some presidents than with others, as you well know. Another fault with the whole discussion about the press is that we talk about it as being a monolith. It is not a monolith. It is as varied, I think, as any profession in the country. It has many practitioners with different views, different attitudes, different philosophies. At the same time, most of us don't conceive of ourselves as taking pot shots at everything the Government does.

It has been said before, and I will say it again, that the relationship between the Government and the press in general ought to be that of an adversary. It is a wholesome relationship. It can be a constructive relationship. Again, I am not trying to promote George's book, but I do subscribe to his view that one of the few channels to reality which the President has is through the press, because he does become insulated by his staff, by the nature of the office. The press is kind of an open conduit to what the country is all about, what people may be thinking.

One final word on the Vice President, although I don't think he even merits it here today. The Vice President was not attacking; the Vice President did not attack the fairness or accuracy of the news report. I think it must be kept in mind that he didn't attack the lack of objectivity. He might well have noted, for example, the distortions of the TV camera. What he did do was question the right of the TV network or analysts to offer a contrary or dissenting opinion of the administration, and that can be dangerous.

WILLIAM J. CASEY: I have a statement as well as a question. I beg to disagree with Mr. Lisagor. What the Vice President did do was to question whether the networks performed a fair and proper function by giving only a critical, and I might say destructive, characterization of the President's speech.

PETER LISAGOR: The President spent 30 minutes outlining a position. The TV networks came back, giving a man 1½ to 2 minutes to express a judgment about that—an opinion about it. I will just simply submit to you as an argument that if in 1½ minutes an Eric Sevareid, or whoever, could destroy the argument, the persuasive argument, the point of the argument that the President made in 30 minutes, then there is something wrong with the President's argument. If you were watching a TV set and you heard the President of the United States speak for 30 minutes on an issue, and a fellow comes along and destroys that argument in 1½ minutes, as the Vice President would contend, then I think we are in danger of doing something to our whole system and our whole idea of what we are all about.

JOHN J. THEOBALD: What happens is that an announcer gives a 1½ minute comment; I agree with you that this cannot be all inclusive. However, I think, then, that the other media all too often pick up that one comment and all their coverage for the next day or two is on the comment rather than the original speech.

PETER LISAGOR: A President's speech makes headlines for days. It is analyzed and dissected for days. If you contend that a TV commentator is the thing that gets the major attention in this country, then you and I live in two different countries!

JOHN THEOBALD: Forgive me. I am not suggesting that an announcer's remarks are remembered as such. Rather I am suggesting that he helps form an interpretation, a mold, out of which headlines are constructed.

WILLIAM CASEY: Let me give you an example of a speech that was handled correctly and of one that was not. In the case of the President's Vietnam speech, commentators took it and distorted it. By contrast, in the case of his speech on welfare policy, he had Arthur Burns on one network and Moynihan on another. They were able to correct, on the spot, the distortions of the critics. That's fair comment. On the other hand, in the case of the Vietnam speech, there was not fair comment. It was one-sided; with distorted comments and with no opportunity to correct.

JAMES HAGERTY: May I say a few words on this subject of network presentation. I have worn several hats: news reporter, press secretary, head of the ABC News department, and now occupy a corporate position. From these several vantage points over the years, I have viewed an evolving process, an increasingly scientific, effective radio and television vehicle. I would defend the right for my network to analyze and to criticize any speech by anyone in the Government from the President on down as long as it is fair.

I need hardly remind you that to a certain point the radio and TV media are regulated by the Federal Government through the FCC. To the best of our ability we do abide by the rules. You may not like some of the analyses or some of the criticisms, but I think you will find over the long run they are constructive and have improved.

These commentaries on Presidential speeches are not instantaneous remarks by people who have just heard that speech for the first time. In most instances, they have read the text two or three hours ahead of air time. There is usually an advance briefing, either by a member of the White House Staff or department staff on what that President or Vice President or Cabinet Member is going to say.

In these Vice Presidential speeches, I think some misunderstanding was a matter of semantics. He was using words that were ordinary to him; that people would be interested in, but which meant something entirely different to us. Let me give you a good example of this: In his Montgomery speech he said: "Just as a politician's words—wise and foolish— are dutifully recorded by the press and television to be thrown up at him at the appropriate time, so their words should be likewise recorded and likewise recalled." Now this raises the image of a nice little room in Washington where some government people are taping and watching everything that goes on the air. They are acting not only the judge, but as jury on what the people on the network are saying.

If such, indeed, were the case, I would disagree with that. I would defend the rights of our television and radio people to make whatever comments they desire as long as their comments were fair. What I believe the Vice President was saying is that communications is a two-way street, and that he and other public officials have the right to respond to those commentaries.

One other point: the relative listener interest ratings for the President *vis a vis* the commentator. The President may attract 75,000,000 listeners throughout the U.S., but once he is off the air, there is a big drop in the number of listeners for even the most interesting commentator. The man in the Government has by far the greatest advantage. We haven't heard yet from Bob Semple, so let's go on to him.

ROBERT B. SEMPLE, JR.: I have a couple of comments . . . very simple ones . . . but I think there is a great fundamental issue implicitly raised in the Agnew speeches. Radio, and particularly television, interpretations were touched upon by Herb in his remarks. He noted the distinction between straight news reporting and interpretive reporting. How is this handled by the most powerful of the media, which is television? The suggestion has been made that an Eric Sevareid in a couple of minutes can set the tone of the news accounts regarding the President's or Vice President's speech. As a writing journalist I would reject that; not only out of pride but out of professionalism. That night I was writing my own story at the very moment that Sevareid, and the other commentators, or whoever was so incensed about the President's speech. To this day I have yet to read a transcript of the comments that were made after a Presidential or Vice Presidential speech, although I am aware of their tone and of their substance. The influence of the TV commentators is not large on the writing press.

At the same time, however, TV has the potentiality to exercise an enormous influence over the American public, and that, I think, lays at the root of the Vice President's criticism. The next day the *New York Times,* and in successive days in a column such as Wicker and Reston, was every bit as tough on the President of the United States for what he has said in his November 3rd speech, as were Sevareid and other commentators on the networks. The Vice President did not make a speech about any of them. Rather, he was concerned about this enormously forceful, powerful media, its influence on the President's posture, and whether the networks had, in fact, made a careful, cautious enough distinction of what is news and what is interpretation.

In a newspaper, it's very easy to see that distinction between interpretation and straight news. The very lay-out of the paper so indicates. When I write a story most of the time it is supposed to be a news story appearing on a newspage with my by-line. On the other hand, when Wicker or Reston write it is clearly interpretive. It is on the editorial page. It is rather clearly labelled as a column, and you know the columnist is expressing his own opinion. I'm not sure in my own mind whether TV viewers are yet sophisticated enough to make a distinction between commentary and straight news on the electronic media.

Readers expect interpretive journalism when they read a news magazine such as *Newsweek* or *Time.* But, they don't know what to expect when they listen to television. Walter Cronkite, who I understand was one of the founders of the Library of Presidential Papers, may be one of the last of the objective TV commentators. It is his view that you should handle the news tonight and the interpretation tomorrow. He clearly labels this distinction.

JAMES HAGERTY: The Vice President has said he doesn't mind the interpretation so long as it is fair and valid. May I simply add the phrase, that as long as it is *labeled*. I think that in a way the Vice President raised a valid issue. My complaint about the Vice President's speech was that, while he *implicitly* raised these issues, which are very delicate, important, professional issues which television network executives have got to come to grips with, i.e. distinction between straight reporting and interpretation, he did not *explicitly* raise these issues. He did not, in my view, discuss the real problems that actually exist. And, I agree, Peter [Lisagor], that Mr. Agnew seemed most upset not so much by the effort to offer interpretation, but by the effort to offer *contrary* interpretation. My own view is that if Walter Cronkite and others had been wholly favorable in their assessment of the President's address, we wouldn't have had Agnew's speech at all!

One other thing. I am expressing my own network's point of view; we do label *our* commentaries, on our TV news shows, and we do keep a sign *commentary* up. I think we are the only ones who do so.

PETER LISAGOR: As Jim Hagerty suggested, many people do turn their television sets off after the Presidential speech, rather than listen to the commentary. As I understand it, a CBS survey after the President's speech revealed 77% of the American people approved that speech. Now, that having been the case, it seems to me that what the Vice President does is to set up a straw man. The President had made his point; the majority of the American people support *his view;* and that is more evident in substance in days and weeks. So, I really don't know what the contention is all about. Now the gentleman who has raised the point is on his feet, so I'm sure he is going to offer us a rebuttal.

WILLIAM CASEY: I just want to say that I have a television set. What really happens is the commentator has the stage for those 2 or 3 minutes commenting when there is the greatest amount of attention focused on the issue, for the greatest number of people. Now what happens, is that the commentator in those two or three minutes has the power to put a label on that speech, to characterize it. I say that it is a matter of the networks exercising their obligation for interpreting and criticism. If it is criticism, it is well and good, but there should be an opportunity to correct the criticism or any distortion made on the President's statement. What is required is balance at the time, with an accurate amount of time, rather than in a capsule to characterize a 30 minute address.

PETER LISAGOR: I accept the Reedy position that the President is insulated. Therefore, he doesn't have access to critical comments that would help to give him a balanced view of the opinions, notions and ideas of the American people. But, I cannot see the reason for all this concern about what a commentator says. I think we underestimate the minds of the American people. As far as I am concerned, they should be free *to speak their minds*. Let them decide whether or not commentary given following a speech is *fair* or valid. The text is there; the newspapers are there; people of this country are literate.

GEORGE E. REEDY, JR.: Let me begin with a remark relating to the theme of this first roundtable. We all become too obsessed about the President's press problems. Frankly I don't think he has any press problems that a student of the press would regard as worthy of any serious attention. Take, for example, this concern about the commentators. I sometimes get appalled over the tremendous argument over something I think is very trivial. Let's look at the facts. The President has taken weeks and weeks and weeks to *prepare the statement* with every bit of writing talent available to him, every bit of public relations talent who can present a massive argument. Then a few commentators start talking about it.

Actually, of course, when the President finishes his speech, his speech ceases to be the news, because you have to assume that no more possible effective presentation can be made than the one he has made that has been heard by an audience that might number upwards of one hundred million. (Whatever those ratings state, I'm skeptical of some of them.) We know it's a mighty big audience. We know that every newspaper that has enough space is going to carry not only an account of the speech but frequently will carry the whole text, and *at that moment,* the story immediately becomes the *reaction*.

Quite candidly, I doubt very much if any President's speech

can be over-thrown in a minute and a half, unless it deserves to be over-thrown in a minute and a half. If this man, with all the massive resources of the Government, including two and a half million civilian employees, plus the armed forces, and a budget of nearly two hundred billion dollars, can have his remarks overthrown in one and a half minutes, they are not very worthy remarks. We seem to get disturbed if a commentator even raises an eyebrow.

What are the President's press problems? He has a few technical problems involving the press. He has to have a technician around who has some idea of press deadlines and some concept of what's involved in getting television commentators to the spot after that.

His real problems are *political.* In dealing with the press, his difficulties are not because the press is something unusual, some weird visitor from outer space, something unearthly! It is a media through which his *political* problems are related to the public. I think that *political* problems are mighty rough to deal with. The press is where he gets to deal with them in a public forum.

In discussions on this subject, as a general rule, those who decide that the press is being unfair or distorting the presentation are the people who strongly support the President. And at that particular moment those who become the most ardent advocates of freedom of the press are those who are against the President. Then about a week later possibly the situation will change; those who were against the President suddenly will be for the President, in which case they will become concerned about the irresponsibility of the press. And those who, *in the past,* were for the President, may suddenly become against him, in which case *they* become ardent advocates of press freedom!

This is quite a syndrome. Presidents like to talk about their press problems! It's a way of personalizing things. It's a way of preparing an alibi for history. You really didn't say *what the press said you said!* You didn't really *hold* such views; it was that ! ! ! *liberal* press! Or, if you happen to be a liberal President, it's that ! ! ! southern conservative press, or to use stronger language, those blankety blanks who used to be out in the lobby and who are now in the swimming pool.

I think we have to take another factor into account. I'm not so terribly concerned about Mr. Agnew's remarks in the sense that they indicate some big conspiracy somewhere to clamp down on press freedom. I don't think there is. I think what you're hearing from Mr. Agnew is what most politicians feel, and it is a very logical, normal thing because they are trying to do something. You don't become a politician if you don't want to do something, and if you want to do something, obviously what you want to do is the good, the beautiful, the true, and the perfect.

Newspaper men, on the other hand, are supposed to report what's happening, and by and large they do. There are professional standards by which they do keep to the facts. I know some newspaper men who are quite capable of writing a conflicting description, such as: "standing 5 ft. 1 in. tall and weighing 235 lbs., he is tall, thin, and handsome!" That doesn't bother me particularly; when the average reader comes across a sentence like that, his eyes sort of opaque at the "tall thin and handsome" and he sees the "5 ft. 1 in." Don't forget you have an audience that knows how to read newspapers.

And if a newspaper *consistently displays bias* over a period of time, the audience learns how to discount it. How many years, for example, has the *Chicago Tribune* been a leading influential newspaper in that town? How many elections has it won in the last 50 years? Few, if any. Yet, people buy it and read it—many people who are against its political stance. They read it for other reasons, including a pretty fair amount of news, interesting columnists, and good comics.

An awful lot of our discussion on so called press bias is totally beside the point. Communication is much more complicated than just the business of the selecting of the news. When I went to college I roomed with a Russian boy, a white Russian and, of course, bitterly anti-communist, but nevertheless understanding the Russian people. He said when a Soviet citizen picks up the official Communist Party paper, *Pravda*, featuring a particular headline or story, he reads something into it. If it says: "Cabbage is wonderful; cabbage will curl your hair; cabbage will make your eyes glow; cabbage will increase your sexual virility and remove body odor," then the Soviet citizen says: "Ha, ha, the wheat crop's failed again!"

A discussion of the press problems of the White House is useful, because it throws a lot of light on the political problems of the White House.

What I believe we are seeing in Mr. Agnew, consciously or unconsciously, is a reflection of frustration on the part of the American people. The American people are very frustrated. The majority of the people of this country is un-young, un-black, un-poor. The real voting strength is somewhere between 43 and 55. Everywhere they, you and I look, kids are growing their hair too long, kids are smoking pot, the blacks are out burning up the middle of the city, and we have a war going on in Vietnam nobody seems to be able to stop. Everybody wants to do something about it. Now they can't seem to change the facts, so they resort to a form of primitive magic. They say to themselves: I can't change the facts; maybe I can change the words; and then maybe the facts will change!

Peter the Great strangled the courier that brought him news of a disaster on the battlefield. Jack Kennedy once cancelled the *Herald Tribune,* or at least somebody cancelled it for him. And, I think, there is a similarity here. I think Mr. Agnew is saying is what the average American is saying to himself. What the average American is saying, unfortunately, is: "By God, if these no good bums—meaning the press—wouldn't print all this stuff and give all these kids and blacks all this publicity, then maybe we wouldn't have this and wouldn't have that!"

That, I think, is a more dangerous thing. I think it leads to a type of public frustration which can really bring about a crackdown on the press. But, I do believe, we have to get away from this idea that all we have to do is remedy White House press relations. Communications, preconceptions, prejudices, and reactions are complicated. The newspapers and the television stations are addressed to an audience. That audience has some of its own built-in preconceptions. You could subject some people to the *Chicago Tribune* for ten straight years, and during that period not let them read anything else; I think many would still be Democrats!

ANNA M. CHENNAULT: Isn't there a great deal of competition among the press? Isn't there a concern for what kind of by-lines, what kind of story, what kind of names you are going to print simply because of competition in the media? Take the Vietnam war, for example, how much do you pay your reporter, say the *New York Times,* to go to Vietnam to write stories? Is he required to do a story once a week or twice a week? Do they have any guide lines?

ROBERT SEMPLE: The basic rule of this business still is that we follow the traffic. I don't write stories at the White House as a rule unless Richard Nixon does something. If it's news, it's valuable. And, I doubt seriously, whether someone covering the Vietnam War follows any other procedure. It's the basic procedure that is drummed into us from the first day we enter the business that we write the news. George Reedy has suggested that the majority of us are capable of doing that with a reasonable degree of accuracy. We are not under any compulsions to fill any quotas. At the same time, if a government official lets reporters stay idle long enough, he is running this very grave risk. There is nothing more dangerous than a bored restless reporter.

In a book called *An American in Washington,* Russell Wayne Baker, who covered the White House for a time under General Eisenhower and Mr. Hagerty, said nobody recognizes this problem more acutely than Jim Hagerty. And, when things got dull for the White House press, Mr. Hagerty, according to the Baker interpretation, made absolutely certain that they had something to do. He recognized full well that reporters with nothing to do would soon start to look underneath the rug, open closets, and worse of all—think, and begin to add two and two together! Then, when they have to write interpretative or analytical pieces, if the writers are in a critical mood, it begins to creep in. As a rule, to answer your question, our main business is still to report the news.

The point I was trying to make in my remarks is that it is incumbent upon television, with its enormous power, to draw careful distinction between news and comment. Although I do not deny the writers the right to comment, by the same token, we cannot deny the same function to T.V. commentators as well.

DOROTHY H. HUGHES: All of us participating in this

symposium read several newspapers; we listen to the networks; we know what we're going to get from the *New York Times,* or if we want to read the *News,* we know what we're going to get. At times, at the end of a Presidential statement, we don't have three television sets, so we rush from NBC to CBS to ABC to hear who is going to say what. I'd like to give a bow to ABC, because I think they do let the public know if it is opinion or it is news.

Speaking for the average person, it would be much clearer in our minds if they would say we are now going to have: a minute and a half of PRO or a minute and a half of CON. I think this is what the main problem is.

JAMES HAGERTY: I happen to be a sentimentalist, but I have an over-abiding faith in the common judgment of the American people. I think they're a lot more sophisticated than you think they are, and I think they're a lot wiser. I have had my arguments with the news media, including my own news department from time to time, and I make no blanket endorsement about anything you read or hear. However, the whole news media, including television, radio, and the newspapers are received by the American public, who make their judgment on what they read.

I don't think, without the news media in recent years, there would have been any honest dissent on Vietnam. I don't think without the news media, there could have been any civil rights—or human rights—movement. It would never have gotten off the ground without the news media and its presentation of both sides. I have a rather lengthy letter from a man who claims that in Vietnam we are conditioning the people to accept war. I think it's quite the reverse. I think, for the first time really, the utter futility of war has come into the home through television. I think all the glory that used to be connected with war has been demolished, because of television coverage, because of that news clip that you actually see. In the coverage of Vietnam, there is no way you can possibly cover a whole war. You can only cover small segments of that war on any given date. All of us had considerable trouble some time ago with the military itself on Vietnam. And, it wasn't until the military got over the first clash with the press that we began to get a better recording on what was going on in Vietnam.

ANNA CHENNAULT: But does the war in Vietnam require first class reporters too?

JAMES HAGERTY: They do require first class reporters, but it also requires young men. I'm too old to cover Vietnam.

ANNA CHENNAULT: That's a problem. Sometimes we have younger men, and maybe they have no experience.

JAMES HAGERTY: That's right. We admit some of the younger men have little experience, but the editors and the men back home are professionals. A reporter isn't going to last very long if he doesn't report accurately and effectively. There have been many instances of this followed by removal from a scene.

JOHN T. CARLTON: I'd like to ask a question of this unique panel, including those who have served as press secretaries. Is it a fact that in the White House Press Room or in the Senate Press Gallery or House Press Gallery there are a few who set the tone of the attitude that the press is going to make? I know Peter Lisagor raised the point that there is no general pattern of operations among newspaper reporters, and this is true. But, there are certain influential reporters and when they all get together, don't they set the tone? Doesn't everyone come out and write the same lead? I've seen this happen a hundred times. You have everyone writing the same lead on a story that has many facts, Herb?

HERBERT KLEIN: The whole view this morning has been on the great variety of decisions that are very difficult: When editing a newspaper, you have to decide the quality of your staff, what you consider to be the main story. Sometimes it's easily picked out, and other times it's difficult, because there isn't that much news. We sometimes overlook the fact that small stories become big ones.

With television you get an even greater degree of selection; how much can you cram into a half hour? Which things do you select and which do you leave out? Another aspect is that I think people on all sides sometimes feel they left out the wrong thing or overemphasized the other thing. And so, it is in the conscience, professionalism, and ability of those who are doing it. People are human beings; it's a problem all the way through. I would like to see under constant study, by the industry itself, problems of human nature like this. We really know very little about how you handle these things.

I think, we agree that there are some people who are greatly respected, but I would like to point out that we are talking about highly professional individuals with independent judgments.

With today's media, time is an imperative factor. Most of the stories you read are written by dead-line, and the reporter has his problems in getting the story out and meeting that deadline. Deadlines are becoming more and more important, and reporters are required to do things rapidly. Radio is on constantly and has the quickest deadline. Television has a deadline that involves a lot of technical problems, and newspapers are also doing it the same way, so the *immediate* story is less likely to be read than heard by what people say.

When you look back at the first 90 days, 100 days, the first year of the new administration, I suspect that there is more of an influence by the news media on some people than on others. Again, it is dependent upon human nature and people whose reporting you respect most in your own profession.

Additionally, as I said at the outset, this type of discretion is a healthy one. No question, we say it's the best press the world has ever seen. We are more able to do things technically, more rapidly. Television, for example, is letting us see the war in film quickly. The recording of history on the spot has increased to a considerable degree. We have a better educated press, and they have a great deal more freedom. With that freedom, and the complicated problems we are looking at, it also means more responsibility in conveying news to the public; what the reporter and the editor feel is happening and what they report.

One final point, lest we forget, the media report on local government matters as well as national. In our system of government on the national level, the people make basic decisions by voting every few years. Actually they make decisions on the local level more often, for example, on such issues as municipal or school bonds. So, in order to cover this adequately, you must have this kind of press that will constantly feel it is on a local as well as a national watch for government, and the public has the right to feel it can get both from the press.

GORDON HOXIE: I understand that we have five minutes before our keynoter, Mr. Klein, has to leave. We see represented here today several distinguished persons who have been related to the position of Presidential Press Secretary. The position that Mr. Klein is occupying, that of Director of Communications for the Executive Branch, is something a bit different, above and beyond that of Presidential Press Secretary. To the best of my knowledge, this is the first time this position has been in an administration. Herb, I wonder if you can tell us a bit about the background of the creation of this position and the philosophy related thereto. Does your position provide a new dimension in this question of the media and the White House?

HERBERT KLEIN: Dr. Hoxie is correct that this is a new position. When the then President-Elect Nixon invited me to join the new administration, I sought the counsel of such persons as George Reedy, Jim Hagerty, Pierre Salinger, Bill Moyers and others. Most of them felt that, in their experience with a total job of press secretary, they had been unable to present many of the recent activities of government. This has not been because of a lack of desire, but because of a lack of time. People who have been on the firing line with these daily press briefings have the tremendous responsibility which is sometimes overlooked by the general public. Whatever the hour, the Presidential Press Secretary has to be sure of each word he says, to be knowledgeable in all subjects. He can't do that job well and then fulfill other requirements related to the increasingly complex government and society.

And so, my office was established with the goal of doing a better job as related to our Federal Government of providing the American public with information regarding the Executive Branch. We are also trying to look beyond Washington, and to provide the background information available to Washington reporters to those who must analyze it in other parts of the country. We do this for radio, television and newspapers throughout the country.

Today, with the high cost of newsprint and media production, the fact remains very fugitive. The full facts aren't always available. I think the key to the positions of press secretaries for all of the executive agencies and departments, and the key to my own job, is to constantly be on guard that you are providing the facts. If you are providing the facts, whether or not the people like those facts, you are fulfilling a basic responsibility in our Republic.

JAMES HAGERTY: We have a welcome addition to our panel in the person of a most knowledgeable working attorney, the inimitable, Thomas G. Corcoran, advisor to Presidents since the days of the Hoover Administration. Ladies and gentlemen, the inimitable "Tommy the Cork."

THOMAS G. CORCORAN: Jim Hagerty, thank you for that introduction.

The reality about you media people is what John Flynn said about you long ago: You're not in the news business: you're in the entertainment business. You couldn't make your money that way. Fundamentally, you have to present the news in a form that is entertainment, and therefore, you just look at the front page of the news—the front page has to be something sensational. The public is not interested in good news, and there is no news with an entertainment value except bad news. So that, in your business, what you are doing is concentrating on sensation; concentrating on the off-beat business in order to sell the advertising contract, whether it is television or newspapers, and that's the honest to God's truth about what you do.

With regard to this controversy about Mr. Agnew and the television and the press, everyone is feeling the elephant at his own point of contact with the elephant. I've been in the television business, and I know it. I have represented at one time or another nearly every one in this business, and you know perfectly well why you're making such a row about Mr. Agnew and his speech: you are fighting a war in France instead of in America. You're very much afraid to see the only privately owned television system in the world under threat of public control. People are getting madder and madder about the amount of money it costs for political campaigns. There is much dissatisfaction with the "media" which you are seeking to fight off. You see in it the threat of a government ownership. You're exaggerating Mr. Agnew because you want to fight the government control issue as far away as possible, before you do come up against the political problems.

As for Mr. Agnew, just as you said, George [Reedy], every politician thinks like a politician, and thank God he does think like a politician. Mr. Agnew is interested in a political position, and he picks up the frustrations of the public right now, who are mad about everything that nothing can be done about. When he picks that up, he helps his political position, and the press criticizes Mr. Agnew, because way out on the Agnew front they're trying to fight this issue of government interference that may eventually become ownership like the B.B.C. and Radio France. They're going to fight it way out there before it ever becomes a fight in Congress about how much it costs to put up the money for political campaigns. We seem to be all talking about different things but this issue is the nuts of the thing.

People are taking seemingly different political positions, but all are using Agnew and this controversy for their own political purposes. Isn't that true?

GEORGE REEDY: I agree with quite a bit of what you say, Tommy, but not with the word entertainment, because entertainment means a couple of drinks on the 19th hole at the golf course.

I started off by saying the President doesn't have press problems; he has political problems and the press is the nearest thing he sees every day which brings his political problems home to him. I doubt whether the television media or, for that matter, the printed media are really consciously adopting the strategy: "If I'm going to fight an invader, I'd like to fight as far away from home as possible." I don't really think there is a threat to the press, and if there is, I don't think it comes from Mr. Agnew; I rather doubt that. I think that it may come from the frustrations of the American people.

Newspapers don't have to concentrate on the sensational; almost everything going on in the world is sensational. There's enough sensation going on every five minutes to keep every newspaper occupied: We've got a few wars going on, city-rioting, bombings, the prospect of guerilla warfare in our cities for the first time in our history. I think there is a public tendency to lash back in rage, and since the people can't get back at the forces that are really doing things to them, the rage is directed at the press. This is an age in which nobody seems to have any answers. It's one of those eras when every leader looks inadequate, and nobody seems to have any answers to the problems.

THOMAS CORCORAN: May I throw in one more dimension? The cohesions that hold a society together are very complicated; a belief, an optimistic belief in life has held America together when we would otherwise be cutting each other's throats. I've been thinking about the kids of this generation, and their Book of Job problem of evil.

Don't take this to mean I'm against a free press, but it wasn't so hard for the kids of my time when you didn't know so much so fast about so much evil in the world. All at once, now, through modern communication you do. When our generation grew up in comparatively rural surroundings and without this immediate communication of the great evil in the world, it wasn't hard for people to have an optimistic view of life. I'm not talking in terms of a specific religion; but maybe God was in his heaven and all was right with the world.

But, now your media drives home the opposite every time the television goes on; fed by the press it feeds out trouble now brought instantaneously to every child's attention. I'm telling you, it is true; to produce sensation, you are dissolving any possibility of optimistic belief. I don't know the answer to the Book of Job; but I do know it is getting harder and harder for children to face this world and the difficulties of it.

I wonder if, unfortunately, our free press with its detailed sensationalism, its detailed evil, isn't breaking up the spiritual cohesion of society? This is particularly with young people who don't believe in anything whether illusionary or not; I'm just wondering if you're breaking the optimistic spirit of these kids upon which any democratic form of government depends?

GEORGE REEDY: I think we're getting to a very basic point here. I think there is a tendency here again to get back to the conclusion that because the news is bad, the best thing to do is to strangle the guy that brought it, especially when you can't get to the basic source. I would agree with you strongly, Tommy, that the trouble with kids is primarily due to the evils of the world. I think it has much deeper causes than the conduct of the media.

What has happened to the family; the way we live? Today kids are being raised for our own emotional satisfaction. There was a time when kids were contributing to the economics of the family, when a five year old was washing dishes, or helping the old man with the plowing; not today. We have kids, all too many of us, for our own emotional satisfaction. In a sense, it's almost like having a pet dog or a pet cat. I believe the kids sense this feeling and resent it. They feel they are not a part of the family, because they are not contributing to the family. The family is doing everything for them, and human beings really do not like people who do things for them. It's the other way around. You know, if there's ever a person you feel good toward, it's the one you could do something for. You felt superior to that person, and that made you feel good. You felt you were bigger than he is.

JAMES HAGERTY: I'd like to talk about one question to which Tommy referred: the increasing cost of running for public office. I agree with him. It has gotten out of hand, with television contributing to it. It's as simple as that.

I am one that believes, that for a Presidential election, once every four years, we can forget public entertainment for part of the night and put candidates for the President of the United States on for free. But, I also urge, at the same time, that Congress gets enough guts to pass appropriate legislation to allow us to do it. They should suspend or revoke Section 315. Last year they did not suspend it; as a matter of fact, it never got out of the Congressional Committee in the Senate. Those who controlled in the administration at that time did not wish it. So, it's very simple. We have to, more and more, give free time to the candidate.

For the Presidency, I believe we should do it on our own and voluntarily. I'd rather do anything voluntarily rather than be pushed. Give time to the men who are appointed by their respective parties to run for the Office of the President. I do not wish to see the saloon-keeper of Weehawken ask for equal time with candidates of the Republican, Democratic, and other major parties. But remember, it is also our dear friends in the Congress who haven't passed the legislation I think is needed.

THOMAS CORCORAN: I completely agree with you, and may I do a commercial. The Twentieth Century Fund in New York undertook a study of the problem of the use of broadcast time for the education of the public and political campaigns. It was a very curious committee; Dean Burch, who was manager of Barry Goldwater's campaign and is now head of the FCC; Bob Price, who was Lindsay's Deputy Mayor; Newton Minow, the Democratic head of the FCC and Adlai Stevenson's friend; Alexander Heard, the Chancellor of Vanderbilt University, and the expert for Kennedy on political contributions. I was there to try to support unanimity, the old ancient mariner.

Today, you go even further than the committee's report did. The committee only suggested that the problem of the education of the public in political campaigns for the Presidency alone was so important that the Congress should pay for it. In respect to Congress, the technical problems you get, when you have so many stations and so many Congressmen in Manhattan, for instance, are difficult to handle. The report of the Fund's Committee is before Congress now. But I noticed that my southern Democratic Senator, Senator John O. Pastore, from my native state of Rhode Island has, so far, rejected the idea of appropriation of money to pay for the public time for even the Presidential elections.

The other day, in a very interesting talk with a very high official in the newspaper business, I remarked, "Why, apart from the entertainment necessity, do you allow to go on the planted story, or certainly the slanted story, in certain of our newspapers with respect to the Vietnam war?" I was picking up Mrs. Chennault's inquiry as to why certain kinds of newspapermen went to Vietnam and whether they were required to bring back a particular slant. The answer I got back was something like this: there is the competition these days for stories in the press that will be as interesting as what comes over television; we policy makers no longer have the kind of control over the employment of reporters or the discipline of reporters that we once did. To compete with the picture tube, you have to have a bright reporter who writes a bright story by his demand under his own by-line; and his attitude is, if you want me to work for you, you'll have to let me write my own story with any shading or personal touch I want to put into it; otherwise, I'll go to a competitor.

ROBERT SEMPLE: I know Peter [Lisagor] has some things he wants to say, so let me address myself to just two points. The first specific point is one Mrs. Chennault did raise. Let's go back in time a little bit to the first wave of reporters who went into Vietnam in the early 60's; it is true they were in their twenties; the most notorious of these, as far as the military establishment is concerned, was a young man, David Halberstam who works for the *New York Times*. Halberstam was not alone in his judgment, for the war was not going as well as the spokesman for the military government officials claimed it was. And, this tension between government officials and the free press we talked about all morning comes to generalities, but it was no better or more clearly illustrated than during that period in Vietnam.

When these young men got there, they were told day after day in briefings that the war was going well; that success was just around the corner; that bales of captured documents proved that the enemy was on the verge of collapse. What these young men did, being hearty souls, was go out into the countryside for themselves and find evidence that produced a certain amount of skepticism about the assertions of the military command.

To me, that was an extremely important journalistic exercise, whatever its excess. To have to deny that information to the American public would have corrupted their understanding today. Far from being a journalistic black mark, I rather think it was one of our finest hours. Successive waves of reporters who have gone to Vietnam, some of them older than the first batch, did not in any way reduce their skepticism. Skepticism, I think, has got to be there all of the time, and that period is a good illustration of it. By and large, our reporting was excellent. Because if things were going well, as the young men were told, then I think we would have felt compelled to double; triple our involvement there.

Let me go on to the broader question, one of the questions that came up earlier and was very well taken. It deals with how the youth of America is being buried under too many layers of tragedy and hypocrisy, as reflected in the instantaneous news media. It is a good point. I feel, that at this point, part of the problem we have with a youth that is far more rebellious than any other, at least as far as I know, arises directly from the constant pummelling they take from the news media. Even though it is not directed to them, there's a sensory impact of the day to day basis of cruelty and hypocrisy which exists in Vietnam and elsewhere.

Scotty Reston writes three or four columns a year in addition to his regular one. He writes one column about baseball and the rites of spring, and one about the population explosion, and another one of his standard columns is a plea for his colleagues of the newspaper business to somehow set up a department of good news; a problem he and other reporters have asked themselves about and wrestled with. Why is it that on page one of the *New York Times* all we see is conflict? Why don't we talk about some of the good things that President Nixon is doing? Or, that President Johnson did? Why don't we talk about some of men's good works in the world rather than just the troubles of our time? It's a terribly difficult question, and I don't exactly know how to answer.

There may have been too much publicity given to a number of issues and conflicts within the Administration rather than on the points on which key members of the Administration agreed; instead of sending Semple out to find out if Attorney General John N. Mitchell is fighting over desegregation, maybe they should send him out to find out what they're agreeing on as to how the Administration ought to move, and the country ought to move.

I can think, however, of one example where bad news may have had a salutory effect, and that is of the whole treatment of the drug problem both on television and radio. If the newspapers had ignored the problem, I am not sure that America, parents as well as the kids who are affected, would be attentive to it, or the Government would be as attentive to it as it is today. The old second hand belief that out of this kind of created tension, comes progress, I am not yet willing to abandon. And, I think other examples of this can be used to prove the point.

PETER LISAGOR: Mr. Corcoran brought out so many fascinating ideas. First of all it is good to know there's an economic determinist and such eloquence left in this country. Secondly, I think you confuse us with Al Capp and Ann Landers and those who make crossword puzzles for our newspapers. You know, it is not easy to be optimistic about this world, but it's rewarding to try.

I couldn't agree with you more about the magnification of our problems by the use of instant mass communication. It has distorted many of our problems; it has magnified them out of proportion. I am not sure that the adults haven't been the chief victims of it because, I think we sell our kids far too short. I think they're far better, the majority, than those that are so magnified, that represent such a small minority.

Any poll of college students today shows that most of them, 80% or more, want the same things that I wanted in college, or that you wanted. Get a good job, get married, have a family, live in the suburbs, have a Buick, although I'm not so sure since my last experience with a Buick.

Let me say one final thing about the nature of our society. I met a friend of mine the other day and asked him if it was really true that we are coming apart at the seams and that we are really collapsing the way I read. Stewart Alsop says there are three nations in this country now: the black nation, the Woodstock nation, and the lawless nation. *The Wall Street Journal* then comes out and applauds the column; says it's great but adds that it blames the wrong people; the people to be blamed are the American elite. And, who are the American elite? Our universities, our newspapers and others in the Establishment who are failing society and helping to tear it apart, and so on.

So, my friend says that No, we are not collapsing. He cited a few things, such as, if you know European history and the history of anarchy in Europe, 1880-1900, the anarchists who had wide, popular support because they came out of the working classes. They didn't come out of Scarsdale suburbs. The statistics about what's going on in the nihilistic, anarchistic area of the youth appear to be not worth dealing with seriously, in this judgment.

If you remember the whiskey insurrection, and the Molly Maguires, and remember that lynchings were commonplace in the south just two generations ago in this country; if you remember the labor strikes; Detroit, and Republic Steel violence in Chicago, then you'll see that we've gone through this thing before. And, it's been far worse than it is today. The television makes it seem worse today. We don't know what television has done to this society, and, if the Twentieth Century Fund wants to do a real study, it ought to do a study of television's impact on the raising of our families, our social habits, our political thought processes, about the whole range of this society.

The generation gap has been caused because we've raised a group of kids who are so much smarter than we are. They know so much more. So, I would suggest in the end that we remember something that my friend also told me about Marshal Foch, what he said in the Second Battle of the Marne. He said something like, "My center is collapsing, my right has gone; the situation excellent. I am attacking!"

L. RICHARD GUYLAY: George Reedy makes a point that the President has become increasingly isolated. I'd like to ask the correspondents here today whether or not they think the policy of hot pursuit of the President that the White House Press Corps follows, pursuing him the minute he sticks his head out of the White House, and driving him into a Cambodia-like refuge, is a correct one? When President Eisenhower was in the White House, he couldn't get to Burning Tree Golf Club without a pack of reporters at his heels. Isn't there some better way to do this?

PETER LISAGOR: Well, what you seem to be suggesting is that we ought to somehow sanctify the President and let him do anything he pleases without raising what I think would be legitimate questions about his activities. I don't accept the premise right away that he is driven into a Cambodia-like sanctuary. I don't know what that means, because I don't think we do that.

I think Presidents struggle all their lives to get that

job; nobody talks them into it. They know what that job entails; and they know the rigors of it, and incidentally, the rigors of it have been overstated. It's supposed to be the splendid misery; someone said that earlier today; but they love it. They outlive their wives, they outlive their vice-presidents, and their press representatives. There's not a thing to feel sorry for about this man who has "suddenly become burdened" with these problems. He fought tooth and nail to get there, and I dare say he is tough enough to be pursued hotly or coldly. If he isn't, he doesn't belong there.

RICHARD GUYLAY: He surely has the right to some privacy.

PETER LISAGOR: Oh, privacy. President Nixon is a past master at maintaining the right of privacy. He's so private, we don't know what is going on in the White House most of the time. George [Reedy] writes at great length about other days at the White House. He says he wasn't talking about any particular White House, but a reasonable facsimile of a man I know that was in the White House comes through in George's book! We knew what went on backstage at the Johnson's; we happened to know too damn much of what went on, from the President's own point of view. He made himself vulnerable by making himself that accessible, and I say this against my own interests as a newspaper man.

Now, on the contrary, we don't know what goes on when President Nixon disappears, as it were, into the Lincoln Study or into the Executive Office Building office; an iron curtain comes down. We've all tried; Bob can substantiate this, to find out what goes on, to find out the thought processes that go into decision-making, what happens after he takes these alternatives and options, that Herb Klein talked about last night, into the Study. What goes on? We don't know. In fact, I think he's done a remarkable job of maintaining his privacy in all three White Houses! Now, maybe, Bob will have another view.

ROBERT SEMPLE: We agree on that. George will be able to substantiate this; from the Johnson Administration, there was a marvelous ritual; something concrete took place, for example, every Sunday morning in Austin. I covered a little bit of Lyndon Johnson before I got involved with this President; and we'd fly down to Austin when he'd go to the ranch for the weekend. Sunday morning was not a day of rest for the press. The President would go to church, and George would call Fredricksburg or Johnson City or some other small town, and we would go at high speed very early in the morning. So every morning, very early we would get up to cover him, and we'd say this is ridiculous.

First of all, we wanted to sleep late, because Saturday night, the night before, the boys were living up to their historic reputation, and we all felt that. Still, we got up, had bacon and eggs and went out at 80 or 90 miles an hour to make sure that we'd be there when the President went into the church. We'd get seats in the back pew and watch him; whether or not he fidgeted with his fingers, if he combed his hair during the sermon, and then we'd try to grab him afterwards; all of this we'd do to report. All of us went out even though we felt this was a mild invasion of his privacy. We ought to leave him alone Sunday morning. Do you know why we didn't? The first four or five times Lyndon Johnson went to church, if memory serves me correctly, he invited every reporter back to the ranch for an impromptu news conference, and those who were not there, those who had determined not to go out to see the President at church, missed the story. In effect, for a year and a half, on Sunday morning we were with the President at his expressed invitation, which I think simply confirms Peter's point. The President can do anything he wants, and we will respond.

Having examined the press policy of the Kennedy and Johnson Administrations, this President has resolved neither to play favorites, nor to deride the individual reporters, nor to berate them, nor to have them in for long chats. Instead, he remains impartially invisible to all. And, there is no policy of hot pursuit. Even if we tried to launch one we couldn't go anywhere. When he goes to Key Biscayne, he disappears behind a hedge and is visible only when he reappears on the stern of Rebozo's boat nine miles off-shore and surrounded by a flotilla of secret service craft. When he goes to San Clemente, he is hidden behind the high walls of his compound, and he emerges only when he wants to. As Peter says, he's a past master of protecting his privacy, and he does this extremely well.

The final point, personally, I would like to move back a

little, not all the way mind you, not even half way, to the accessability of Lyndon Johnson, because in the end, as Peter suggested, the rigorously self-enforced privacy of President Nixon is going to hurt him.

I've covered him since October 29, 1967 when I first saw him speak in a low-ceiling room before the Laconia [New Hampshire] Chamber of Commerce. During those early days of the primaries there were only five or six reporters around.

The Presidency is a very real problem. You get to learn quite a bit, and everybody's always said that Mr. Nixon is a very impressive fellow in private conversation, although in his big elaborate circus-like press conferences he doesn't come off that way. The problem he's defined then is how do I capture that rather interesting personal relationship I have with a few reporters when I've got 70 or 80 of them, without getting into the same problems that Lyndon Johnson got himself into? And, he really hasn't found the solution.

Until recently, I hadn't spoken to President Nixon, personally, which, of course, is an enormous blow to my ego, because if only I could tell my mother I had spoken to the President! Well, two week ago today, at 5:30, I was in the shower where I hate to be interrupted, and my wife came in and said the White House is on the phone. I said it was probably Ziegler and say I'll call right back after I finish shaving. My wife came back, the shower was still going, and said it was the President. I came out stark naked, water dripping off me. My wife said I sat bolt upright talking to the Commander-in-Chief throughout the entire conversation. Early in the day he had held his first impromptu news conference, FDR style or LBJ style, with no cameras, and it was a rather interesting and productive day. Nobody watched the clock; you knew you were not on television; it went on 35-40 minutes, and we were able to ask all the questions, and he was able to give all the answers.

I think that now, far from resenting the pursuit of the press, President Nixon has found such pursuit practically nonexistent, and he is beginning to worry about the ways to incur more direct contact. I think as a result, we will see more of these informal news conferences; and fewer of these stylized presentations.

SEVERAL PARTICIPANTS: What did he call you for?

ROBERT SEMPLE: Oh, he said that he had been getting some beef from the television people for having had this informal news conference around his desk in the office. The TV people insisted that their cameras are their pad and pencil, and he gave out a lot of news that day without them. He had upstaged Bill Rogers completely on the Arab-Israeli issue; he said I don't want to tell you what Bill's going to say, but here it is ... in effect. And he came out with a couple of more good stories including reaction he might take in the postal strike, i.e. two days before he called out the troops and sent them to New York City. So he was asking—what do you think about this? Do you think this is a useful exercise, because I'm getting some beef from the TV boys.

Defending my own interest, I said I think it's wonderful not to have those cameras around just once in a while, Mr. President, and I said there's nothing to prevent Herb Kaplow or Bill Gill of ABC or Dan Rather from standing up that evening and telling the American people what you said. It is all on the record though they may say it won't be used. I just put in a plea for this option. At the end I just said once you do that, there remains just one more thing you haven't done and that is to have an exclusive interview for the *Times* . . . and he said . . . "Oh, oh, I'll give an interview any time . . . about my daughters."

PETER LISAGOR: I just want to bring up one point I disagree with Bob [Semple] about. You said the President had discovered he can make himself more available or accessible to the press. I, for one, support this detachment on both sides. I think an arm's length attitude between the President and the press is a good one. I think if he destroyed it a little bit we might see more warts by a look up close. That's what happened in the case of Lyndon Johnson.

So I think in his own interest he might well consider not doing what he has suggested to Mr. Semple. And in our own interest, we preserve a good deal of our own objectivity and detachment when we have a crack at him in public circumstances like a press conference. So I would tend to disagree on that point. I just want to make one other point. You now can see the difference between the *New York Times* and the *Chi-*

cago Daily News. If the President were to call me, heaven forbid, if he would then tell me he was going to Chicago, thinking I might be interested in that.

CONFEREE: I noted Mr. Lisagor's indictment of the Vice President's celebrated speech and the reaction here this morning to that indictment. There was another active newspaperman whose reaction to the Vice President's speeches was quite different than yours; his rationale was quite interesting. It was Howard K. Smith, and his comments were on the bias and prejudices of the news industry.

PETER LISAGOR: I can save you a little time. I read that article. Is this the one that appeared in *TV Guide?*

CONFEREE: Yes. He accused his colleagues in the news industry of bias and prejudice, and he said that practically all the working press are liberal. He went back to a time when liberalism was a necessary good thing; he says most reporters' intellectual occupation, by definition, have a left bias.

PETER LISAGOR: You put me in a position of defending the television commentators; they're sworn enemies of mine; I hate to do this, but you don't leave me much of a choice. First of all, Howard K. Smith is a friend of mine; I've known him a great number of years. In that same article, he defines himself as a left of center liberal. There's something strange about conservatism in America. Nobody wants to admit he is a conservative. I went to see Attorney General John Mitchell; in the first 20 minutes of a 40 minute discussion he was trying to persuade me that he was a liberal. And he cited evidence: the fact that he was a bonds lawyer working on public housing; "If that isn't in the liberal spectrum," he said, "I don't know what is."

I think it's perfectly reputable to be a conservative and wholesome, and I don't think Howard K. Smith should try somehow to cop a plea by saying he's a left-of-center liberal himself! I think the question really ought to be answered by Jim Hagerty, because Howard K. Smith is with his network, and he knows Howard K. Smith. I just want to make that the preliminary comment.

JAMES HAGERTY: Let me try without going into personalities. I think what is basically at the root of Howard's article is what normally happens when an Administration comes into office that is trying to move that Administration and the country from labels—if you wish to call it by labels—from the left to the moderate center. This is nothing new in our history. But when you try to do that, the proponents of left-of-center are going to be the vociferous opponents of any move that the President is trying to make. I think this has been really the basic question in the Supreme Court decisions or the Supreme Court appointments. And, when you try to move from the left to the center, you get this dialogue and this discussion within our country.

My friends in the Washington Press Club are to a great degree left of center, but I don't quarrel with that. That is the way it is. But the honest ones, and there are a great many of them, don't think there are not; the honest ones are reporting and interpreting without their own personal thinking in their stories. You may disagree with this, but I think I know them; I think I know most of them.

I am quite sure then there is a political argument of a shift of the Government from one force to another force. Historically, it has always been the kind of debate and dialogue that you get in these circumstances.

JOSEPH P. B. McMURRAY: A little question of history which you may be able to shed some light on: the Cuba situation. You recall that President Eisenhower, I thought, invited Mr. Castro up to the United States, and I always wondered to what extent the White House was aware of what really was going on in Cuba. Why, if they knew as much as I believe they must have known, why did they not share this with the American people?

JAMES HAGERTY: Well, you are wrong on the facts. The President of the United States did *not* invite Mr. Castro to come up to the United States. The newspaper publishers did for their convention. And Mr. Eisenhower was just as surprised and indignant as quite a few other people were. He came up on invitation to a convention, and *not* by invitation from the Government. While he was in Washington, D. C., there was no conversation formally with Mr. Castro, although someone in the State Department did see him informally and briefly.

Then he went to New York, and he and his staff did a lot of chicken plucking in his hotel room on 125th Street. He moved from one hotel, and went to the Hotel Theresa in Harlem where he tried to make headway with what he thought was a sympathetic black population. He found out it was quite the other way around. So he was not here by invitation of the Government.

I would think the Eisenhower Administration, the Kennedy Administration and the other Administrations had very good knowledge of what he was up to. The intelligence apparatus of the United States is getting better and better. It's a pretty darn good outfit. Even though our CIA is much maligned these days, they still know their business. So you can't blame any Administration that Castro came to the United States.

JOHN H. MARTIN: About nine o'clock this morning we had a quote with regard to the ability to make abstract that which is concrete; it occurs to me we have been doing a very good job of it, and it is extremely interesting, here at the seminar on the Office of the President. However, I would like to hear the distinguished gentlemen of the press table make comments as to what would they do differently if anything. How does the Office of the President adjust to all the real facts in the real world, and the way the job is being performed?

JAMES HAGERTY: One of the arguments that I have with some people, including the news media, is that it is completely ridiculous to try to compare one Presidential term, or one President, with another. Situations change. Problems change.

Let's take the Administration I was associated with. After President Eisenhower made a settlement regarding Korea, there was no place in this world where we had the international problems which the Administrations have been involved in from 1961 on. The same thing was true of domestic problems. Our major . . . MAJOR . . . civil rights confrontation was Little Rock. And Little Rock seems to be way in the past and rather minute compared to a Watts, to a Newark and other confrontations you have at the present time.

So each President determines the tone and the policies of his Administration. He is the indisputable leader of his Administration. He makes the basic decisions—no one else. I've heard a lot of talk aimed at me to the effect that I made policies. I did nothing except what my bosss told me to do—and say. And if I didn't, I wouldn't have been in that job very long. You just can't compare the present day to the 50's or the early 60's. So in the Executive Branch of the Government, it is the President who decides the policy, and it is the combined members of his Administration that carry it out.

The news media has the right and obligation to try to write honestly and think honestly. It is necessary to the decisions made . . . so that the American public can know what is happening and be informed from day to day. Every National Administration is called to account by the public every four years. Each President has an entirely different situation to face; he decides which way he wants to go, and then *he* is called to account every four years.

GORDON HOXIE: I'm glad to hear the question from our friend John Martin of California, because it was precisely what I wanted to say. May I just pursue it this much further. I agree with what Jim Hagerty said, i.e. each President is dealing in a different environment with a different set of problems, and, therefore, comparisons do indeed become dangerous, sometimes invidious. However, we have in this room persons who have dealt rather closely with Presidents at least from the FDR period; FDR, Truman, Eisenhower, Kennedy, Johnson, Nixon. Granted the difference in problems, I wonder if we could speak a little bit to the matter of attitudes and style between these people from a certain historic perspective which many of you can give to this. Could we give just a little bit of historical perspective and comparison on the style of these Presidents and their attitude towards their office as viewed by the news media? Maybe it's unfair to ask for a report card as to who came out the best, and I am not suggesting that, but could we get a little historic comparison from FDR on?

GEORGE REEDY: There's one very important point which I think is absolutely basic to the whole discussion. Herb Klein said last night that the Presidency is a very personal position; this is not a remark to be tossed off lightly. If you don't understand the full meaning, you'll never understand anything about the Presidency. The point is the President is one of the few men in the world who owns his job. He only owns it for about four years, and I think there are times when he thinks he made a bad deal. But, as Pete says, nobody drives you into the White House; you have to go freely. And to try to get an idea of how the White House reacts to a press problem is a complete waste of time and utter futility. What it amounts to is how *one man and one only* reacts to a problem. The way the White House will react is not as an institution that automatically evolves a policy towards a press problem, the way a corporation will evolve or for that matter the way a government agency will evolve.

Government agencies are institutions, but I don't think there's much institution-wise in the White House—except for such things as the press office, and that's largely because of the airplane schedules or the complications of the electronic equipment. Also, there are institutional characteristics in the protocol arrangement and formal banquets and that sort of thing.

But, if you start rating Presidents on the basis of how they reacted to the press, or how their style differed—you have to realize that in a very peculiar sense this is a man, not the institution responding to outside stimuli. We live in an institutionalized world, and it's a little hard for most of us to comprehend that there's one institution so big, so powerful—two and a half million people—budgets nearly 200 billion . . . that sort of thing, and which one man, in a very peculiar sense owns.

I can recall the FDR press conferences. I didn't cover many of them because I was a cub reporter in those days, but I covered some of them. And I think if you are talking about style, FDR had it. He was able to take this banter back and forth. Of course, he could get pretty mad; he gave a correspondent an iron cross once right in the middle of the war. And there were a few other occasions when he got right irritated. He wasn't afraid of the press and often played games with it. I can recall the third term—he delighted in leading reporters into a blind alley where they would come out speculating from some remark he made that he was going to go out for a third term. And once the story was printed, he exploded in derision and demonstrated to the press that the remark had an altogether different meaning.

Harry Truman was very direct; very blunt. I don't think he

loved to fight with the press, but he came in and fought if there was something he didn't like. But somehow I don't think the press was ever really mad at him. In my experience in Washington, I think the President who, as a person, was most popular with newspapermen was Harry S. Truman. They all liked him deeply and personally. There's a lesson here a lot of Presidents could take to heart, because President Truman had a press that was almost unanimously against him during the 1948 campaign. I've never seen a campaign in which the press was more unanimous. And yet, individual reporters thought Harry was a great guy. Those who were around him in those days and covered him were extremely warm.

In terms of President Eisenhower, Jim Hagerty is quite correct; as Press Secretary he certainly didn't do anything Eisenhower didn't want him to—and why should he? He's not there to be a minister of information, nor was I . . . nor was any other press secretary. You are there as the President's spokesman. When you get to the point where you can no longer speak for the President in good conscience, you leave; it's that simple. But as long as you're there, you aren't there to give some version of something that's not the President's version—or the White House version, if you want to call it that. The only reason for the press secretary's job is that the President cannot deal with the press 24 hours a day. You have to have somebody that acts as a stand-in for him.

I think that in President Kennedy's case you have a man that did a brilliant job of what you might call press relations. He certainly had a lot of devoted followers among the press. I'm not sure his press relations, which really were excellent, weren't poor public relations; I'm not so sure he did too good a job where the public was concerned. I have a strong feeling that he would have been in grave difficulty in 1964 . . . in many parts of the country.

President Johnson, who, I think, was the strongest of all men and an individual of great will power, had an extremely explosive relationship with the press. Because he was less likely than others to back away from a mistake, he accentuated bad reactions. He would insist on pursuing a number of things which another man wouldn't have pursued. It's too early to rate President Nixon. What has impressed me so far were some inspired stories that appeared a few months ago explaining how good his press relations were. I have one rule of thumb—when there are stories about how good your press relations are, you haven't got any. When you really have good press relations, nobody notices it. What they notice is what a good job you're doing.

PETER LISAGOR: I like the question because it comes from a general interest in the President, the man and his style. We in the newspaper business tend to confuse style and substance. I said we probably practice more psychiatry without a license than any other profession in the world. If the President sweats on the upper lip in a press conference, by God, we're going to read meaning into it. People don't sweat on their upper lip unless there's something wrong.

It disturbs me a great deal, because what you really want to know about is the difference between, say a swash-buckling administration and one in which the President and his family like meat loaf for dinner or how Jackie's souffles came out . . . and those kinds of things . . . and it's fascinating . . . it's interesting; we like to find out about it ourselves. But, you don't want to let that get in the way of your real judgment of the President and what he's doing in his job.

Let me just tell you a story that might amuse you: Harry Truman was an earthy little fellow. He once went to a horticultural show with his wife and a friend of his wife. Many of you have heard this story—I see the anticipatory smiles. He would stop and say this is a wonderful plant; you must use wonderful horse manure on this. After three or four times, the lady accompanying them said, "Bess, couldn't you get the President to say fertilizer." She said, "My God, it took me 25 years to get him to say 'manure'." But we don't remember Truman just for this story. We remember Truman for the Marshall Plan and for the many other things he did, and I think that's the way it ought to be.

In George's [Reedy] presence, let me also say most of the press have a very hard nose about Lyndon Johnson. They reported all sorts of things about him, outlandish things. You know about them, because he made himself vulnerable by making himself open, but I daresay if we sat down and wrote a thoughtful piece about his Presidency, we wouldn't write about that kind of thing. We'd really write about what he tried to do, very constructive things he tried to do, very destructive things he did. And I think, as Jim [Hagerty] said, there's a very great, wide, deep element of professionalism in the press in Washington, and it overcomes and surmounts all the bias, liberal or conservative, that's there.

Now there are people whose job is to purvey opinion, liberal, conservative, or what have you—anarchist, socialist, nihilist. But most of us are newspapermen with certain standards for our craft, and we know how responsible it is; we know how necessary it is, how crucial it is, that we do a responsible job. I don't want to make a brief for the press in Washington; there are some real bums among us; we know that. There are people who thrive on the kind of stories I've related here, only the worst stories; they thrive on gossip. But, basically, we are concerned with what the President does, what he says, what his motives are, what his purposes are. And we have, despite what many of you may think, we have a sense of professionalism about reporting.

GEORGE REEDY: Pete, [Lisagor] there's one little point I want to make. I used to derogate from myself all of these gossip stories. I still don't like gossip. But I think there is tremendous interest in the little things about the President—what he likes to eat, how he talks, how he dresses, what his wife is like. I think this is a matter of absorbing interest to the American people, and I think they are right in having an absorbing interest in him. What they're really trying to do is to get a picture of him, and there is a form of folk wisdom that holds that the way a man acts and the nature of his family, tells you something about the man's character.

Now, for instance, consider the story you have just told about the horse manure. I don't regard that as just a piece of gossip; it does tell something about Harry S. Truman. He was earthy; he was a man of strength and determination and even his wife couldn't force him into a style that wasn't *him*. He was going to be Harry S. Truman all the way. He was not going to concede anything—even to a gentility he thought was not in him and in fact was not.

I'm not quite as sour on this idea that these little stories about the President are just trivial chit chat, or that a correspondent shouldn't pay any attention to such matter and what the people should have are only the serious and profound analyses. I think Lyndon Johnson's style tells about the man—I think Nixon's style tells a lot about the man. I think Eisenhower's style told a lot about him. I don't think this style thing should be derogated.

PETER LISAGOR: You misunderstand, George. Whether he beats his wife tells a little about character; what he wears in his study tells less. I read with great fascination and I'll report as much of it as I can, but I just wanted to make the point that we shouldn't confuse style with substance in the President's public acts. And that often happens, and I think it happened in a major way with your boss.

JAMES P. McFARLAND: I'd like to supplement Mr. Martin's question and make this preliminary remark directed to that question. One, I would like to say that any institution grows and becomes strong by reason of constant testing. Second, I can't visualize the democratic process or our free enterprise system without a great opportunity for communication. And that must be through the media and, in my judgment, through free media.

I get to the point as to whether we can judge ability for the press to survive by its credibility or by the Administration's credibility on how well it performs its assigned function in the society. I'd like to direct the question related to Mr. Martin's question. How do you foresee any Administration, forgetting the style for the moment, better organizing to use these great capabilities of free news?

JAMES HAGERTY: I think we have to get back to what I referred to before. Each Administration takes advantage of the advances in communication which are really increasing in geometric rather the arithmetic progression over the years. Let me look ahead a little and make a prediction. In FDR's time, the press secretary had to face the radio. In President Eisenhower's time I had to face TV to take advantage of the increased facilities and technical advances that were developing in mass communication. By contrast, we are now in the international satellite age—there are two, one over the Atlantic and one over the Pacific, 23,000 miles out in space, and they work. Finally there will be a third one, the triangle, over the Indian Ocean.

In 1968, the opening and closing ceremonies of the Mexican Olympic Games were watched live around this world by 500 million people—between the tape and the film, we guess about 750 million people. How many people do you think would watch the President of the United States sitting in his office in Washington, providing the climate was right, and the leader of the Soviet Union sitting in the Kremlin, discussing world affairs? It's going to happen—it's going to happen sooner than you think.

We have instantaneous capabilities in television, but we have no permanent record. You can see a World Series on TV but you also like to read the story. You can hear the President speak, but you like to have the text of that speech through the printed media to analyze it after you hear it. Each Administration since Mr. Roosevelt—which is really the start of the modern period of communication—has spent a great many hours studying, consulting with the news media, and on their own on trying to increase the flow of information from the White House or other sections of the Administration, not only to the people of our country but much more important to the people of the world.

Each man who heads our Government does things in his way, but he has professional assistance in the communication field. What we did in the 1950's is going to be elemental for what the next President is going to be doing and the next and the next. In our own country, it's not just the networks; you're going to have CATV, cable TV; you're going to have many other facilities that are going to be added to the communication capabilities of Washington and the President of the United States. All of us in the news media, in newspapers, in magazines, radio, television, constitute a whole. If any are taken out or weakened, it blemishes the information that is available to the people of our country and the people of the world. So this is an evolving process. Ten years from now you are not going to recognize the communications possibilities in our country; it will be so different and so extensive.

We can move anything on communications satellites. For

example, you don't have to move word by word over tele-graph wires; you can move a page of copy at a time. You can move photographs, anything. This is going to happen. That's about the only way I can answer your question. The people who work for the President and the people who work for the news media, are not too distant from each other. There are many times when we sit down and talk these problems over. All of us are working for one major thing—the advancement of com-munications to the people.

PETER LISAGOR: Bob Semple has a more direct answer to your question. My thoughts on July 20, 1969; I realized then how obsolete the printed word had become. You sat in your living room and watched men on the moon, and you watched the President of the United States pick up a telephone and talk to them. Just think about that for a minute.

ROBERT SEMPLE: I was just going to try to address myself to the concrete question dealing with the theme of the confer-ence; how does the White House organize itself to get various jobs done? This question deals with how does the White House organize itself, how does the Executive Branch organize itself to take advantage of, make the best use of, the media that presently exists without going into Jim's vision of the fu-ture which is perhaps going to require a whole new set of arrangements.

I should mention this one thing that Herb Klein does. This unusual office, the Office of the Director of Communications, is to service a lot of people who simply do not have the money to have Washington correspondents. And I think the President recognized where his constituency was—a lot of them are out there in the small towns with newspapers where they can't afford to send a man to Washington. He recognized also that these fellows had to rely for many years on the ma-jor wire services: the Associated Press, United Press Interna-tional. What he has really instructed Herb to do is to make certain that these smaller institutions get all the background material they need to make some kind of an informed judg-ment on the policies the Administration is viewing.

Now this is a major institutional change in the way the White House goes about dealing with the problem of com-munications. That's my only point. I think to a certain extent,

Herb concedes he's not in the business of disseminating unflattering news about the President of the United States around the country. And, therefore, it has not made reporting an obsolete skill. At the same time for complicated issues, such as the welfare issue, he does derive an enormous amount of information. Admittedly, it's the Administration's own information about what the program is designed to do; thereby making the job a little bit easier for the small town newspaper editor in Colorado who is seeking to explain an issue to his readers or the local TV station in a small town someplace else. This is one concrete response to the problem, and I just thought I'd throw that in.

GEORGE REEDY: Bob, I would like to add one cautionary note. As stated a little while ago, the White House is not really a body that has evolved in these things in an institutional sense. The next President is entirely capable of abolishing the post. The next President is entirely capable of going back to a sole press secretary and abolishing even that if he wants to, because these things do not persist as they do in most institutions.

Let me give you one concrete example. When I was Press Secretary, one of the things done was to set up this TV room in the White House—the thesis being we were going to have warm cameras ready all day long. This cost the networks quite a bit of dough to set up, and keep the crews there. I think that if that had happened in any other institution, it would have developed into a tremendous factor in the communications process in our country. It certainly would have developed in any government agency, because obviously the facilities are useful. What happened? There was a flurry in which it was used quite a bit for three or four weeks; after that the networks just went on paying for crews that sat there and cameras that were kept warm, with neither being used to any significant purpose. The President had decided he didn't want to use it.

With regard to Jim Hagerty's point, we will have a day when the President of the United States holds a discussion with the Prime Minister of the Soviet Union. I think that might demand quite an audience, might even outdo the men on the moon. Who knows? But if at the last minute the President de-

cides not to talk to him, he doesn't talk to him; it's that simple. This is not an institution where somebody sees that something is worthwhile and therefore, it goes on.

There is in this institution the capacity for a type of change,
a change that can be made whether it's wise, or it's stupid, or
it's simple, or it's forward, advance, or going back. You must
not forget that point.

JAMES HAGERTY: On behalf of Bob Semple, Peter Lisagor,
George Reedy, Herb Klein, Tommy Corcoran, and myself,
thank you very much for coming. We stand adjourned until
the afternoon session on Domestic Policy.

CHAPTER III

The Office of the President: Formulation and Implementation of Domestic Policy

GORDON HOXIE: This afternoon we turn our attention to something of the heart and substance of the matter; to the White House and the Formulation and Implementation of Domestic Policy. In doing so, we have a panel bringing breadth and historical perspective to the subject.

It is my pleasure to introduce the moderator of the panel, my very good friend, Judge Leonard P. Moore, Second Circuit Court, United States Appeals. Judge Moore is a native of that community in the middlewest which has its own unusual qualities, Evanston, Illinois, home of Northwestern University and the National Headquarters of the WCTU. But the good Judge is associated with neither. He is an alumnus of Amherst College and of the Columbia University School of Law.

I can personally attest that the Judge has been described in the annals of the Columbia Law School as one of its most brilliant alumni. This is no mean feat when you recall the history of that law school, numbering as it does among its alumni at least two former Presidents of the United States and two former Chief Justices of the United States.

After thirty years of the practice of law, he served from 1953-57 as United States Attorney for the Eastern District of New York. Since that time he has been a most distinguished member of our second highest federal court. The warmth of Judge Moore's friendship and his musicianship (as a jazz band member) is matched by his illustrious community service in the Brooklyn Institute of Arts and Sciences and other cultural organizations. Members of the Conference, I present Judge Leonard P. Moore.

LEONARD P. MOORE: After Gordon's introduction I was about to say, who me? I had prepared a preamble for our discussion. It was somewhere between 30 and 45 minutes long, as I recall. After reading it over, I realized how well I had done, because the preamble for any discussion should be one that ends in utter confusion! Out of that you are then supposed to solve the problem.

We have Mr. Lee C. White. Coming from Illinois, as I do, I think it's a very fine thing to be born in Nebraska, where he got his electrical engineering degree. Well, you think that might be enough for anybody; in my books it's too much, but no, he then goes on, also at the University of Nebraska, and gets a law degree as well. At that particular point I said to him, you must obviously be a patent lawyer, but he ended up as Chairman of the Federal Power Commission, and I don't think he was personally responsible for that blackout we had in New York!

A practicing student of government, Mr. White was a member of the Hoover Commission on Governmental Organization in 1954-55; also during the Eisenhower Administration he served as administrative assistant to Senator John Sherman Cooper, a Republican, lest you forget. Then he made the transition to Assistant Special Counsel to President Kennedy and Counsel to President Johnson before assuming the position of Chairman of the Federal Power Commission. Now with the return of the Republicans to the White House, he is practicing law in Washington, D.C., and like another member of our panel who was already introduced this morning, he is the distinguished counselor to many.

Then we have Dr. Charles L. Clapp, and he's been around political science all over the countryside from Florida to California. Rich in governmental experience, he has taught Political Science, written a book on Congress, served on the Government Studies Staff of the Brookings Institution and has had considerable Capitol Hill experience, most recently as Legislative Assistant to Senator Leverett Saltonstall of Massachusetts. Now he has a most important position on the President's staff, in charge of the Task Forces.

And we have Professor Louis Koenig, New York University, author of learned books relating to the Presidency; he will probably be willing to inscribe any one of his books that are available. Dr. Koenig is a member of the Educator's Committee for our sponsoring organization, the Library of Presidential Papers, soon I understand to be renamed as the Center for the Study of the Presidency.

Next we have another member rich in governmental experience. Long with the Air Force and then with the Federal Power Commission, Mr. Murray Comarow is now Executive Director of the President's Council on Executive Organization.

Without further ado, I would like to call upon Mr. White.

LEE C. WHITE: Judge Moore, fellow panel members and participants in this seminar. This morning's panel is a tough act to follow. They had at least three advantages that I am aware of. The first is that everybody was fresh; the second is that they were talented, bright, clever, humorous, witty and charming; and the third is, they were talking about a topic that has broad general interest to all people. People in Sioux Falls, South Dakota, wake up thinking about television, thinking about news, and thinking about the conflict that sometimes comes between the Government and the information media. They rarely wake up thinking about domestic policy formulation and how it takes place in the White House.

But, quite obviously, as was clear from this morning's discussion about the contrast between style and substance, and the way they meld or in some cases repel; it becomes extraordinarily important to think about the *purposes* of our Government. And, our Government, obviously, is not set up to afford an individual the opportunity to manifest his style, as attractive or unattractive as it might be. Rather, it is keyed to the accomplishment of governmental *objectives*.

This is the topic, of which we this afternoon have one subtopic, and there will be others who will follow in this seminar on the accomplishment of governmental objectives. It's a highly interesting and fascinating pre-occupation for those of us who have participated in or who have observed the process. I should note for you that I had the pleasure of working for two Presidents: President John F. Kennedy and President Lyndon B. Johnson.

The role that I played had a title, but as George Reedy's book suggests, it's a misnomer. I was Assistant Special Counsel to President Kennedy and Special Counsel to President Johnson, but please don't be confused by the names. They really mean extraordinarily little; far more important is who does what? And, I think I can characterize my role in the Kennedy White House by saying that I was a part of the [Theodore C.]

Sorensen apparatus. Ted Sorensen, who was Special Counsel to President Kennedy, had an informal portfolio known as "the domestic policy and program bag."

In this particular "bag" were all the activities that you would expect; it was the preparation of legislative programs; preparation of special messages to deliver those programs to the Congress for its consideration; working with the Congressional liaison segment to see to it that those programs were moved along; it worried somewhat with the policy issues that arose out of old programs as well as new ones that were being formulated; obviously concerning itself with some of the problems, or dilemmas or crises that inevitably arise to take the time and the attention and the skills and the wisdom, and, if he has any, the good fortune of the President to handle. No President, obviously, can perform all of the functions that are assigned him by himself, and he, of course, requires, therefore, a staff. In this particular spot in the Kennedy White House, I had the good fortune to be in that particular part of the apparatus which concerned itself with the domestic programs.

We did not then have a Domestic Affairs Council, along the lines of that proposed by President Nixon to the Congress. We had, however, an informal mechanism which served roughly the same function as I conceive the more formal proposal for a Domestic Affairs Council. Many ideas came to that little body of men, and let me indicate how small it was. Ted Sorensen, who was the Special Counsel, had in his immediate office three people, Mike [Meyer] Feldman, Dick [Richard W.] Goodwin and myself. This isn't to say that there were not others who contributed. But, in the White House Staff proper, that was the cadre, the small funnel through which an awful lot of material, a lot of programs, a lot of substance, was compelled to pass.

Many of the programs came from the campaign of the winning candidate. Quite obviously commitments made by the Presidential candidate are the starting points for his program to be put together, and that was certainly the case in the Administration of President Kennedy. Many of them came from task forces along the lines that Dr. Clapp will discuss later and that are now being used by President Nixon to help formulate some of his views; and, indeed, there is nothing so unique or creative about the idea of setting up task forces. Many of them in the early Kennedy years flowed from groups that had worked with Candidate Kennedy; their ideas and recommendations moved into the governmental blood stream, and it was our role to keep them clean; refining, modifying and in some cases outright rejecting.

In addition, there are other sources of program idea and content, not the least of which is the Congress which proposes a great body of legislation every year; some of those proposals ultimately become a part of the President's program; but, even if they don't become part of the President's program, there is a need to have an administration position and attitude on them. And so, this, too, was one of the responsibilities of this group.

I think I may mislead you slightly if I suggest that all activities of this character were performed by this small core. Quite obviously, the role played by the other people in the White House Staff, by the Budget Bureau, the Council of Economic Advisors, and, far more importantly, by the Cabinet Officers and Agency heads, had to be folded into it.

I'm talking now in the narrowest sense about the White House Staff that worked most closely with the President in the formulation of these programs. Putting them together was comparatively easy during that period for the reasons I suggested. Many of them were put together in that fashion; namely from an outgrowth of the campaign.

President Kennedy also had another advantage that I don't quite see in the Nixon White House. Let me tell you what the advantage was. That is that *Senator* John Kennedy had picked up, through his Senate career and his campaign for the Presidency, a group of people with whom he had worked very closely, and who themselves had worked closely with each other; so that, by the time that he was President-Elect, it was possible for him to designate a small group to serve as liaison with the Eisenhower Administration; and let it be recorded, as it has been more formally many times before, there was great cooperation from President Eisenhower's staff. There was some sense of delight on their part as they handed over all of these problems to the new Administration!

The programs that emerged had to come through a couple of other refining processes. We regarded our role as that of coming up with the perfect, the ideal, the unflawed approach to each of the major problem areas. This took the form, as I suggested earlier, of special messages, but we had to also work with those whose political instincts, whose jobs, involved an assessment of the practical reality of any particular proposal, and there was an extremely close liaison with Larry O'Brien's group. Larry [Lawrence F. subsequently Postmaster General of the United States] O'Brien was the President's Special Assistant in charge of Congressional liaison and a man who was consulted not only after a message was prepared and a bill was submitted and the trouble had arisen, but also in the preparation. And, there was, and I don't think there's any mystery about it, nor should there be an embarrassment about it, there was always some trimming, some moving away from the ideal to what was hoped to be the obtainable, i.e. the achievable.

As to the success of this operation, I'll leave that to you. I don't know if I'm the best one to judge. I think that many of us feel that a superb set of programs were submitted to the Congress by President Kennedy. There was not a great deal of accomplishment of legislative success in some regards. In others there were notable achievements. Certainly a great deal of housing legislation, economic relief legislation, was enacted; and, of course, we had a great deal of pride in the fact that the economic situation did brighten and continued until recent months to be on an upswing.

There is, I think, a tendency on the part of many observers to regard the accomplishments of President Johnson in 1964 and 1965 as being attributable to his legislative skills. May I say that he does have tremendous legislative skills, and I think in large measure that assessment is correct. I think it's also reasonable to assume that a great deal of the program that was enacted had come through an excellent refining process, if I may say so, and I think I can, because my own role was relatively minor.

One of the great advantages of being on the White House Staff is an opportunity to see what is going on, and in a sense to observe what is taking place. As I viewed it, there were rings around the President. The President has all the authority assigned to him by the Constitution and by statutes, and it simply isn't in his ability to do everything; this requires him to rely on helpers, aides, and staff. So the tight inner ring is there; they're the ones who get wet when the President sneezes; they are the ones who feel guilty if they are away for a weekend; they are the ones whose telephone systems at home have to be altered so there will be no delay when the White House or the President calls; they are the ones who, indeed, carry the heavier burden.

Then, there are a few other rings, concentric to the President, that afford the opportunity to participate but not in such an intense fashion. Fortunately, I happened to be in one of the close in rings but not so close in that I felt the great heavy burdens and problems. This may, therefore, to some extent, weaken my objectivity or power to observe, and, quite obviously, anything I do say this afternoon is limited to what I have seen myself.

That, I think, goes to a very recent dispute that has emerged in the press. That is the role of various individuals, including the President, in handling of the Vietnam turn around. I think it is fair to say that many people have a piece of what happened. But no one knows all of what took place better than the one who decided. The President himself was certainly standing in the best position, and thus his assessment should be most valuable. This isn't to say that his powers of observation or recollection are flawless. Indeed, I've heard some criticism leveled at President Johnson's assessment of precisely what did happen. But, nevertheless, the principle is valid: namely, that you must take any thing that any one individual gives you about the Presidency and recognize that he is limited by where he stood and by his own capacity for narrowness.

After President Kennedy's death, a project was undertaken which I think will be of interest to you in your Library of Presidential Papers, i.e. the Center for the Study of the Presidency. I refer to the so called "oral" history in which individuals who had played any particular role in the Kennedy Administration were asked to record on tape and then edit their observations; what they saw, how it happened, how a particular thing came to pass. I was both interviewed and served as an interviewer, and I found in both instances a basic problem. That is, when you ask somebody, and I was one of the somebodies asked, too, it is very easy to begin to talk about what *you did*. Now, what I think is more interesting is what the *President did*. The tendency to always translate things into a personal, first person, subjective description has to be overcome to the extent that these oral histories and studies will be of any value.

There are a couple of points about the White House Staff of a general character that I would like to refer to. These have to do with the characteristics that I think are of great interest in terms of who served on the staff. Organizational charts are extremely important, and how the work flows is significant, but I would urge those who are in the appointing business to really pay an awful lot of attention to *ability*. I refer to ability in terms not only of natural intellectual equipment, but experience, and judgment and personality characteristics that permit a man to serve in a staff role and to recognize that his function is to serve the principal and not necessarily to establish his own individual identity and become a force in his own right.

I suggest that a White House staff man is only a reflector; he is only a user of another man's power, another man's authority, another man's responsibility. Parenthetically, let me note the great pleasure that I sensed when I left the White House staff and assumed a job in which, right or wrong, it was mine. It was a great lift to me personally to recognize that whatever decision was rendered in my name, was in my name. It was my vote, and I didn't have to worry about the impact on somebody else. This, as far as I'm concerned, was a great step; although, quite obviously, as staff roles go there is no better staff job than that of White House staff.

I would comment on a couple of points that were mentioned this morning. First, with regard to the Presidential job: I too, agree, having had the chance to observe both Presidents Kennedy and Johnson, that I don't think the job is so horrendous. I don't think it is beyond the capability of one individual. Obviously it is a very tough and demanding job, but there is no reason for me to have concluded that it's incapable of being handled by any single individual. It simply is not. Many of you run extremely complicated corporations. The principles of management and decision making are different, but only in specifics. The basic concepts are, in my view, substantially identical.

Secondly, there is an aspect of White House staff developing, building, or assessing that has to do with how broad or how narrow the assignments are. One of the jobs that fell to me, in the case of President Kennedy and President Johnson, was to work with them on civil rights matters, but that was only one of the assignments. There is, I think, a danger in having an assistant for a particular or a very narrow activity which has a constituency. I think that a White House staff man's constituency ought to be limited to one individual, namely his boss, the President.

It should be comforting to the individual to know that if one particular group, for example, just to use them: If the Veterans' organizations believe that this staff man is doing a lousy job, I don't think that they should have a right to go to the President and say that this guy is doing a lousy job and you must fire him. Let me take that back. They have the right to go, but I don't think that the President ought to believe that this is the judgment that he ought to accept at face value. The head of the Veterans' Administration has that job. He has the job of catering to, listening to, and working with the Veterans' organizations. The White House staff man ought to be, as I see it, standing in the President's shoes. He ought to view things from the President's view point.

I remember clearly that one of the earlier responsibilities I had was handling District of Columbia matters. President Kennedy called me in and said that he had a suggestion from a very prominent newspaper man in Washington that what Washington needed was a full-time District of Columbia assistant. And he asked what did I think. And, I said that I thought it was a very bad recommendation for two reasons. One is that the poor guy is going to have to satisfy this city, and you've got a whole group of commissioners to do that, and perhaps more importantly, the commissioners would be undercut. If the city believes that they can go to a White House staff man and avoid the normal processes, all the business will wind up there. President Kennedy grunted, and I walked away; the next thing I heard was a phone call from him about two days later, and he said, would you please work up the press release, Charlie [Charles A.] Horsky's going to be my Assistant for District of Columbia Affairs!

I had quite an excellent record, particularly with President Johnson. He liked recommendations to be on memos rather than in person, and there were a whole series of them in which he checked the "disapproved" box. There was one time when I felt so strongly about something that I reversed my recommendation in the hope that it would continue and that was the only time that month he took my recommendation! That, incidentally goes to a somewhat more serious point, which is the role of the staff *not* to remake, at least as I view it, the President into the staff man's image of what the President ought to be. Whenever you start in a staff role to begin to save the principal from himself, I think you are courting trouble.

George Reedy has written copiously about the difficulty of telling the President, "No." We had a standing gag in President Johnson's time, "Of course I told the President 'No,' just the other day. He asked me if I had any complaints about the way he was running things." There are devices, tactics, techniques that are developed by people for telling the President that his fly is unzipped. It is particularly difficult to tell a President, particularly a strong, strong willed President— as was the case with President Johnson, and is true of most men who wind up in the Presidency. These aren't just run of the mill people who are selected at random. Most men who get into the Presidency have passed through a selective process and, for the most part, they are strong men. Well, nobody makes a career of telling the boss that he's wrong. But, there are techniques, not the least of which is to push all the blue chips out on the table on those big ones, when you think you must.

I, personally, believe that people should not only go into the White House with some background in government, deep background if at all possible, but they should go there with a willingness to leave soon, soon meaning 3 or 4 years. Also, they should recognize that on the big issues if they can't live with their President's decision, then what they better do is walk away. It's tough, and I, myself, never got to the point where I thought there were some decisions that were so basic to the nation and so wrong that it was up to me to resign in protest. And that is, of course, a drastic step. But the concept is there in terms of the mental attitude that the staff man should take to the boss if at all possible and feasible.

I've spent a little time about the way the Kennedy domestic problems and programs were formulated, and were fully implemented. In the Johnson era, there were sort of successors to Sorensen, although there is hardly ever a one for one replacement in a staff job. People are different, and the President uses them in different fashions. But in a rough sort of fashion Bill [D.] Moyers took over the Sorensen role of coordinating domestic programs and policies. Then Joe [Joseph A., Jr.] Califano served to the end of the Johnson years. I gather from news accounts that Mr. [John D.] Ehrlichman, who was to have been with us today, was the direct successor in that chain, recognizing if you must, the inevitable differences.

As to whether or not the formulation of this into a highly structured council would be useful, I really have serious doubts. I'm sorry I won't be able to listen to tomorrow's discussion, but my own instincts tell me that it'd be better not to be so structured. But that's all right because the President will operate the way the President wants to operate, and he should. He is the President.

As we said earlier today, Presidential personality fuses itself into the staff, and that's the way it should be and must be. It's hard to know how good a job you do in those spots. There aren't conventional measuring devices. Hits and misses are not usually available, in such an imprecise and amorphous type of assignment. I guess the ultimate test is the success of the particular administration of which you are a part.

Another aspect of White House staff responsibilities to which I'd like to devote a minute is that of knowing how to relate to the President in terms of what goes to him and what does not go to him. I think one of the activities that this proposed Domestic Affairs Council will concern itself with is which issues must go to the President for his personal decision. Obviously, this is a gray area; in the middle is where all the trouble is. There are some that clearly should not and some that clearly should go to the President. That gray area sometimes gets pretty large; it's not so narrow a band, perhaps, as you imagine it or you would like it to be. I really don't know if there is any formulation that helps, but again there is the ultimate test of what happened.

I remember a call from President Kennedy who said to me: "Did you tell the Defense Department that they could," and then he listed a policy; it was clear to me that I wished to hell the answer to that question were "no." I would just like to have been under the table, although I'm sure you can imagine that it frequently gets crowded under that table, whenever a President is trying to find out who did what. Well, my answer to him was "Yes," that I told Adam Yarmolinsky that what they proposed to do in that particular situation at 4 o'clock on Friday afternoon sounded reasonable to me, but I certainly didn't think this was going to establish a department-wide policy. The President then said, "Why didn't you ask me about it?" And as soon as he asked the question, it was perfectly evident that I should have asked the President about it. He was not inaccessible, and I don't even remember whether I had a good excuse like "I tried to but O'Donnell [Kenneth O.] wouldn't let me in," or that "I was told you were busy." There wasn't any point in it. The lesson was crystal clear to me on that one that a mistake had been made. And it was also rather evident that the President would have reached a different decision on the question had it been put to him.

I point this out not to suggest that there's a whole series of these; I don't know how many of them one particular staff man could stand; I hope this is out of a spirit of candor that if you make a few, you learn your way. If you make too many, you better find yourself something else to do, because that's not your dish of tea, and you shouldn't be there.

This, I think, goes to what I said earlier about the selection of staff. To the extent that the President is able to pull in people who know him, who read his signals, who have access to him, I think he is better served. Frankly, I am somewhat concerned to see the large numbers of staff people that President Nixon seems to have, partly because it must inevitably breed bureaucratic processes and problems of communications. That in itself is not as productive as it ought to be. I hope that I am misreading that, and that somebody will either this afternoon or tomorrow shed some light on it, because I am limited only by what I have read. I have no personal knowledge about it, but it doesn't quite fit comfortably with my own personal experiences and observations.

I think I have used much more time than was allotted to me; I see that all of these copious notes where it says say something humorous and use an old joke such as was used this morning; well, it does not make me think I ought to continue.

Even though, the introduction was very limited, we are very privileged to have Mr. Corcoran here on this panel as an extra starter. The question was put to me this morning, "Do you think it would be possible to get Mr. Corcoran started to say something?" I said that, "to my personal observation, that's not the problem." The reason that one can kid Mr. Corcoran is that his own activities are so legendary; he really is one of the early strong staff people, and we are privileged to have him here. Dr. Clapp, I've known for many, many years as a distinguished political scientist who not only teaches it and writes it but undertakes to practice it. He seems to do it more often with Republicans than Democrats; frankly I feel they need people of Charlie's caliber to help them out.

Dr. Koenig, of course, has the detachment the others of us on the panel do not have, and he has the critical responsibility of informing, inspiring and guiding his students. Mr. Comarow, I, of course, have known from the Federal Power Commission when I was there, and is now deeply involved in trying to reorganize the Federal Government. As many of you may know, there is a special wing of St. Elizabeth's Hospital in Washington, D.C. for government reorganizational specialists. One ward is for the horizontal types, another for the verticals, and the diagonals have their own separate facilities. There is one saving grace, and that is the nation has proved over a couple of hundred years to be able to withstand reorganization commissions, and I have every reason to believe that we'll still survive.

Let me solicit, if I may, any questions.

STEPHEN J. WRIGHT: What is the relationship in the formulation of Domestic Policy between the Staff and the

White House on one hand and the domestically oriented groups like labor, ATW, and so on the other?

LEE WHITE: It varies somewhat from department to department and, as you might imagine, on the basis of who happens to be the head of the particular agency. I keep going back to something quite basic, and that is that a lot of this depends on Who is there, not What is there. A strong Secretary of Labor and an effective Secretary of Housing, or an effective secretary or head of anything else can make a difference, but that's kind of general response. Let me talk a little more about the mechanics of how it gets done.

STEPHEN WRIGHT: Does that mean that the effect of the Cabinet is also in decline, or if I may borrow, in "the twilight," as reflected by the growth of the White House staff?

LEE WHITE: I think the answer to the question is a qualified yes. There is some movement in that direction. The reasons for the qualification are, that if you talk about the Cabinet, and if we're talking about Secretary McNamara, that is one thing. Now again I'm the prisoner of my own experiences and observations. Secretary [Robert S.] McNamara had no trouble getting right through to the President, whether it was President Kennedy or President Johnson. On the other hand, Secretary [Abraham A.] Ribicoff made it abundantly clear that he didn't like that job. He thought he was the Secretary [of Health, Education, and Welfare], and he had a bunch of punks in the White House that he had to work through. Well, it wasn't that bad. You can imagine the uncomfortable attitude of a Cabinet Officer who calls to speak to the President and gets a return call from Ted Sorensen or, heaven forbid, Lee White. He begins to chafe a little under that.

And yet, again, from personal observation, each President has his own set of priorities. Normally they go into what he thinks is the most important to the nation at that particular point and time, and so he will fluff off, if you will, that's too harsh a term, but close enough. Some of the people who are in the Cabinet, need not be, and this is one of the great challenges for the White House Staff. And again I hark back to what I said before, not only should you have skillful and experienced people, but also people whose personalities and capacity to work with others will permit them to work with the Cabinet and not ruffle their feathers and not get them going cross-wise, and not having felt that they're left out. That staff man, then, better serves his President.

GEORGE REEDY: I've made one observation that might be helpful. I think you have to make a distinction between the Cabinet Officer as an individual and what the specific job is he performs by virtue of his office. You must also consider the meaning of the Cabinet as a whole. You can say the individual Cabinet Officer may be a man of tremendous effectiveness with the President; that's both because of the individual and specific duties he performs. Beyond this you must consider the meaning of the total Cabinet. The Cabinet as a whole is less than the sum of the parts. Now you might have one Cabinet Officer who has far less influence than a member of the White House Staff. On the other hand, you may have one or two Cabinet Officers who have tremendous influence, much more than the White House Staff people. I think you have to stop thinking of them as Cabinet Members per se. Rather, you have to consider their specific duties and their relationship to the President.

LEE WHITE: I don't disagree with a thing George has said. One point that kind of emerges from that though is again with regard to the operation of the White House Staff. I suggested, for a considerable period of time I was the staff man who was assigned civil rights matters, but each President likes to operate with his first team when the crisis or when the problem or the subject is uppermost; and so I was not surprised, offended, or disappointed when Oxford, Mississippi comes along and all of a sudden the President wasn't consulting with me, but with the Attorney General and with Ted Sorensen and O'Donnell and O'Brien and everybody else, because this was now way up at the top of his priority list.

That's the way it ought to be as far as I can tell. There's a man who used to work with agricultural problems, and all of a sudden the question was whether wheat was going to Russia, and that guy became a spectator at the discussions. This is the way it should be, because the President himself operates the way that he can be most effective; he's entitled to have the guys that he is most comfortable with and can rely upon. What he ought to have is a process to make sure that the problems get to him in time, and well documented, briefed, and argumented.

LEONARD MOORE: I don't know if the moderator is permitted to ask a question. You noted that the President and his Staff create program ideas. I suppose ultimately they will go into laws passed by the Congress, but does the Office of the President transmit to Congress that which the President would like to see accomplished in contrast to the idea of it originating in Congress and eventually being passed back to him?

LEE WHITE: Well, the first approach is the triumvirate of messages that come in January. The State of the Union message, the Economic Report, and, of course, the Budget. In preparing the Budget, the President establishes his priorities and normally suggests where he thinks the money ought to go. That is customarily followed by a series of more specialized messages which spell out his thoughts and normally will be accompanied by specific legislative drafts. This is the conventional and traditional fashion in which the President proposes to Congress what he believes they should do.

CONFEREE: You pointed up the problem of knowing when to approach the President regarding a question and when to go ahead and answer it yourself. As a practical matter, it probably depends, as you indicated, on the personality of the President. But, how much does a major staff member, such as yourself, feel at liberty to disagree with a Presidential view and go to the President and say "look Mr. President, I'd do this in a different way"? You are supposed to be there because of your expertise in a particular area.

LEE WHITE: As you might have guessed, the answer is, it's up to you. Each individual sort of makes his own drum beat, and he does what he does best, both by way of initiative or suggestions for change. And, if an old college classmate of yours calls you up, and you go out for a drink, and he comes up with a great idea, and you look at it and check it and run to the President and say look, here's what I just thought up! Well, you know, it may be a good idea. It may have come out of a policy planning apparatus that the Department of Interior may have been working on for five years. This is somewhat unlikely, but it could have happened. Where do ideas spring from? They spring from experience and men's minds.

LEONARD MOORE: We thank you, Lee White, for this incisive essay based upon your own experience. Now if I were to ask, "Is there a doctor in the House," doubtless 50% of you could rise, but few could tell whether the appendix is on the lower right or the lower left side. No exception to this is our next distinguished speaker.

CHARLES L. CLAPP: My charge is a narrow one: To discuss Presidential task forces, domestic ones at that. When you consider the tons of input which are made from committees reporting to the Executive Branch, you can see that those task forces form a very small portion of the total. For example, today there are about 850 inter-agency committees. There are something on the order of 1400 public advisory committees serving the Federal agencies, and 50 or 60 Presidential committees, some of which are task forces. Some of these Presidential committees are continuing organizations, while others are one-shot short-term bodies.

Presidential task forces are established for a variety of reasons. They may be used to provide visibility to the President's interest in a subject or problem, to elicit some new ideas, to evaluate on-going programs, to provide a view independent of that of a department or departments concerned with the subject matter, to provide support for a program important to an Administration, and to encourage citizen participation in the problems of the day in a direct and meaningful way.

They may be confined to summarizing or reviewing existing information on a subject and recommending action, directed to concentrate on short-range and/or long-range recommendations, requested to evaluate a particular program, or established on a "crash" basis to study a particularly timely and serious problem. Since there are wide differences in the purposes for which task forces are established, the nature of the problem they seek to alleviate or solve and the kinds of results desired, there should be opportunity for variety in the task force structure. There is no one way to organize task forces or so it seems to me.

The use of Presidential task forces reflect something of the shift that has been taking place in recent years in the policy-making process at the Executive Branch level. For many years, the departments and agencies themselves provided the overwhelming majority of new legislative proposals, forwarding them to the Bureau of the Budget and to the President and his assistants for consideration and modification. Then, the people around the President, as well as the Bureau of the Budget, began taking a more active role in suggesting new proposals and activities.

President Kennedy has been credited with developing the idea of a series of Presidential task forces. This was really a continuation of informal advisory committee systems on which he had come to rely as a Senator and which other Senators, such as [Jacob] Javits of New York, had used to great advantage. Kennedy set up about two dozen pre-inaugural task forces, most of which had reported to him by the time of the inauguration. Later, after he became President, he continued to create task forces although the membership tended then to come from within the Government, rather than from without. President Johnson continued the use of Presidential task forces and, indeed, expanded tremendously on the number, believing them to be an important mechanism by which to get new ideas. In the task force system as it functioned under LBJ, the reports were regarded as personal and confidential to him, so that the task force membership tended to be secret and the task force reports themselves were not made public. They were available to the President and his staff. In 1967, there were said to be 50 such groups in operation.

As the Republican nominee for President in 1968, Richard Nixon decided to create a number of working task forces to provide him with ideas for programs if he were elected. If he failed to win, it was planned to turn the materials over to the victor. Paul McCracken, now Chairman of the Council of Economic Advisors, was asked to assume overall responsibility for this activity. The results of these task force meetings were made available to the President and his advisors. Names of the chairmen of the task forces were released as was a list of the individuals who served on one or more of the groups. This public identification of participants represented a break from the policy followed by President Johnson. However, the list was an alphabetical one which did not specify the specific task force to which individuals were assigned. President Nixon was much pleased by the results of the pre-inaugural task force operation and decided last summer to use this technique again.

Responsibility for this new undertaking was given to Dr. Arthur F. Burns, then Counsellor to the President and now Chairman of the Federal Reserve Board, and I joined Dr. Burns in August to carry it out. The goal was to get ideas from the task forces which could be used in developing legislative programs for 1970 and beyond, and to get suggestions which might be useful in preparation of the State of the Union message and the various messages that would follow that one.

Seventeen task forces were organized in this group. I should say parenthetically that, of course, there have been other White House task forces, and one should not think that this list of seventeen is all inclusive. For example, there have been task forces dealing with international problems, rather than domestic ones. There also have been individual task forces in the domestic area not included in this group.

Let me mention, very quickly, the seventeen task forces for which we had jurisdiction so you can get an idea of the scope of them: Aging, Air Pollution, Business Taxation, Economic Growth, Higher Education, Highway Safety, Low Income Housing, Mentally Handicapped, Model Cities, Oceanography, Physically Handicapped, Prisoner Rehabilitation, Rural Development, Science Policy, Small Business, Urban Renewal, and Women's Rights and Responsibilities. The size of the task forces varied from 10 to 16 members, with a total of about 225 individuals participating. All of them were private citizens. There were no governmental personnel serving as full-time members of the task forces.

Some of the task forces were suggested by members of the Cabinet and the various departments and agencies. The President himself asked that task forces be established on several of the subject matter areas. Members of the White House staff suggested others. In one or two instances, the departments concerned were not particularly enthusiastic about the creation of a particular task force and in at least one instance, the department was somewhat hostile. There always is the fear, I think, on the part of the departments that the establishment of a group at the Presidential level is an effort to by-pass the Department itself or ignore the recommendations of that department. There is also a concern about the effect of the creation of a Presidential task force on various advisory groups which function at the departmental level. Some members of departmental advisory committees feel their own group is being downgraded. Also, there is something of an air of mystery about these Presidential task forces.

The charge to the task forces deliberately was a broad one, although the groups were advised that because of time limitations they probably would have to be selective on the issues they chose to emphasize. But, the choice was theirs. They were to look for new ideas, new programs, concentrating on 1970, but also considering long-range policy. They were asked to evaluate existing programs, too, and to keep in mind present budgetary constraints. They were given three to four months in which to do this, with a request that at least a preliminary report be provided by December 1st, so that there would be an opportunity to consider it when decisions were being made about the State of the Union and other messages. A number of the task forces met every other weekend for the three or four months, and maintained a very high rate of participation. Members were told that both the reports and the membership of the various task forces would be made public. As a matter of fact, as each task force was organized, there was a public announcement of its membership. Members were also told that they should not hesitate to file a minority report, if in the course of task force deliberations they found themselves disagreeing from the majority of the group.

A conscious determination was made to provide only small staffs to the task forces, although in one or two cases, supplementary staff assistance was required because of the nature of the subject matter or the desires of the members. Budgets were limited, too. What we wanted from these knowledgeable people was their ideas, their reactions to existing programs, the benefit of their experience, and their full participation in the deliberations. We didn't want a staff report submitted to a group of individuals merely to have them react to it, nor was there, in fact, time for extensive research by a large staff.

A great deal of discretion was given to the task forces as to the time and place of meetings and, as it turned out, meetings were held all over the country, although most of the sessions were in Washington. Each task force was provided with an executive liaison person, a responsible official in the Executive Branch, who met with the task forces, provided them with necessary reports and materials and suggested governmental experts and outside experts who might meet with them. The choice of the chairman obviously was crucial in the success of a task force, and we were remarkably fortunate in that respect.

There was no standard format for the task force operation. Some task forces held meetings around the country; some had few meetings but sent staff around to interview individual task force members and other citizens; some divided into sub-committees; some had a large number of witnesses appearing before them. Virtually all sought written statements from interested organizations and individuals. Only two or three people who were invited to serve on a task force declined and then only for very good reasons. The groups were bi-partisan, although one could say that there were more Republicans than Democrats serving. The chairman of the Scientists for Humphrey-Muskie in the 1968 campaign served on one task force, as did other members of the Scientists for Humphrey Committee. Former Secretary of the Treasury [Henry H.] Fowler was a member of the Business Taxation task force. I. W. Abel, President, United Steelworkers of America, and other prominent Democrats served on other groups. One could not always predict, on the basis of his organizational affiliation, how a particular individual was going to perform in a task force group. Some, indeed, took stands which were surprising. One might say that they rose above the interests they might have been expected to represent. Certainly, the vast majority became deeply involved in the work of the task force. Only one or two of the participants were casual in terms of attention and participation, or tried to send substitutes. That's a poor practice, I believe, and one, if permitted, which tends to diminish the dedication and interest of the other participants.

The reports of two of the task forces—those of Rural Development and Small Business—have been printed and others will follow soon. Not all of the groups have completed their work—at least two got a late start, for example—but most of them have.

In my discussions with task force members—and I sit in on as many meetings as possible —I find them concerned about the brief period they have in which to accomplish their work. They are afraid they can't prepare the kind of document they want to produce in the time allocated. They sometimes also observe that their coordinator gives them too much background and reading material to absorb and make judgments about between meetings and even at the sessions themselves. Another comment is that the staff is too small and that there are often disadvantages in having it associated with the executive department or offices which have great interest in the particular issue and sometimes strong positions on it.

Meeting dates occasionally have aroused criticism. The members are busy people, and it is desirable to give them as much advance warning as possible about the sessions of the task force. We suggested that at the initial meeting the dates of subsequent sessions should be determined. Most chairmen did make those decisions at that time, thereby reducing prospects of low attendance.

One of the most important questions for task force members, understandably, is whether there will be any payoff for their endeavors; whether the end product will be considered seriously and whether the recommendations will be implemented. Certainly, they have every right to expect that careful attention will be given to the reports.

One thing is very clear; the experience is a most educational one for the participants. Even the individuals who were considered most knowledgeable learned a great deal in the process of the task force deliberations.

The basic question over which there has been considerable difference of opinion in recent years is whether the reports should be public or private. As I have indicated, President

Nixon decided to make this group public, while President Johnson preferred that his task forces be confidential. Perhaps the policy should vary depending upon the purpose or purposes for which a task force is organized. Inevitably, some members of these groups are representatives of organizations which are extremely interested in the outcome. If, for example, someone in the field of mental health, such as the past president of the National Association of Mental Health, sits on the Mentally Handicapped Task Force, the constituency that person turns to is the National Association. It's not the White House. It's not the agency. And, there's a feeling that at some point, perhaps at the last meeting, people who operate as a part of the majority all along, suddenly announce they intend to file a minority report, possibly because they have to live with a group to whom their professional life is tied. If the report were not to be made public, there might well be less pressure for this.

There's another matter which relates to the question of public versus private reports and that is the consensus that seems to go on in a group. You can make it clear to the members that you don't mind a minority report, but the participants like to avoid that, so most of them try to compromise their differences. Too much compromise, of course, often results in a lowest common denominator document, full of generalities, a document, in short, that is acceptable to the group but not particularly specific or innovative. In some cases, that may be desirable. If, however, what you want is ideas, new approaches, alternative paths, then perhaps the best thing to do is to put on a task force people with widely divergent views and let them sharpen their ideas in combat with colleagues with conflicting views. Such a task force might even come up with two reports headed in quite divergent directions.

It isn't always easy to coordinate the task forces and their efforts with those of other groups in the Executive Branch working on similar problems. As I said at the outset, there are something like 850 agency committees and about 1400 public advisory committees. Inevitably, there are other groups within the Executive Branch working on similar problems. One report may undercut another. Timing, then, can be extremely important. I think that members of task forces and people looking at task force operations must recognize that they are but one of many inputs to executive policy-making. How effective each one will be depends upon the particular issue, the timing, the alternative suggestions that have been made and the reaction of the policy-makers and those with responsibility for making some political input. The composition of the groups, their short lives, the nature of their staffing, the kinds of meetings they hold, make it unreasonable to expect that every recommendation will be implemented or should be implemented. On balance, however, I would say that task forces are valuable assets to any Administration and that they should be continued by whatever name one wants to apply to them.

LEONARD MOORE: Thank you Dr. Clapp. Our next speaker likewise has an earned Ph. D. and is likewise a scholar in the field of political science. Dr. Louis W. Koenig.

LOUIS W. KOENIG: In looking at our subject today, I thought that one way I might look at it was inspired recently by a question I had from a student. He asked me when a President picks up a social problem or economic problem, when does he deal with it seriously? Now there is an interest and concern shown here in the apparatus that is evolving in the Nixon Administration. We've had reference to an apparatus which has long been in previous Administrations, but I would like to suggest, on the basis of the inspiration from that student, a test which I think is quite relevant. There is a relevance which I think is derived partly from some of the program we have had this morning. It is a relevance which I think has very much to do with the nature of our students today, and their citizenship role in the future.

I think one of the consequences of the age of television is not only a vast increase in the audiences and the immediacy of the audiences that was made very clear to us this morning, but also, I think one of the consequences is that we have a population which is much more sophisticated, better informed, more interested than I was or the generations that I know were. It's easy for me to make some comparison, because I have a daughter who has begun college as well as contact with a number of students. The problem as I see it is that these students have achieved new sophistication in the main;

perhaps, I should preface all of this by saying I'm a little bit loath to talk about students as such because there is so much diversification on a huge mixed campus. On the other hand, this is a general impression not relevant to our discussion.

I specifically argue this, if we are looking at how presidents function, if we explore revisions, administrative mechanisms, if we listen to speeches, watch television, I think maybe the aspects of what I call the old political game are not going to pass with the present sophisticated student body. That is to say that one test that any machinery we talk about will have to face is its *genuineness*. It's not a cover-up; it's not a sham; it's not a half-step.

My question is what respect the students would have regarding this machinery, whether it's past administrations or in the future, if it were the ability of that machinery, in the White House Staff or executive offices; if it were the ability of that machinery to give adequate attention, adequate access to groups in our society that by traditional standards have inadequate access to public policy in governmental affairs. This is a major challenge of our time.

The students, I think, will be interested in groups and individuals in our society who cannot afford to retain lobbyists in Washington, who cannot afford to plead their causes in court, who do not have the money, and will begin to apply these prescriptions around in our population.

There is a pertinent number of groups that find it difficult. I think, for example, the aged who are notoriously lacking in organization in our society and who are, by and large, grieviously affected by inflation which has risen. Policy will be affected, for example, in terms of the added income data that we have on these people. I think of the ill in our society, the poor, the consumer. If we have percentages and give totals, we've got a pretty good picture here. Some of the structures of the present administration and also of the past represent groups or task forces that concentrate in problems that deal with some of these groups.

Important strides have been made in the consumer area in recent Administrations. Whether the pace will be kept up, and what the White House structure watching over it these next years as we move to the 70's will be, remains to be answered. We have the projection that Herb Klein gave; whether that *structure* then may be relevant, not only to the groups which have had particularly good access to governmental policy, but also to that portion of our society that has had much less access, remains to be proven.

One thing I do realize, and, that is, there is a trend or rule of progress of optimism that one can apply. Certainly when we compare, say, the days of the late William Howard Taft or Calvin Coolidge with those of Dwight Eisenhower or Richard Nixon, and the agendas of these Presidents, we have a sense of progress in social concerns. In other words, we are witness to an evolving concernment of policies which, not so long ago, and groups which, not so long ago, would not have been represented, who are interested in public policy. Well, I'll leave that particular point. My own interest in referring to it is that students seem to tend to discount traditional politics. In other words, if they don't believe the concern is genuine, instead of merely preempting problems; or if they feel those taking a position on these concerns will not follow through, this won't catch.

This is secondary. Let's get back to a question that was raised before, I think in Mr. White's presentation, and this has to do with the relationship of the departmental bureaus, the civil service with the White House organization. The other day, I was with a group of Federal civil servants and we got into some of these matters which are coming before us here, and I got somewhat of a picture from that which I think is probably characteristic of any Administration, regardless of which one they might choose to talk about. There is a perennial problem that in a government there is a kind of barrier between the career civil servant, as against those, say, in the White House organization. There are other kinds of barriers, too, which confront these people. But, this group that I got some feedback from, gave me a picture of a feeling of being shut out, of being frustrated, of not being sought in terms of ideas, information, response to issues.

I'm sure this is nothing particularly new, but at any rate it seems to me that one problem we face as we build a White House organization, and executive office organization, is to maintain access of those in the departments, to the President or to the staff working for the Presidency. There's nothing particularly new in this contention; we can go back to the Brownlow Report, back in 1937, in which we have the suggestions of some of the early White House staff; one of the items in that report was that we ought to be very careful as we move along that those around the President should not become a barrier to the access of those further removed. Now, there are several books on this question. I'm interested in just throwing this out as a kind of question or a kind of proposition.

One other area that I also want to touch on very quickly, by the way of comment, is the preoccupation with organization, with re-organization, revising structures and so on. This sometimes can be a diversion from the serious business of policy. In other words, that organization and reorganization represents motion, movement; it gives an illusion of activity; it gives, apparently, an expression of concern, but one to bear in mind. Again, I'm using my students as a reference point. It's the policy action that counts. It's the final policy output that counts. I suppose one can argue that organization or reorganization is not a substitute for a policy, and even though we may elaborate on the structures and processes and so forth, that perhaps, this is a caveat that might well be considered.

The last point that I would like to touch on is that I think it is very clear that what has transpired so far in the Nixon Administration is most needed. Particularly, Mr. Herbert Klein referred to last night the problem of moving us away from some of the cliches of the New Deal era, 1930's, which are so much outworn. It's high time that we had some of the extensive re-evaluations of programs which we are in. There's a suggestion of new approaches and fresh approaches; all of this, indeed, is very much in order, and the Administration is performing a great service in taking these approaches.

On the other hand, I'm depressed in watching all this business over the past decade. When we talk about domestic programs, particularly social programs, one of the big gaps that we have to struggle with is the matter of *action*: having a reasonable approximation between what was accomplished and what our goals were; what the goals are that are incorporated into the preamble of a particular statute; that, compared with what actually happens when time lapses after a program has been in effect for a spell. Then What?

One problem that I think is very serious in our total society is that in these last years some programs had been oversold by Presidents; then they have raised false expectations. The political rhetoric has been too soaring, and it has raised in many parts of our population expectations of results that are far beyond availability. So, again, I think the present Administration is to be praised in this respect. It is making a very valuable curb on political rhetoric.

There is, though, a second half of my contention here, and then I'll stop. I think one of the big struggles we have ahead of us is *not* organization at the White House level or the executive office level, but it's organization at the implementation level. Here, I'm thinking of the bureaus and departments, the neighborhoods, the back country from Washington. Here is where I think we have had a general fall down in one Administration after another, and all of it is perfectly understandable; it's most difficult to do this. But I just wanted to throw this out as an oversight that I hope a Presidential Administration will get around to very soon to looking at very seriously.

LEONARD MOORE: Thank you very much Dr. Koenig. Our next speaker, Murray Comarow, is the Vice President of a very large nationally known firm, Booz, Allen and Hamilton, management consultants. But, like so many public spirited persons, he has decided to let that go by for awhile, and he is now serving as the Executive Director of the President's Council on Executive Organization. Now, when he says there's not a chance that he'll tell us what it means, that does not surprise me. I've never known anyone who has been able to describe what they do in a title as long as that, but I'm sure we'll be very interested to hear it in any event.

MURRAY COMAROW: Thank you. I'm going to be brief for several reasons; first of all it's ten after four. This is supposed to terminate at 5 o'clock, and if we yak at you for 50 minutes, you won't have time to ask questions. Secondly, I just don't want to get in the way of the great Tom Corcoran. Let me explain my presence on this stage, notwithstanding the absence of my name on this part of the program. As I understand it, from our fearless leader, Dr. General Hoxie, there is some connection between John Ehrlichman, scheduled to appear, and my sitting on this dais. This is extraordinary. If there really is a concept of a political coming together in this country, this has got to be it; because I'm not only a Democrat, but worse from John's point of view I'm sure, and in spite of my distinguished connection with Booz, Allen and Hamilton, I'm essentially a bureaucrat, having spent most of my time in government.

I was complimented on my courage in coming here and participating, but that has never been the issue. The issue was my intelligence. You know, Rufus Miles said something which could become famous: "Where you stand depends on where you sit." There has been a lot of talk about elephants and how you get hold of the tail and think it's a rope. It is always the speaker, of course, who sees the elephant in the round, the whole elephant, not a wall, not a rope, not a snake. From where I sit, as Executive Director of the Council, of course, we see the elephant as a whole. I'm going to tell you a great deal about that tomorrow, probably more than you need to know. Also tomorrow, Walter Thayer will be here; he's a member of the Council and Assistant to the President, and he'll catch me up on any lies.

One word about the Council and one of its functions. The Council deals with organization, and in order to do any kind of a job on organization, you've got to understand how policy is made. Since we've gone into that in great detail, I can give you the answer: Policy is made with difficulty. Policy making is an enormously complex thing involving the interaction among three parts: the White House, the cabinet agencies, and the independent departments. Between these agencies and the White House policy is made in many different ways. Anything anyone says about it must be at least partially true.

I would like to draw a distinction, between the *institutional* staff of the President and the *personal* staff of the President. This distinction has not been made today and ought to be made, because of its importance. The fact that the Bureau of the Budget exists makes a difference. It is there; Presidents use it. I hate to admit it, with Dwight A. Ink sitting in the audience, but it's even useful from time to time. The fact that the National Security Council exists makes a difference. Some Presidents didn't like it at all. Some did. But it always makes a difference. It gives each President an institutional memory, a tool which he can use in his own way.

So it doesn't get us very far, you see, to say, "every President has his own personal staff." Who's going to take the other side of that one? I will stand courageously for the proposition that every President should have his own personal staff, as several have told us in this symposium. But it doesn't answer the questions: "How do you improve the making of policy? How can institutions help?" I hope we get into these questions later today or tomorrow morning.

LEONARD MOORE: Thank you very much, Mr. Comarow. I was appalled that if I were able to get everybody on base that my friend, Tom Corcoran, would hit a home run. I hadn't any doubt about that at all, but I have done something that very few people have been able to do. It looks to me as I look back and forth that I've gotten 4 men on base, and therefore, when he hits his home run, he will be the uniquest person to have scored 5 runs on one hit.

THOMAS CORCORAN: I was a classmate of Adlai Stevenson, and I never forgot what he said during a campaign. You should *appreciate flattery,* but you shouldn't inhale it. You know, as you listen to all of this, you come back to thinking about *what the nature of this government is,* and I completely agree that every institutional device created which can help in the great problem of government should be tested and tried. But at the same time you can't avoid what the great problem is. Unless you have a military dictatorship, there is only one way to use government and insure domestic tranquility; that is to *balance* constantly, at every point; it changes almost from month to month, the *effective* forces clamoring for attention and for a piece of the pie. Within the American scene we never really had to face that, until Franklin D. Roosevelt came along.

When Roosevelt came along, as somebody said today, modern government started in the United States. Because the real issue in coming years, as it was from Roosevelt to now, is the same: how and whether the Government would take responsibility on a large scale for social situations which the vastness of the country's resources had hitherto abandoned. Once that recognition came, you had created a pattern which became more and more intricate as more and more special groups with more sophisticated intelligence got into the game. Now all are claiming attention for what *they* think is their legitimate share of the pie or their legitimate share of attention. It's almost as if you had a lot of electrical forces that converge on a point at a given time. And the effectiveness of those forces changes from time to time.

I was very interested in hearing Dr. Koenig tell what parents were saying about children. I happen to have put six children through college, and I listen a great deal to what their generation is saying. Theirs is one of the forces that is involved in what I term the *balance of forces*. These children do not necessarily have any political sense at this time. Nonetheless their compassion, even though it is a compassion that they will have to ameliorate later on with practical facts of life, their compassion must be reckoned with; it is a force in the political payments that have to be arranged by whoever governs.

I remember Mr. Roosevelt saying once: "I am the captain of this ship, but the seas control the captain." What he meant was that the strength of forces, impulses, opinions at any given time determine what he had to do. Now, what was his function as a leader? The other powers in the Government, about the relations of which, as you said, there is always a struggle, the powers in the Government which deal with social problems, are the Congress and lately the Supreme Court.

I first went into Washington in 1926 in the time of Coolidge as Supreme Court Justice Oliver Wendell Holmes' Secretary. Holmes used to tell me that "the prime purpose of government in this kind of a democracy is to avert civil war. Few people understand that, but I understand it. I was a captain in the Civil War, and, I know what our business here is. For this reason we should keep away from great social changes *as a matter of decision by the courts*. There is no use talking about a law that will not be willingly obeyed by at least 90 percent of the population." And all of us who lived through prohibition in New York know in an extreme way what that meant.

Now, the legislatures don't respond to these great social changes until those forces have worked themselves up to a point where the legislature, responding in a kind of bungling way, understands and is convinced that 90 percent of the people will obey a change which the legislature orders. But is it perfectly possible—because you can't define an exact line between the separation of the powers of the judiciary and the public—for a smart lawyer to bring up the issue of change through the judiciary not the legislature, and thus prematurely change that balance before the legislature has worked it through to what you might call a consensus. Constitutional issues before the Supreme Court interpreting the Constitution can thus precipitate an issue; the Court may thus propose change before the public is ready to take the change. Therefore, in Holmes' court and Louis D. Brandeis' court, and Benjamin N. Cardozo's court, the Supreme Court very carefully never put itself in the situation where Justice Roger B. Taney helped bring on the Civil War in the Dred Scott decision.

Right now this is what the puzzling thing called Constitutional government is all about. It's about the Court assuming judicial functions. To emphasize: I've always known from my days with Holmes, after the row that Teddy Roosevelt had made about Holmes' decision in the Northern Securities case, what judicial risks meant; so also after the political furor about the recall of judges following the Court Plan of Franklin D. Roosevelt; so also in the wake of the risks that the Democratic Supreme Court has taken in the last four years. Such experience tells me that this kind of problem of judicial risks with a legislative function was going to be the cause of accelerating social difference in our time.

Since the Supreme Court has, contrary to the advice of Holmes and Brandeis and Cardozo, ventured into what we call the political ticket, who goes on the Supreme Court becomes a judicial competence issue. And who is appointed to the Supreme Court is from now on just as real a political issue as who is elected to the Congress of the United States.

I'm sorry, I shouldn't have gotten onto that subject. Nevertheless, the *most important job of all these assistants in the White House is to do something to help the President do this balancing of forces and demands.* Everybody who's in Congress, assuming, of course, that he wants a political future, has his own particular ax to grind. He comes from a people and a district that have a certain view of the world, and, necessarily, the Congress have to think that the views of their constitutents are the views that should be considered. But a President is supposed to look at the whole picture. He tries to lead the Congress, and he tries to lead the people. As the balance of those forces change, he must seek to readjust the balance and lead the electorate to understand that you have to make changes when the balance of forces has changed.

The wise President understands that he first has to lead the people in putting the pressure on the Congress by making evident what they feel about the changes; then he has to persuade the Congress to devise some decent equilibrium between their own demands and other forces. Then he has to take the initiative when he presses those changes in the form of recommendations of law. After the enactment the wise President administers the new law in such a way that the resulting change of a balance of forces remains within the purposes his administration seeks.

If you think about the political process that way, you understand and can see it lives in a constantly changing balance; you can see how the balance of forces has changed since Roosevelt's time; how our history has been made by its changes. I happened to have served in the United States Government under Mr. Herbert Hoover. I have tremendous respect for Mr. Hoover. But, Mr. Hoover was so certain of a certain ideology that he never could see that the circumstances his Administration had encountered had changed that balance of forces, and he wasn't happy to see that balance of forces be changed. By contrast, Mr. Roosevelt was willing to let it be changed.

But if you ought to be willing to do these things, you have to accept the reality that necessary changes are always attempted first imperfectly for lack of sufficient knowledge how they will work; little by little, you improve on them. Many of the "answers" and new institutions that were initiated in the New Deal in immediate response to the immediate change in the balance of forces, are now outworn, because the balance of forces has since changed; one indicator of such change is the aforementioned attitude of today's children. Whether these children know what they're doing or not, the very weight of their interests, as you saw from the last political campaign, has become a force to be reckoned with.

Now, how does a President handle this sort of thing? He handles it in many, many ways, among other things by facing the demanding problem of the Constitutional separation of powers. We're going through an acute phase of that problem, not only in the George Harold Carswell appointment struggle, but also in the James W. Fulbright attack on the State Department. What is Fulbright doing? Basically Fulbright is trying to re-establish that relationship between the Foreign Relations Committee of the Senate of the United States and the Presidency that William E. Borah achieved when he took on Wilson—which Roosevelt reversed.

Always within the divisions of government this struggle for power goes on, because the line of separation in the Constitution is so necessarily blurred; at any given time the true separation of powers is defined by the strength of the protagonists of the particular division of government, whether it's legislative or executive or judicial. This, too, is from the President's point of view a force behind constant change.

Now the President has to ride all those forces of change like a circus rider. He's the only one who has to think all at the same time about the proper division of powers within the Government, about the comparative effectiveness of forces outside the Government, and the equilibrium of the total demands of all the people in the country.

Not all Presidents have the same skill and technique by which they lead the country to appreciate in time the necessity for change in the balance. The wise President devises statutory and administrative techniques by which that change in balance is effected in a way to do the most good and the least damage; he realizes it can't be all good or all bad.

I've always been proud of the record of service of the

lawyers during the period of the Roosevelt Administration. (I say this recognizing that there are many lawyers in this room.) I think Roosevelt's lawyers did the best legal technicians job that's ever been done by a President's lawyers. The changes that had to be made were too big to be simple and asked more of this Administration's lawyers than ever before. If you will recall the Securities Act, the Securities and Exchange Act, the Public Utility Holding Corporation Act, the F. H. A. and many others—you will appreciate the unparalleled details of operation of profoundly changing business which were put through with such meticulous attention. At that time, in the early 1930's, there were four precedents in state laws on which to build in putting these changes up to the Congress.

None of the organizational detail that has grown since ever existed. Sometimes programs didn't come about in the way the President originally wanted them or first thought of them. For example, the FHA revised the building mortgage business of this country, but the idea was originated by William G. McAdoo in the Federal Reserve Board. The Public Utility Holding Act originated in an idea of Roosevelt's, but it eventually took a different form. In the case of the Securities Act—about 15 different lawyers took a crack at drawing it, and every draftsman had a different idea about how it should be drawn. Finally, in desperate necessity of getting a bill before the Congress in the first hundred days, three young lawyers were put in a room in a hotel by the Democratic National Committee and told to produce a program in five days, and that was it. I also remember that after the Democratic Committee saw the draft it wouldn't pay the hotel bill!

Therefore, as you listen this afternoon to the place in which the official organization of the Presidential Office fits, it's only a part of a whole process of the machinery of everlasting change.

And sometimes the Administration with the best of interest makes beautiful miscalculations. Take, for example, the Alliance for Progress which was being trumpeted in the 1960's. Those of us who ever worked in the Bureau of Economic Affairs were sure that if the generality of its promises were ever translated into specific economic terms, it would cost 3 trillion dollars to implement it! We knew the U.S. Congress was never going to pass a bill authorizing 3 trillion dollars for Latin America or any other place. And so what's developed is an over-promised Latin America.

So in the excitement of political campaigns candidates over-promise things to people in this country and sometimes to people abroad. We are fresh from that type of promising done in the last campaign; everybody tried to outpromise everybody else; the people of the U. S. were promised things that won't be done if they could be done—things that the rest of the country were not willing to pay for to grant the beneficiaries of those promises. Mr. Nixon is now dealing with that problem of settling these promises at a discount. And the Democratic Party will be dealing with that same problem of discounting dreams if we ever get reorganized.

You'll remember that story in the *Arabian Knights* where the fisherman went down to the beach and found a strange bottle and opening it in his curiosity let a geni out of the bottle. We've let the geni of over-expectation out of the bottle, and now we're not going to get it back in the bottle. And we'll be working out the disconcertment of our political promises for a long time to come.

That's part of the problem of a President's dealing with the Congress. The President has to get the Congress to meet these same past and perpetual expectations. Somebody has to pay the bill.

I have a lovely daughter at Radcliffe, who's all excited about environmental controls; so am I. But I gave her an old hand's advice: "Darling, before you get in too far, please go down and work in Senator Edmund S. Muskie's office and find out that the environmental problem is not a matter of a difference of objective to save the environment. The problem is a whole succession of specific problems of who is going to pay for each specific improvement. Who's going to vote what bond issues; who's going to pay for the arresters on the utility smoke stack; who's going to invest in the chemical additives to purify the waste from the pulp plant?"

These payments have to be measured against other demands, and, therefore, above all things, the President has to maintain a relationship to Congress *so that it will try for him*. I need not tell you, Congress is hard to handle if a President doesn't try hard enough to educate both its members and their constituencies.

That's where Cabinet members have a particular importance. Whether a Cabinet officer is helpful to a President depends largely on his own political firepower. Nowadays, Mr. Nixon has decided not to have the kind of fire-power Cabinet Roosevelt had. Mr. Roosevelt was lucky, I always thought, in having to take into account the barons of a political party called Democratic. When Mr. Roosevelt came to power, the barons decided to divy up the Cabinet jobs between them. Thus Harold Ickes became the Secretary of the Interior, because Hiram Johnson was entitled to a place in the Cabinet and didn't want to take it and substituted Ickes. Homer S. Cummings became the Attorney General because he represented the old Wilson crowd, i.e. the old League of Nations crowd to which Roosevelt belonged and was politically indebted. Jesse Jones of Texas was there because he was a representative of the Kingmaker Jack [John Nance] Garner.

I first began my work with Mr. Roosevelt with Mr. Jesse Jones, as I had with Mr. Hoover. I can tell you that working with Mr. Ickes and Mr. Roosevelt and Mr. Jones all at one time, as I had the luck to do, was a most sanitary and expansive experience.

Mr. Nixon picked his Vice President; Mr. Roosevelt didn't. He picked Mr. Garner because that was Jim [James A.] Farley's Hearst-Texas deal that obtained the nomination for Mr. Roosevelt, and so we had Vice President Garner whose ideas were not always FDR's.

One of the first jobs I ever-ever had for Mr. Roosevelt was to carry to Mr. Garner personally, as a trial balloon, a measure Mr. Roosevelt was not sure Mr. Garner would like. I was just a boy, but I went down to see Mr. Garner as ordered. Mr. Garner received me very nicely about 10 o'clock in the morning, and I proceeded to tell Mr. Garner what Mr. Roosevelt wanted him to do. Mr. Garner got the drift very quickly, and didn't like it. Before I was half-way through, he stopped me and said, "Tom, would you have a drink?" I replied,

"No, sir." He said, "But I've had a drink and you know I find it very difficult when I have a drink to understand a fellow who hasn't had a drink. So help yourself and have a drink." I countered, "But Mr. Garner, I don't drink."

Then he put me right on the spot: "Well, I'm afraid that I can't talk now, but son, I've got an idea. Come around again before I have a drink. I begin to drink at sun-up. So you should come around to my apartment and see me at 5 o'clock tomorrow morning." I collapsed: "Well, Mr. Garner, I have to get this to you today; so, all right, I'll have a drink."

He pulled out a big tumbler and some famous red-eye, Wild Turkey, the native distillate, 180 proof, before it was watered down. As I drank, too hurriedly, he teased me along about my family, my antecedents and all of my relatives for about fifteen minutes. After that Mr. Garner never got my message: I couldn't remember what I came for!

But in later days he tutored me well on the balancing theory of government. "Listen," he would say, "the members of this Congress individually have completely different ideas why and what it's willing to go along with Mr. Roosevelt for. For instance, the liberal North is not interested in financial reform; you'll find nobody up north is going to bloody his banner for you; they're all too tied in with the business interests who put the money in Northern political campaigns. But we Southerners will do that job for you. We'll be the heroes of the New Deal. But do you know why we're doing it? It's just that we people down in Texas and Georgia are sick of being in hock to the New York banks and Chicago banks. We go along with your beautiful ideological financial reforms just because we want to get rid of the colonialism in our relationship with the North. For that reason, we'll be your heroes."

Another day he tutored me with this example: "Son, when you talk to this Congressman remember: you can say exactly the same thing in one of two ways. For instance you can say to a homely woman, 'My lady, when I look into your eyes, time stands still.' Or you can say: 'Woman, your face would stop a clock.' You see, when you are trying to change the balance of things, you have to know which crowd will play with you for what reasons. Maybe they will vote right for what you think are the wrong reasons. That's what the South's going to do about your financial bills. But son, it makes a difference how your President approaches it. And understand, my boy, that you are the representative of the man in the White House. How you handle his ideas with our committees depends on how well you remember my story about stopping the clock."

Now, what I'm trying to say is—agreeing for the moment with everything that's been said here today—ideological right or wrong is not determinative in the political process. What is determinative is the skill to work among conflicting forces; as Holmes expressed it, a bartered price of not having civil war. What Mr. Nixon can do with what he has on his hands right now, and to what degree all the apparatus in the White House can help him, depends upon a realization of this. If a President makes a decision that shocks the life out of the Congressional apparatus, as FDR did with the Court Plan, he will not get the results he is seeking.

On the other hand, sometimes asking too much is a deliberate Presidential tactic. I was on the President's liaison team in the push for the Minimum Wage Act and the Child Labor Act, what we now call the Fair Labor Standards Act. We tried to put it through in the closing days of the Congress in '36—just before the election. We did get it through the Senate. We had hard goings in the House. Why did we have a hard time in the House? Because the Southerners who were willing to help us beat Wall Street in '33, '34 and '35, did not intend to decelerate their recapitalization of their country up to the point of capitalization of the North, by not using the labor of their people at lower rates.

My friend, Joe [Joseph D.] Keenan, I've always thought has been one of the most perceptive leaders of labor; in understanding labor's problem he has tried to extend the standardization of economic relationships all over the country; he always understood this as he understands many things. I'm glad Dr. Hoxie invited him to participate in this symposium; he is one of the most able servants President Roosevelt and many Presidents after Roosevelt ever had. He will appreciate my example.

I was deeply interested in this bill partly because Justice Holmes had been overruled in Hammer vs. Dagerhart in the Supreme Court. He had written such a brilliant dissent against the position of the Court that the State of New York did not have the right to regulate the hours of work of children. In the House the Rules Commitee had decided that they wouldn't let us have a vote in the House. There was only one way to handle that, to get a petition signed by enough members of Congress to overrule the Rules Committee. So the day before the House was to adjourn, the President ordered me, "Tommy, I want you to get enough signatures on this petition to overrule the Rules Committee and get a House vote." So I went down and I sweated all day long and into the night getting the needed signatures.

About 11 o'clock at night a call, from Mr. Roosevelt, caught up with me. He said, "Tommy, ease up, will you. I sent you down to get names on that petition but I didn't think you'd work so fast. I sent a more subtle man, Mr. Charles West, to take them off as you got them on. At this time I don't want the vote this year. I want the issue instead, and you're down there only to get it on record that we tried like hell. So lay off, boy; you've done wonderfully, but you're working too hard." Now, I am sure that no normal White House staff member would have understood any better than I did at the time such consideration of political strategy; of the application of "I am the captain of the ship, but the seas control the captain."

So in this business every executive assistant has to understand: there is only one man who completely understands this balance of forces, and that's why he's the President of the United States. All you can do is give him all the help he asks for. The increasingly institutionalized memory in the White House is one thing: but a still more wonderful thing was the magnificently performing "chaos" of the Roosevelt Administration. Ultimately, a President has to read the seas himself and make the judgment which ultimately achieves the necessary equilibrium to avert civil war. We're the only country in the world now like this.

I tell my precocious children: "You can't learn about democracy in a political science course. When I took political science up in Brown University, I learned that the Argentine constitution was an exact copy of the U. S. Constitution. Then thirty years later dealing with Evita Peron in the Argentine it just wasn't the same thing."

Institutions and technicians help, but they are not enough; there still stands the political skill of one man and his political, *not* technical, advisors: the balancing instincts of his experience; his sensing of what his people will take in a further redistribution; his sensing of what the forces are that will compel a different distribution; and the batting odds. Right now, the President of the United States never had a tougher job in making that evaluation and then convincing the people how he is going to establish and carry it out.

Joe Keenan and I were talking at lunch. We remembered the hassle whether we could keep civilian production going at the same time we re-armed the nation. Joe had been serving in 1940-41 as the labor advisor to the Associate Director General of the Office of Production Management. The motor companies, in particular, didn't see why we couldn't do both—go to war and do business as usual. Even the President couldn't break the deadlock. But, as Joe said, along came Pearl Harbor, and that ended it. For his part, Joe went on to become vice chairman for labor production of the War Production Board.

I hope it doesn't take a catastrophe of the magnitude of Pearl Harbor to effect the next equilibrium, and I sincerely hope that all these new devices that have been added since the chaos of my time will help the President to make the right decisions.

LEONARD MOORE: Thank you, Tommy Corcoran, for that eloquent presentation. I guess you realize by now that we have four panelists who can handle just about any question you throw in their direction. Any one who has a question that he'd like to direct to a particular panelist, do so.

EDWARD W. MILL: I wanted to ask Dr. Clapp about the Task Forces. What happens to the Task Force Report? I think that basically the idea of the Task Force is a very good one. I'm not questioning that, but what is likely to happen to it? Who is going to *use* that report? What is the system of evaluation of the findings of the Task Force group?

CHARLES CLAPP: It is clear that the use made of previous task force reports has varied significantly, and there will be significant differences in the extent of the use made of the recommendations contained in the reports that are filed in connection with the present series. But, for example, the Rent Supplement Program and the Model Cities Program are said to have been developed in Presidential task forces.

In terms of the Nixon Administration, two of the 17 task force reports in the group with which I have been concerned have already been released—Small Business and Rural Development. The one on Small Business, after being studied in the White House and by the Commerce Department and the Small Business Administration, resulted in a Presidential message on Small Business to the Congress, which incorporated many of the recommendations made by the task force.

As far as Rural Development is concerned, subsequent to the organization of the Task Force on Rural Development, the Rural Affairs Council was organized. The Task Force then was directed to report to the Rural Affairs Council, which it did. The Council has studied, and is studying, the results of the Task Force Report. There is no question that very serious attention is being given to the recommendations contained therein. The press conference for the Task Force was conducted by Secretary of Agriculture Clifford M. Hardin. The Department of Agriculture has established a committee of assistant secretaries within the Department to implement certain of the recommendations immediately. One major company in the country, after studying the report, asked about using some of the people who participated in it, in an advisory capacity, in an effort to develop a program which will result in the transfer, or if not the transfer, then in the placement of new plants in rural areas rather than in urban areas.

It's going to take time, for a total picture of the impact of the Nixon Administration task forces, but certainly the two reports that have been issued so far have received careful consideration and have been useful in the determination of policy.

LEONARD MOORE: Any more questions?

JOSEPH McMURRAY: I wonder if Tommy and Charles would react to this: Has the balance of power shifted since the establishment of professional staffs in the Congress, and indeed, professional staffs in the Congressmen's and Senator's offices? Hasn't it changed considerably since the Roosevelt days, the expertise in the Government? And, hasn't it shifted much more power to the Congress? Hasn't it effected, somewhat, the ability of the President to operate in the independent manner Roosevelt enjoyed when he was President? Wouldn't it be smarter in terms of getting the results that come out of the Task Force to have some kind of Congressional representation, either their staff or members of Congress themselves operating on those task forces, rather than come in after the act has been performed?

THOMAS CORCORAN: The balance of power has shifted way over to the Executive, because, first of all, it is continuous; secondly it isn't fragmented among the committees in Congress. There's only one really completely staffed Congressional committee, i.e. the Proxmire Committee. Then there's a Joint Economic Committee in Congress that has a complete staff; there is the Joint Committee on Taxation for both the Finance Committee in the Senate and the Ways and Means Committee in the House.

JOSEPH McMURRAY: How about the Committee on Appropriations?

THOMAS CORCORAN: They don't have as much as they need. Lister Hill (who has just retired as the Senator from Alabama because of the Wallace business, which resulted in the loss of one of the finest Senators in the United States) was number 2 on the Appropriations Committee. He used to say, particularly in relationship to the big scientific projects that came before him, that "We have nobody on our Committee who matches the expertise of the Executive Department. I'm voting in faith for things that I don't really understand."

The last time there was put through an administrative assistant supplement for Congressmen there was talk about taking a third of the funds authorized for such new assistants and using them to man a largely expanded Legislative Counsels' Office of the kind which functioned effectively to some degree in the Roosevelt times. I'm unhappy to say, and I'm not saying this by way of criticism of the Congress, that every Congressman has been thinking if necessary he can be his own lawyer. As a result the money was spent, *not* on adding expertise to examine the multiplicity of things that were coming up from the Executive, but on answering ever-increasing constituents' mail.

You would think the work of Congress sufficiently important to give each Congressman enough to answer the mail and for the expertise, too. Furthermore, the institutional *continuity* of expertise that has been built up in the Executive has way over-matched that available in the operation of individual Senatorial and House Committees. The House needs much more expertise than it has, but the first priority is to get some sense of institutional unity in the Congress itself. So long as we're divided, as we are now, I'm afraid that's a long way ahead. I'm sorry, I wish it weren't so.

CONFEREE: What do you think of the wave of anarchy that's taking place in this country? And do you see anything in the way of methods being taken in Washington that could curb it?

THOMAS CORCORAN: I talk like a lawyer: Lord Mansfield said in the 18th century, and it is true today, that no law was a law that 90 percent of the people wouldn't willingly obey. I was in the New York District Attorney's office in the days of Texas Guinan and the prohibition law in New York; I saw then the necessitous disposition of cases for lack of personnel. There was a Bargain Day on Monday on which anybody who would plead guilty could get off for five dollars because the D. A. didn't have the money to provide for demanded jury trial.

If 10 percent of the people choose not to obey a certain law, it is practically unenforceable. So the first cure is to make sure that you've reached a certain point of acquiescence before you pass a law; you must make certain you are not trying to push down people's throats laws that they're not willing to obey.

In Washington, D.C., we have probably the highest crime rate of crimes of violence of any place in the world right now. We're trying to get through, a so-called crime bill initiated by the President, in which we're trying to get an appropriation of enough money to have enough judges, enough district attorneys, and enough police to handle the monetary problem so that there won't be a three year lag between the time a prisoner is arraigned for robbery and gets to trial. And under the present law a prisoner can go on probation for an extended period, and while he's waiting for trial he can commit two or three more robberies.

There is something else which could be done. How far are you willing to go in the protection of a criminal's constitutional rights? I'm a Holmes' secretary; I'm not interested in derogatory constitutional rights at all. But the Constitution while requiring a jury trial also gives the Congress of the United States the right to regulate the appellate jurisdiction of the higher federal courts. One of the things that could be done right now, if there were the guts to do it, is to have the Congress legislate that in a felony of violence once a jury trial has been had the convicted defendant has no right of appeal to an intermediate federal court. If he has a constitutional issue he can go upstairs directly to the Supreme Court on *certiorari* issue. But there should be no right to stall punishment in an emergency situation such as we have; constitutional protection should not require over an extended period appealing from the District Court to the Circuit Court of Appeals and then to the Supreme Court on the grounds of constitutional issues. Such a reform would short circuit much unnecessary litigation.

If my confreres in the legal fraternity had the energy, through their Bar Association, to have the grievance committee step up to proper criticism of those lawyers who participate in and are confederates in the kind of brouhaha that took place in Chicago and before Judge John Martin Murtagh in New York last week, a lot of the dramatics of the criminal bar would stop. The legal profession is itself to blame for the inefficiency of the law in handling the criminal problem. Because it's good for lawyers, I suppose we hesitate to halt the stringing out through too many courts; and we don't discipline our profession enough so that the entire profession will desist from engaging in the kind of tactics that is bringing the profession to contempt now.

In brief, the enforceability at least of the federal criminal law can be improved even without more money. There are a lot of things you could do if you wanted to do them. Holmes said once, "Any man can have anything in this world he wants, provided he wants it hard enough. But the trick the good

Lord played on the universe was that he made a few men who could want what they wanted hard enough." If the society wanted to pay enough, and if the legal profession wanted hard enough to do its work, it could be done. As yet the society doesn't want its own protection hard enough to pay for it. But pretty soon, we'll have to pay enough.

LEONARD MOORE: Instead of interpreting your remarks as trying to put me out of a job, I agree with you 100%. I have observed the enormous increase in the appellate calendar. Well over 50% of that increase is in criminal cases, of which there are appeals because of the laws that we do not make.

Lest we forget, we are here to discuss the Office of the President, and the Office of the President is still one of the most unique features of our Constitution. We have seen the Office of the President; we have seen the division of powers undergo many changes for the many years that you and I have been around. It reached its heyday, from a legislator's point of view anyway, probably in 1932. We saw a very strong man, hated to be sure, make changes by the temper of the times and the social conditions; for some 12 years, he was very responsive to those needs.

You all remember that we have gone through a period where the judiciary has taken over and is perfectly satisfied that it has all the expertise to run the country. And, the Supreme Court has been perfectly willing to run the country by a vote of 5 to 4. In other words, one man, for all practical purposes, is running this country. And, it's not the President of the United States; it's just that "swing" man who happens to be in that position in the Court.

But, this is no time for me to put forth any ideas that I might have on that subject. Let me just add this, of all the phobias that I have, this is the greatest; I'm against the Judiciary thinking they know all the answers, when in their more humble moments they, certainly, realize that they do *not*.

JOHN MARTIN: Something that has bothered me has to do with the matter of formation of policy in the executive offices to the cabinet departments and other branches of government. I refer to that layer below the great issue, the problem of policy being made by the 4th, 5th level staff, on small things. Over a period of time this kind of nibbles you to death, and you get great policy growing out of little policy. Is there anything that this distinguished panel could comment on? What, if anything can be done? How do you meet that problem, i.e. the nibbling policy?

MURRAY COMAROW: You mustn't look at it though, as if it were necessarily a bad thing. For, while the word nibble, may be pejorative in this context, in other context, in the case of a good steak, for example, it might be a good one. And, nibblers sometimes make good policy and sometimes they make bad policy. And in any event neither the President nor the White House staff, nor the top Cabinet Officers, nor anybody in the top echelon of government can make most policy decisions; there's too many of them.

The question is one of special assistance and the development of a reasonably good screening process which will attempt to force decisions at the point where they ought to be made. Of course, there are a great many decisions that ought to be made at the 4th level, and it would be a mistake to force them up to the Cabinet level, much less the level of the Executive Office of the President. And to the extent that we can keep the decisions at the lower level, and yet within the guidelines established by the people who ought to be running our government, we'll have a better government, and we won't have a White House staff overwhelmed with the necessity of making a great many decisions that they have no business making at all.

LEONARD MOORE: With Dr. Hoxie's permission we can adjourn now to other activities perhaps better calculated to resolve the world's ills.

CHAPTER IV

The White House and Foreign Policy: Formulation and Implementation

GORDON HOXIE: We started our first session last evening with the somewhat formal: "Ladies and Gentlemen." This evening I hope we may begin: "Good friends."

First, I would like to offer an explanation about a few names on the participant list who are not with us. The list was based on the acceptances as of April first. Subsequently the blizzard in the Middle West and the air traffic controllers' slow down took their toll in a few cancellations.

Secondly, I would like to invite your attention to two of our colleagues here whose names do not appear on the participants list. I refer to Dr. George Benson, the former President of Claremont Men's College, who is now Deputy Assistant Secretary of Defense in charge of educational affairs. I refer also to Dr. Stephen J. Wright, the former President of Fisk University, now serving with distinction with the College Entrance Examination Boards. My apologies to both of these friends for this omission.

Before introducing the moderator for this evening's distinguished panel, may I point out the obvious. There are many of you who are not listed on the program as panelists who have had White House experience and some considerable expertise on the roundtable subjects. For example, I see a gentleman here, and I mean a gentleman, who is both a general and a scholar. I refer to Brigadier General Robert N. Ginsburgh, Commander, Aerospace Studies Institute, Air University. General Ginsburgh earned his White House spurs as an aide to President Johnson.

Let me briefly review the Symposium to this point. Only last evening our keynoter, Herb Klein, set the pace, answering the arresting question, "Is Government Governable?" Then this morning we had that memorable session on the news media and this afternoon on domestic policy.

Now, this evening, we turn our attention to foreign policy,

and I say in sincerity our cup runneth over with the talent of this panel. The moderator, William J. Casey, Esq., will introduce the panelists. Just a word about Mr. Casey, distinguished author and publisher and a senior member of the law firm of Hall, Casey, Dickler, and Howley. Although Mr. Casey's principal office is in Manhattan, he is in a very real sense "Mr. Long Island," the President of the Long Island Association. He has done so much for so many. While I was Chancellor of Long Island University he played, for example, an invaluable role as the Chairman of the C. W. Post College Associates. He is today a Trustee of his alma mater, Fordham, and also of the sponsoring institution for this symposium, the Library of Presidential Papers (Center for the Study of the Presidency).

Mr. Casey is a discerning student of foreign policy, a long time friend, and a trusted advisor to the President of the United States. Presently, he is a member of the Presidential Task Force on International Development and a member of the General Advisory Committee of the U. S. Arms Control and Disarmament Agency. With warm regard, I present a dedicated student and public servant, William J. Casey.

WILLIAM J. CASEY: Thank you, Gordon, ladies and gentlemen: First, may I introduce the very distinguished panel that Dr. Hoxie has assembled for this session. At my left, your right, at the extreme end of the table is Ambassador Richard F. Pedersen, who was formerly deputy United States Representative on the United Nations Security Council and is currently Counselor in the State Department, Ambassador Pedersen. To his right is Ambassador Robert D. Murphy, who in 1942 was in North Africa to greet the American forces when they landed in Algiers. He has served as foreign policy advisor for General Eisenhower in North Africa and General Clay in Germany. He was the first United States Ambassador to Japan after the peace treaty, subsequently becoming Under Secretary of State for Political Affairs. Presently, and for the last nine years, Ambassador Murphy has been a member of the President's Foreign Intelligence Advisory Board; he served as advisor to President Nixon in the transition from the Johnson to the Nixon Administration. An eminent business leader, he is the Chairman of Corning Glass International, Ambassador Murphy. To his right is Professor Koenig whom you met this afternoon, the distinguished scholar of the Presidency at New York University.

And to his right is the Honorable Gordon Gray, formerly Secretary of the Army and presently, like Ambassador Murphy, a member of the President's Foreign Intelligence Advisory Board. Secretary Gray is the fourth of seven men to have served as the President's National Security Advisor. First it was St. Louis insurance executive, Rear Admiral Sidney W. Souers, under President Truman; then Boston attorney-banker, Brigadier General Robert Cutler, the first of three to serve under President Eisenhower; then Dillon Anderson, a Houston lawyer; followed briefly by Cutler serving again; then Gordon Gray for the final three Eisenhower years; then McGeorge Bundy; followed by Walt Rostow; and now Henry Kissinger. Secretary Gray, in an illustrious career, served as President of his alma mater, the University of North Carolina, and is a member of the Board of the Brookings Institution.

At the extreme right of the table is Helmut Sonnenfeldt, senior staff member of the National Security Council at the White House. A distinguished scholar of Soviet affairs, he was formerly director of the Office of Research and Analysis for USSR and Eastern Europe in the Department of State. Since 1958 he has been a lecturer in the School of Advanced International Studies at his alma mater, Johns Hopkins.

As I think of myself as the moderator of this knowledgable, distinguished and experienced panel, I am reminded of the story of the man from western Pennsylvania who had survived the Johnstown flood. For the rest of his life every chance he got he would get two or three people together and he'd tell the story of the Johnstown flood and how he survived it. Finally, he passed away, and he knocked on the pearly gates. Having been a good man, he was admitted. After he was there awhile, St. Peter said to him, "We try to make people comfortable and happy here. What did you like to do when you were down there on earth?" He replied, "Well, the thing I think I enjoyed most was to get a few people around and tell them about the Johnstown flood." St. Peter said, "Well, I think we can arrange that." In no time Peter had a fairly substantial assembly of spirits there and arranged for this chap to tell about the Johnstown flood. He warmed to the task; just about the time he had the dam break and the water started to rise, St. Peter tapped him on the shoulder and whispered in his ear, "By the way, I ought to tell you; Noah is in the audience."

That's the way I feel with this panel. It has only one rule; that is that there are no rules. We hope to kick it back and forth; anyone here is free to comment or question. I know that a moderator should moderate, but I think I will also spend a few minutes in laying a little background. So far as the organization of national security affairs is concerned, the modern Presidency began in 1947 with the enactment of the National Security Act. This legislated the unification of the Army, the Navy, the Marine Corps, and the Air Force under the Secretary of Defense. It also created the Central Intelligence Agency (CIA) and the National Security Council (NSC). Prior to that, Presidents did have advisors like Harry Hopkins in the case of President Roosevelt and Col. Edward M. House in the case of Woodrow Wilson. There were roving emissaries like Norman Davis, and there had been a special relationship with someone other than the Secretary and the State Department, such as President Franklin Roosevelt had enjoyed with Sumner Welles. But it was all very informal. The late Senator Robert A. Taft was a particular advocate for the establishment of the National Security Council.

Harry Truman and his successors had not only the new National Security machinery but a whole range of new instruments of foreign policy. There is, for example, the Central Intelligence Agency, the U. S. Information Agency (USIA), a different foreign aid agency every eight years or so, the President's special trade representative, and the Arms Control and Disarmament Agency. He has all these instruments of foreign policy to direct and control.

At the same time the task of the President as the molder and implementer of foreign policy became increasingly complicated by the expanding range of our global interests, rapid communication, instant news, multiple levels of conflicts, psychological, unconventional, conventional, and strategic. He has had to cope with competitive foreign policies developed in Congress and by some newspapers.

There is the greater role, and some will say the intrusion provided by domestic politics and Congressional forces in the formulation of foreign policy and its conduct. Recently Otis Pike, who is the Congressman representing this Eastern end of Long Island, I thought, put it rather neatly. He pointed out that Senator Charles E. Goodell is against intervention in Vietnam and for intervention in the Middle East, which, he said, shows how carefully Senator Goodell has counted the number of Vietnamese votes in the Bronx.

In any event, we have seen the great crises of the post-war era, Cuba, Korea, Berlin, Quemoy and Matsu, the Dominican Republic, brought into the White House, with the Secretary of State serving as one of several principal advisors. We have seen the President and his National Security advisors become increasingly important. The White House National Security staff has increased in number, stature, and influence. We're told that President Kennedy, frustrated by the cumbersome machinery in State, would call desk officers directly and dream of leaving State to its own devices, while he operated with a mini-state department under Mac Bundy.

The role and the need for the National Security staff are clear: the awareness and anticipation of problems, the identification of issues, providing full information, a full range of options, evaluating alternatives, getting a full reflection of the views of the various agencies, forcing decisions, following the full implementation, and finally coordinating the agencies. This reminds me of World War II definition of a coordinator as a fellow who can tell you the time if you showed him your watch.

Each President used this security instrument according to his style and background. Eisenhower, accustomed to orderly staff operations, had staff papers on policy for each country and each issue with committees to monitor the execution. Kennedy came in as a Senator, used to a small free-rolling staff; he dismantled this machinery pretty much, reduced the paper work, and functioned with small informal *ad hoc* groups. Johnson, likewise a former Senator, had a similar style.

With President Nixon we seem to be seeing a restoration of the staff system, with a high degree of personal participation on the part of the President.

Each of these approaches has the defects of its virtues. The elaborate system tends to get musclebound, the informal approach tends to get sloppy. I look to our panel for a deeper evaluation of these alternative approaches.

Before putting our panel into operation, I'd like to just indicate the increasingly important role of other segments of the President's Office in foreign policy. There's the President's Advisor on Science, increasingly important in weapons and arms control policy. There's the Budget Bureau, which in reviewing the defense budget and relating it to other needs, certainly has great impact on foreign policy. There's the intelligence community, tending to become a policy battleground. Some argue that it is not the capability but the intention of a hostile power that must be assessed and established before the President can legitimately establish a policy or defense. Then there's the President's Congressional Liaison staff. It can be exceedingly critical, whereas in the ABM debate, defeat for a Presidential proposal could deprive a President of trading chips and the Soviets of any need to agree to reduce their level of arms.

Then there's Herb Klein's communication function that we discussed this morning. This can be critical in an era when we're engaged with a foe which counts on weakening our public opinion and morale more heavily than on attacking our troops. Last October the media created the impression that the moratorium more nearly reflected public opinion than it did. And there was a time in late October and early November where there was tremendous pressure based on this assessment for the President to call a cease fire and otherwise effect a unilateral withdrawal. In this age of modern communications, a President to formulate and carry out a foreign policy must have the facilities to measure the real state of public opinion and to explain his policies and his purposes to the people.

In addition to these more or less formal instrumentalities there are advisory boards like the Foreign Intelligence Advisory Board, of which we have two members here, and the Arms Control and Disarmament Agency's General Advisory Committee. President Johnson had an informal panel of senior statesmen whom he called in prior to the decision to halt the bombing in Vietnam. As a final and more recent instrument there is the position paper, the foreign policy position paper, which Gordon Hoxie has provided for all of us, "The Foreign Policy for the 70's." This for the first time formulates, codifies and presents the whole range of our foreign policies as the President sees them.

Now, with that brief background, I'm going to join the panel. I'm going to ask Gordon Gray to tell us something about the structure and functioning of the National Security Council and Staff during the Truman and Eisenhower years.

GORDON GRAY: Thank you, Mr. Chairman, I think I would like to make some general observations first, if you will permit me, arising largely out of this fine summary the Chairman has just given you. But first I should remind myself as well as you that it's now been nine years since I've been connected with any of this machinery, and my views and participation are largely a matter of history. Fortunately, we're going to be brought up to date.

Of course, the National Security Act of 1947, as the Chairman has told you, established the beginnings of the modern machinery. It was brought about by the hard experience we had in World War II. Many of you will remember there was put together in the war years a group known as the State-War-Navy Coordinating Committee or SWNCC (SWINK), as it was popularly called, because there was no existing coordinating mechanism in the government such as was later established by the National Security Act.

As the Chairman pointed out to you, this Act not only sought and, to a very considerable extent, succeeded in unifying the various services, but also very importantly, it established, for the first time, a statutory based intelligence agency recognizing intelligence as a necessary ingredient in the formulation of foreign policy. I won't dwell on this except to say that in recent years, and for some unfortunate reasons, intelligence, in the minds of some, has become a dirty word;

nevertheless, however you wish to refer to it, it remains an essential ingredient. This was importantly recognized by the framers of the legislation.

The Chairman has said to you correctly that I'm one of seven who have served as special assistants to the President on National Security Affairs. I think the number is correct. Since the passage of the 1947 Act, I think it's fair to observe, and I should like to say it to you so that someone else won't have to, that the position of Special Assistant to the President for National Security Affairs has undergone some considerable change through the years. I won't dwell on this at any great extent except to say that when I held this position it was not one of such breadth and depth as it is today under Henry Kissinger or indeed was under McGeorge Bundy and Walt Rostow. It's a bigger job now than when I held it.

I'm glad that the chairman mentioned also both formulation and implementation of foreign policy because it is clear that we must talk about *formulation,* and I'm sure that we will be much involved in that in this panel. But also for the purpose of this symposium, it's equally important if you're thinking in terms of the Office of the Presidency and its responsibility to consider whether once foreign policy is formulated, it really is properly implemented in accordance with the wishes of the President.

Now, in turning to the Eisenhower Administration, I'm sure you all know that for the formulation and implementation of foreign policy he looked to the National Security Council machinery, consisting of the Council itself created by the statute and also consisting of various components of the Council which he established by directive order, such as the Operations Coordinating Board.

My responsibility was primarily to serve as staff officer for him in the operations of the National Security Council. Now, when I say the National Security Council let me avert to one principle which I urge upon you; perhaps some of my colleagues will differ but what we are really talking about when we mention the National Security Council is the *President in Council.* The National Security Council does *not* exist apart from the President himself, and if there is to be a meeting of the National Security Council in the absence of the

President I submit that it is not, indeed, the National Security Council. This is really the President in Council; the National Security Council has *no* power but to advise the President.

My own personal view is that a President who uses it is a wise President, but after all it exists only to serve him as Commander-in-Chief. Now I won't go through all the detail of the operations of the Council. They were touched on quite succinctly and clearly by the Chairman, but again let me state a principle or two if I may. One thing that the new machinery accomplished, or hopefully should have accomplished, was to eliminate what I would call the "yo-yo" form of government, the yo-yo form of arriving at policy decisions.

The yo-yo form is exemplified in a case such as the following: The Secretary of State goes to the President and says "Mr. President, because of the climate of world opinion we must cease atmospheric testing of atomic weapons." I see a member of the audience smiling because he remembers one of these occasions! The Secretary of State makes a very persuasive case, and the President says "Bill," "Dean," or whoever the Secretary of State is at the time (maybe he's "Oscar") "You're right; we'll stop testing atomic weapons in the atmosphere." Then the Chairman of the Atomic Energy Commission gets wind of this. He asks for and gets an appointment with the President. He says, "Mr. President, you remember a particular series of weapons we decided were so important to our defense; if you stop testing now, there goes the series of weapons!" Well, the President says, "Well, gee, John" or "Glen," "perhaps you've got a point."

About the same time the Secretary of Defense hears about this, and he has a different point of view. So he goes to the President. Well, what happens? In the end the President has to call together the Secretary of Defense, the Secretary of State, the Chairman of the Atomic Energy Commission, and perhaps the heads of other departments and agencies that are affected and thrash this thing out. And that, in a sense, is what the National Security Council is all about. You don't have this kind of *ad hoc* piece-meal business of arriving at a decision.

Mr. Chairman, one final statement and, perhaps, we can get back to some of this in more detail, if there is interest. The value, as I see it, of the President in Council is this: that when an important foreign policy decision is to be taken by the President, all those who are affected and will be somehow responsible for actions flowing from this decision are present when the decision is made. They proceed from the same information base. Presumably, there will have been a briefing of the Council on the appropriate intelligence involved in this decision.

If there are different opinions, the President hears them expressed by those who hold the differing opinions, and in the presence of each other. When the President makes his decision in Council, those present know the reasons for the decision. Finally, and almost as important as any of these reasons for the Council, is the fact that it provides absolute clarity in the minds of those present that this is the decision that has been reached. None of these things can be accomplished by shuffling notes or by several *ad hoc* meetings. None of this total can otherwise be accomplished.

So although Presidents have used this machinery in different ways, as they should (every President must run his business as he chooses to run it), my own conviction is that it is important machinery and deserves the continued consideration and use by the President. I believe I'll stop at this point and pass this on to someone else.

WILLIAM J. CASEY: Thank you Gordon. Ambassador Murphy, I think we'd be interested in what you can tell us about how some of these coordinating and related procedures were carried out before the creation of the formalized National Security Council. In doing so, assuredly you speak from rich experience.

ROBERT D. MURPHY: I hesitate to talk in front of Tom Corcoran and many others here who can talk on any of these subjects. I watched Gordon Gray operate for quite a few years and know what a constructive job he did in the White House to implement the purposes of the National Security Council. I've often wondered what his innermost thought was when President Kennedy, on advice of, I think it was Richard Neustadt, decided to suspend and abandon the Security Council for the time being. Perhaps that was a wise move at the time; I never thought it was.

I do know before the institution of that organization we were dependent on a very *ad hoc* treatment of national security decisions.

If you will pardon a personal reminiscence extending back over 50 years, I began with the Foreign Service at the ripe age of 22 back in World War I. When I came into the service I was assigned as a code clerk in the American Legation in Bonn. Allen Dulles was then the Third Secretary there. His uncle, Robert Lansing, was Secretary of State. Woodrow Wilson fell ill, as you know, at a very critical time. Mrs. Wilson, I think, did her best to cooperate and carry messages between the sick President and the Secretary, but Mr. Lansing was put in a rather impossible situation for nine months or so. He had a very difficult time. It ended up rather unhappily for him because, after all, the Secretary of State has only the amount of authority and power that the President is willing to give him. Apart from that he has no status whatsoever. At a certain point I think Mr. Wilson withdrew any authority from Mr. Lansing.

Mr. Foster Dulles had that very vividly in mind; I know; he told me so; so that his relationship with President Eisenhower was based on one that had developed through the years. His was one of the closest intimacies which a Secretary of State has ever received. Yet he never made a decision without prior consultation with the President on an ever larger basis. Even so, with that close association during most of both terms of the Eisenhower Presidency, the development of any important foreign policy principle or rule or intention would require more than just those two men. There must be, and there was, a much broader consultation.

Of course, each President operates differently, and you can't lay down a hard and fast blueprint to which every President is going to follow. This President is no different than any other. He has his own methods of working. Its invaluable, I think, to the President to have a certain staff, as a base for his operations. He doesn't always follow them; he doesn't always agree with them, but he does have the benefit of that valuable consensus which any group of men in different walks of life, who are presumably loyal to the President and patriotic Americans, can give to him. So that if it is properly managed, with the President's full support and cooperation, I think this, too, this instrument that is the National Security Council, is very necessary in our Federal Government.

I'd like to just mention one other thing, having seen Jim Hagerty here this evening and bearing in mind that Gordon Hoxie said that we were to talk on "foreign policy operations." One time during the Eisenhower Administration the press took hold of the President's tendency to play golf. He had established a putting green behind the White House. He liked to play golf, and I think it did him a world of good. It didn't harm his foreign policies, but the criticism about too much golf got pretty hot for a couple of weeks.

Jim Hagerty thought that something ought to be done to rectify this situation and let the reporters understand that the President was really on the job even if he did play a little golf every now and then. So that Saturday morning Jim called up the State Department saying, "You might get into the Sunday editions a little reference to item so-and-so;" Herb Hoover, Jr., who was then Under Secretary, always was very cooperative. He took the Hagerty call which was in reference to some tanks to Saudi Arabia, which was a rather difficult item in Brooklyn at that time. Seeking to be agreeable, Herb said "fine." But then a few minutes later, after consulting with some of us who said, "this would not be a good thing to publish now," Herb called Jim back and said, "No, I don't think it would be a good thing for you to run this particular item." Jim said, "Oh, that's Okay with me. All I was trying to do was to show that the President was not sitting around on his fanny playing golf."

WILLIAM J. CASEY: Hal, I wonder what you could tell us about the use of this foreign policy and national security machinery, based upon your own experience both at the Department of State and the White House.

HELMUT SONNENFELDT: Thank you Bill. Let me first emphasize a couple of points that have already been made, not only about this machinery but about any other aspect of the operation of the Presidency, if not indeed of the Executive as a whole. The point is that the President of the United States is an enormously powerful individual for the four years that he is in office. Probably there is a greater accumulation of power and authority in his hands than in any comparable hands today, in a head of government. That means he is also able to shape and mold his machinery very closely to what his own wishes and desires are. That is to say our system is sufficiently flexible and sufficiently capable to being tailored to the man. Thus the President can put his imprint on it, at least in the White House itself. Some Presidents wonder whether they succeed in putting their imprint on all facets of the Executive Department, and they probably don't even when they are around for eight years.

There's no question that in the White House, the Presidential imprint and the Presidential personality is all pervasive. So Presidents have molded and reshaped and tailored the rather bare bones machinery in respect to the NSC that was established by the 1947 Act. Moreover, the longer I labor in this building the more conscious I am of the need to make the President as comfortable as possible, in the machinery he has.

The responsibilities he has are obviously so enormous that if he constantly finds himself fighting his own machinery and his own system because of rigidities this is going to be utterly debilitating and will detract from his ability to focus on the real issues. Therefore, a crucial function of the White House operation and all its facets is to make the President as comfortable a chief magistrate, a chief executive, as possible. There are people who criticize that particular point.

I don't know if any of the journalists that were here today said anything like this, but I've heard it said by some of our columnists, who sometimes believe that they are the President, that obviously Presidents are only human and the function of their staff is to prevent them from going wrong. They would tell the President that if he sees too few people, well, by God, it's his responsibility to see more people, because it's dangerous to see too few people. They also say that it is a supine or spineless staff that will accommodate itself to the Presidential whim. According to some journalists the staff ought to be there to teach the President how to do his job and how to do it right. Well, that's a concept which has a nugget of a point. If someone sees the President obviously and evidently making some error, it ought to be prevented. But the basic function of the White House Staff is to make the President operate in comfort, and with a sense that he has support, and *not* have to constantly fight against some sort of resistance.

Therefore, inevitably the Staff's setup and the various conceptions that have operated in the national security field have been reflections of Presidential preference and of Presidential desires and of Presidential will. I think it's a very important point to remember. I would be surprised if a great deal of machinery that has either been restored or newly set up in this Administration is going to survive the life of this Administration. Undoubtedly, a future President will want to make his own arrangements, even though hopefully we have discovered some devices and some techniques which will serve other Presidents. Obviously, none of these things start completely new. Every President inherits something from his predecessor as far as machinery is concerned. Of course, he inherits a great deal as far as his policies and his options are concerned. But it is not likely that the particular machinery is going to reappear in its present form in the case of Mr. Nixon's successor.

Now, I'm not going to try to rehearse the intricacies of this machinery, because I think Dr. Hoxie has given you the February 18, 1970, President's report to the Congress on foreign policy called: *U. S. Foreign Policy for the 1970's*. There is a rather detailed treatment of this machinery in there. Certainly, if you have questions or comments on it later, I'll be delighted to say something about it from my perspective and probably Ambassador Pederson will certainly be able to say something from the perspective of the Department of State.

Let me make a couple of general points. The example that Mr. Gray gave, which he referred to as the "yo-yo" form of government, is a very telling example of where the decision-making process or where the orderly making of decisions can be placed in great jeopardy. That is to say if the President is exposed to individual advocates of a position, of a policy, of a strategy, he is not likely to get all the information he needs in order to make the policy himself. The advocate, being human, is most likely to present the evidence in such a way as to march to the conclusion that he is going to give at the end. That is only normal, and advocates are expected to do this.

The President is also likely to be confronted with something that Presidents are ordinarily reluctant to do, which is to have a head-on collision with their own Cabinet Officers in such a way that they are obligated to over-rule in a crass and clear manner. If you do this too much, obviously, the relationship between the Cabinet Officer and the President becomes a very difficult one. For this reason Presidents in general have preferred to have some sort of machinery where positions can be argued out. They prefer this to a system where individual advocates will come in and buttonhole him and perhaps persuade him through the vigor of their argument, through the force of their reasoning, to make some particular decision, perhaps even quickly before someone else who may have a different slant on this particular problem can make himself heard. All Presidents, I think, have attempted to protect themselves against that kind of advocacy and that way of making decisions.

Now, the candid example that Mr. Gray gave is very unlikely to happen in this Administration; the President, as you will see from his *U. S. Foreign Policies for the 1970's* (if you haven't read it or those of you who have) has established a machinery and a system for orderly advocacy and opposition. Not only is a particular position advocated in the presence of all the interested members of the Administration, but he has established a system whereby each advocate of a particular line of policy is obligated to state not only the advantages of that policy but also its faults and disadvantages.

In this Administration, the NSC system is designed to make sure that any particular policy option that is considered by the President is presented in such a way that the President can be made aware of the gains that he can achieve by following this line; the system also sets forth the disadvantages that he must in some fashion seek to compensate for, in some way to allow for, or in any event be prepared for.

Advocates have a way of not stating the other side of the case. In the NSC system as presently established, any one or several options in any issue, whatever it is, are defined. The President is presented the pros and cons. Normally we give the advocates the opportunity to state the pros as vigorously as they wish; and we give the opponents the opportunity to present the cons as vigorously as they wish. Thus, we can be as sure, as one can humanly be, that the President has before him a clear and fair statement of what it is he is about to let himself into.

Now another aspect of the present system, and I think in some respect that this perhaps is true of the system as it operated in the past, is that in the present system the decision that the President makes is not in fact announced at the council table. The NSC machinery serves, so far as it deals with the policy formulation aspect, as a clarifier of the issues, as presenter of the options that are open to the President: together with the advantages and disadvantages that he can expect from each option. The President either reads or hears the issues and options. (Normally Mr. [Henry A.] Kissinger will have presented the issues and options.)

The President will then ask the other members of the Council to state their preference and any considerations that they have at all that bear on the particular problem. He will ask for any criticism of what the NSC machinery has produced in the way of presenting the issues. Then normally the Council will be recessed, and the President will then take it upon himself to choose. He normally does not do this in the Council, at least not in the present Administration. Historically, Presidents have acted differently in this regard, but a number of Presidents have withdrawn to make their decisions in their own way, in their own time, in their own manner, rather than in the presence of their advisors.

Now this President will then insist to have that decision recorded on paper for all to see, for all to know about. Ideally the decision that the President makes is one of the options that was presented to him through the system. There may be occasions when other factors have influenced the President's decision. These somehow did not get into the system, such as the domestic factors of one kind or another, or political factors or what have you; there may be occasions when the decision may come out differently from the options presented through the system. But in many cases it does come out as one of the choices, as it did, for example, in the decision on chemical and bacterial warfare made last year. That is a model case in marching through the system.

Let me make just one more point, then stop. I think it is

important in measuring the effectiveness of a President to distinguish between *decision-making* and *implementation*. Presidents, like other heads of government, have traditionally found it somewhat easier, or a good deal easier, to establish a congenial mechanism for decision making. They found it far harder to find ways to get those decisions implemented. After all, the decision making process is one that involves relatively few people in the end. About six or seven people that go to the NSC meeting can sit around the table. Ultimately, that is where the end of the process is. These people can be reasoned with; they can present their views intelligently.

On the other hand, when it comes to implementation, you deal with the mass bureaucracy. Particularly when a decision has gone against some interest group in the Government, you deal with a problem of getting the faithful implementation of an adverse Presidential decision from the standpoint of that particular interest group. Now, what I have said is that you have to distinguish very clearly. I don't think that a President is a great President only if he makes wise decisions. He becomes a truly great President only after he has succeeded in enforcing those decisions.

The so-called Under Secretaries Committee of the NSC is the implementing arm of the NSC; it receives Presidential decisions and is instructed to translate them into operating policy and to supervise the actual implementation. This is somewhat along the lines of the OCB in Gordon Gray's period of the White House. There are, of course, enormous problems in implementation and in follow-through in the Administration in the Executive Department, not to mention the problem of getting Congressional support and so on and so forth.

This matter of support and execution is an entirely different facet of the labors of the White House staff. It is in the monitoring of Presidential decisions that White House staff can manage to make themselves most unpopular because they have to crack the whip and get people to abide by Presidential decisions. And machinery itself is not the answer for this very crucial problem; the implementation of the Presidential will.

I leave this as a problem for the moment, and, we can, perhaps, come back to it. I'm sorry I've taken more time than I should have.

WILLIAM CASEY: Well, thank you, Hal. With this obvious increase in the size and the effectiveness of the White House foreign policy staff and function, I wonder what Ambassador Pedersen can tell us of the impact of this on the operations of the State Department.

RICHARD F. PEDERSEN: One of the favorite parlor games in Washington for twenty-five years, no doubt longer than that, is to talk about the demise of the State Department; it hasn't happened yet. It reminds one of the man who read his own obituary in the newspaper and termed it "a little bit premature." I don't think we need to be concerned about the disappearance of the Department.

The Constitutional authority that has been stressed by every speaker here regarding the formulation of foreign policy is that it is Presidential authority. The Secretary of State is the President's principal advisor on foreign affairs, but he has very little statutory authority. His basic authority was set out in 1789. It was essentially to have control of the foreign correspondence of the country and to do such other tasks as the President wished him to do. And that essentially is his authority of today. His current statutory authority is in areas which are really secondary to this primary task. He has statutory responsibility for foreign policy guidance to the Arms Control Agency, and to the U.S. Information Agency, and to aid the Peace Corps, which are agencies within the department; he has responsibility for the coordination of foreign, economic, and military assistance. But his basic authority is the delegation from the President.

Now the key word is that the Secretary of State is the principal advisor; he is not the President's sole advisor on foreign affairs, nor should he be. From this point of view of the Department of State, I would say that if we did not have a national security staff in the Presidency, we would be among the first to want one. We do a great deal of business every day with the White House. A number of memoranda recommending policy actions or policy decisions or simply providing the President with information go from us every day; there is a larger number of information memoranda simply to keep this staff informed. If we did not have a focus of staff in the White House to process these matters, if we could not test attitudes in the White House so that we could then go ahead and do our business for the President, if there were no one in the White House who was there to work with the President on a day-to-day basis, it would be extremely difficult for us to work.

In an informal way I serve a similar function within the State Department itself. Often other people in the Department will consult me as to what the Secretary might be thinking about a certain subject at a particular point. In many cases, not always, I have more direct knowledge of his attitudes, and I am often able to avoid a lot of bureaucratic problems. In brief, I can short circuit some of the arguments that might otherwise take place, so that when papers go forward, when action is taken, they are done with knowledge of the policies of the Secretary. The same thing is true in the White House. The staff of the White House is closer to the President on a day-to-day basis and knows factors that we cannot know a few blocks away.

The other thing that I would comment on is that people often think of the National Security Council and its staff as functioning only in the foreign policy field and thereby as overlapping almost coterminously with the responsibility of the Department of State. In fact, of course, the NSC function is broader than that. It is an attempt to pull together and to coordinate political considerations and military considerations in particular but also to encompass other considerations into one common national security policy which takes into account political, military, security, and economic factors.

This coordination we seek to do at all levels of the Government though inter-departmental committees, most of which are chaired by the State Department. But much of this can only be done at the White House level, and it can only be done effectively if we have structure of this sort.

In the long run, the input of the established agencies of the Government in the formulation of policy and in the execution of policy are inevitably and, in my opinion, will inevitably be very large. The input of the Department of Defense into the formulation of defense policies has to be the major input because it has the expertise; it has the knowledge it has the direct responsibilities for execution. The input of the State Department into the formulation of foreign policy derives from the same sources.

For example, the Assistant Secretary of State for Middle Eastern Affairs is the man who is looked to by the President and by the Secretary of State for assuring that all relations with the Middle East are in as good a condition as they could possibly be. His recommendations directly through the Secretary of State are bound to carry a very considerable weight in the thinking of the President as he decides on policy.

The man responsible for the implementation of our policy in the area is the ambassador; who is the ambassador of the President of the United States, but is ordinarily a member of the State Department. He is the one who is responsible for our overall relations in the area, and, therefore, what he recommends is bound to be given considerable weight in the formulation of foreign policy. His recommendations ordinarily go to the Secretary of State in the first instance.

So just as the military services and the Defense Department are the principal advisors of the President on the formulation of military policy, so the Secretary of State, in my opinion, will continue to be the principal advisor to the President in the area of foreign policy. So also will there continue to be a National Security advisor at the White House.

In conclusion, I might just say that I think that the present relationships and the present manner of working are functioning rather effectively. I agree entirely that the system of establishing foreign policy has to be a system which is in accord with the desires, the interests, and the way of working of the President. There is not one system which is better than any other system.

Having said that, I rather like the present system that is being followed. I like it in the sense that it is fairly formal, and in the sense that different possible policy decisions, not just one, are put forward. Thus, the President can see the range of choices which government agencies would regard as within the national interests of the United States. One department of government might regard one choice as more in our national interest and another department might regard a second choice as more in our national interest. But when various alternatives are put before the President, it seems to me it is easier for him to think about the matter; it is easier for him to come to a conclusion; and you are more likely to get the issues fully explained; than in a case where a single recommendation is put forward, where critical elements may be obscured by departmental compromises.

WILLIAM CASEY: Professor Koenig, from your detached and scholarly viewpoint how do you feel about the evolution of this machinery and its value?

LOUIS KOENIG: One thing, I think, deserves to be emphasized. In dealing with national security, we are dealing with one of the most politically risky areas that the President has faced since the Second World War. In all the Presidential elections and in many of the Congressional elections in that era, this subject has been in the forefront. One can identify a couple of the Presidential elections as instances where the Presidential candidate either was unavailable for a further try at the office, or out of the office, or his party went out of the office. What I am getting at directly is that in 1952 the Korean War was costly to the Democratic Party and that in 1968 the Vietnam War was also costly to the Democratic Party. Among the arresting things in the next couple of years that we will have to watch will be the current swift developments in Southeast Asia. What will hold forth for the future of the Nixon Administration?

One thing I'm concerned about, therefore, is the fact that the machinery related to national security affairs has great political consequences for the President. In the workings of this machinery we do have a hallowed doctrine which has heretofore been stated in this Symposium, that this machinery should be shaped and adjustable to help the President to do things.

Bill Moyers had some things to say about this formula and this machinery in the *Atlantic Monthly* a couple of years ago, when he wrote regarding the development of the Vietnam decisions in 1965. This, of course, was the year that President Johnson was virtually preoccupied with his great legislative program. Moyers' analysis regarding the development of the Vietnam decisions suggests a kind of sliding operation being developed rather incrementally. Because of the absorption then in the domestic legislative program, there was an atmosphere then of second class citizenship so to speak for the decisions related to Vietnam.

Now what I am getting at is simply this: it is true the President has to make the final decisions. It is true that he goes off in some privacy normally, although it is not always the pattern, to make these decisions. To me one of the fascinating and elusive things about the matters so expertly and lucidly presented here tonight is this lingering question: Are there ways to help the President to get the most mileage out of this machinery? Are there ways to reduce as much as possible the risks, the hazards to the President, in these final hours or days after the presentations have been made when he may act without the full benefit of this machinery?

Just one other illustration of what I have in mind. I was rather fascinated by the content of President Nixon's Vietnam address in November. Now public opinion polls indicated a most effective address in terms of the impact on public attitudes. From the accounts that I saw, it would appear that very few key members of the President's staff had any idea much before hand as to what the substance of the President's address was going to be. In other words, this was largely Mr. Nixon's personal effort assisted only by instant foot-work in his rather extended privacy. There is thus engendered an atmosphere of unpredictability among the staff as to the ultimate outcome of any of the decisions. This is a slippery kind of problem; yet, as I say, in view of the purple hazards and costs involved here, this is a very crucial problem related to this machinery process.

A second matter that our moderator indicated at the outset, I should just like to underscore, too, in reference to the machinery. I was impressed from the studies made of President Nixon's methods on world affairs by the extent of the machinery. I have followed this subject for years with a pretty full development of the picture as it spans the attitudes of the various Presidents preceeding Nixon. In all of this it seems to me one of the haunting elements is this matter of *innovation,* making innovative foreign policy where you have elaborate machinery; as you build on it you reach the point where innovation becomes quite difficult. It is O. K. to move along with policy which has some roots in present Presidential decisions and past Presidential decisions, but there is this haunting question: Can there be reasonable good innovations if we have this rather elaborate structure?

In the last point that I would like to make, one of the sources of inspiration I would use would be the Townsend Hoopes book, *The Limits of Intervention.* I don't know whether I am citing an heretical source among present company or not, and I grant, of course, that still part of the story might be President Johnson's TV broadcasts and other sources yet to be revealed. But here, too, we have an old problem which has always surrounded Presidential staff, and this is the question of access. The odyssey of access begins with the assembling in the structure of persons at the second and third level who figure pretty seriously and pretty importantly. The most dramatic aspect, I suppose, of the Hoopes story is the discussion among the people at the second and the third level of the Defense Department and the State Department as to whether several of them should resign in order to bring impact on the President and on the public and, of course, above all on public policy as to the course of the war.

Now in making these references to the war, I am not myself intending to make any value judgments one way or the other. In other words, I am simply using that as an illustration of another of the kinds of problems which arise related to the war or other situations; that is the limit of my intention. Well in the Hoopes thing, this again would be the kind of evidence of the question of the adequacy of access of those people who are important to the machinery. Do they have adequacy of access to serve effectively?

WILLIAM CASEY: Dr. Koenig. I think that you put your finger on this question of how far and how useful this machinery can be. There's a point at which the machinery has done its job, and, as President Truman used to say, the buck stops. In the case of the Vietnam decision, the President clearly had to consult only his sense of the political position and the amount of maneuverable area he had together with an overriding consideration for the credibility and the security of the country.

I would like to put out for discussion the problem created by a kind of asymmetry between the activity of democratic methods of the U.S., particularly how we reach our foreign policy decisions, and the way the totalitarian countries are able to do it. We're limited and restrained in our policies by public opinion. Public opinion does not always have full information and does not always take a long view. The totalitarian powers don't have that problem at all. They can get the staff work done from a sense of reality, and can go on facts. Our leaders have to consult public opinion and Congressional opinion. There is also the question of secrecy: How much they know about what we're doing, and how much we know about what they're doing. The fact is that through the budgeting and the appropriation process and the operations of the press, everything that we do is more or less an open book. Quite the contrary is the case with the Soviet Union and the Asiatic powers. Now I think that this makes the conduct and development of foreign policy in a democracy extraordinarily difficult. And I just don't know how the staff machinery gets at this kind of thing. Hal, do you have any light you can shed on this?

HELMUT SONNENFELDT: Well, just let me be sure that I understand the problem, the problem of asymmetry, the difference of our methods and theirs, and the problem of our operating in effect in a gold fish bowl. Well, obviously, there are disadvantages associated with the fact that you have to operate in the full glare of daylight and that you are subjected to a great many pressures, quite articulate pressures, compared to people who can operate in a much more sealed or concealed form of government.

On the other hand one ought not to underestimate the problems that, for example, the Soviet Government has in making its own decisions. It isn't that just five or six or eleven men sit around a table and get the yellow notepad or red notepad out and make their calculations coolly and then reach an agreement either enforced or otherwise, and off they march. They have interest groups as well. They don't express themselves in quite the way that ours express themselves, and they certainly don't have the enormous noise level with which American policy making has to contend. But there is plenty of evidence to indicate that the Soviet system is far from the monolithic and smoothly honed machinery that one sometimes associates with the totalitarian government. The Soviet Government, not to mention the disagreements and backbiting and political maneuvering among the eleven people in the Politburo, is not without its peculiar pressures and countervailing arguments and pullings and haulings. Thus the asymmetry isn't quite so stark in some respects as one might think.

I think also that there are significant advantages that accrue to us in functioning in our system. I think when all is said and done, the vigor of the press, the vigor of Congressional involvement, all of these things go into the system of checks and balances that we have in our system that can frequently prevent grave error, not always obviously, and they certainly do not prevent problems. Dictatorships have a way of perhaps reaching a decision somewhat more easily in their conspiratorial fashion. But if they divorce themselves too much from the political hinterland in which they operate, they can get quite far out of tune with their own country; that is precisely why they are totalitarian, because then they have to ram things down the throats of their population, including by terror and by coercion. And they must do so precisely, because their decisions do not very often flow from the wellsprings of popular attitudes and interests. That is one of the characteristics of the totalitarian government.

So then I think that there are pluses and minuses. Although quite obviously in a tactical sense it is very difficult for us to make quick decisions or even to make surprise decisions which sometimes might help us in a situation, because we are likely to read them in the newspaper the next morning, and that is a distinct disadvantage that we have to contend with. But I don't think that we are all that badly off compared with the communists, for example, in the decision making process because I think that there are strengths and assets that stem from this system in which we operate that they don't have the benefit of.

WILLIAM CASEY: Of course, once the Soviet Union has

thrashed out the pros and cons and the decision is made, it's the decision.

HELMUT SONNENFELDT: Yes, but it not necessarily implemented. That is what I think was Khrushchev's experience. He was great at manipulating the machinery to get the decisions he wanted. But he was far less successful, at least in his later years, whether it was on agriculture or it was on his particular ideas on military policy, in getting the people who really didn't want those decisions to implement them. That is one of the interesting facets of Khrushchev, and contributed to his downfall. Stalin, of course, got his decisions implemented, but in ways that Khrushchev was not prepared to use, to quite that extent.

GORDON HOXIE: This splendid panel here has made only passing reference to the role of the Department of Defense in the formulation of foreign policy. True, passing reference was made, by way of example, to an Under Secretary of the Air Force, Mr. Townsend Hoopes. Parenthetically, may I say it would appear that Mr. Hoopes, a deputy in a sub-cabinet post, took his own foreign policy role too seriously. Nonetheless, there is suggested here what is the foreign policy role of the Department of Defense. The role of the Department of State has here been made manifestly clear, as in a sense has the role of the National Security Council which includes representatives of the Department of Defense. Does the Pentagon play a significant role in foreign policy? I should like to address this question primarily to a former Secretary of the Army who is with us, Gordon Gray.

GORDON GRAY: I'll just make a couple of comments about it. It has been, indeed, touched upon when it was pointed out earlier that the inputs into the formulation of policy which are largely of a political character must come from the State Department. Now to the extent that military policy is deeply involved, and these days as it is very deeply involved, then inputs may indeed come from the Defense Department. I think that nobody has mentioned the fact that under the statute the Chairman of the Joint Chiefs of Staff is a statutory advisor to the President and to the National Security Council and does, or used to, always attend meetings of the National Security Council as does the Secretary of Defense and I suppose someone assisting the Secretary of Defense. So by statute the Security of Defense is a full fledged member of the National Security Council. There is no question that these days no President would in the Council or otherwise approach a foreign policy problem without seeking the views of the Secretary of Defense and, I suppose, the Chairman of the Joint Chiefs of Staff, where military considerations would even in a remote way be involved.

Just for half a minute it might be amusing for you to know that I am one of two living persons who has been kicked off the National Security Council. I will show you how there has been some evolution. Under the National Security Act of 1947, both the Secretary of Defense and the three Service Secretaries were made statutory members of the National Security Council. When the Act was amended in 1949, perhaps to reduce military influence, the three service Secretaries were taken off; so Stuart Symington [then the Secretary of the Air Force] and I have the "honor" of having been kicked off that Council. But the point is well made, though no one has mentioned it particularly, that the Secretary of Defense speaks with a powerful voice in Council deliberations.

ANNA CHENNAULT: May I ask a question directed to Mr. Sonnenfeldt? How do you distinguish the responsibilities of these two organizations i.e. the Office of the President (NSC) and the Department of State? For instance, in recent happenings related to Cambodia did the President talk to Dr. Kissinger first or to Secretary Rogers?

HELMUT SONNENFELDT: I don't have the telephone log. But the chances are that the President talked to Dr. Kissinger first in chronological terms because he's there. But I don't think that in itself is necessarily significant.

But that is the sort of issue that the machinery that has been established is supposed to deal with. This is in the sense that when a fast moving development of this kind occurs, the facts can be gathered as rapidly as possible, and you can get agreement among the various agencies concerned as to what the facts are. Also the possible American responses to the events can be rapidly canvassed, much as we would do when we had more time, and we were looking at a long range problem. There is the machinery for this.

Now whether a problem like this comes before the full National Security Council, or whether the findings of the machinery are presented to the President, depends on the issues and the schedule and various other factors that are sort of unpredictable. But I think as a whole, wouldn't you say, Dick, [Ambassador Pedersen] whether its Cambodia or the shooting down of an American plane over Korea, or some rapidly changing set of events in the Middle East, that by and large the machinery has now established itself sufficiently in the year and a quarter or so since this Administration has been in office, that it can move in rather rapidly to get the President the considerations that he needs to have in trying to decide how to play that particular issue.

RICHARD PEDERSEN: I think that's right. There isn't any one answer to a question like that. Probably the President spoke to Mr. Kissinger first. He also spoke to the Secretary of State. And before the Secretary testified in private session before the Senate, he spent a considerable amount of time with the President in discussing what our policy position ought to be.

We have a formal mechanism for handling crisis situations called the Washington Special Actions Group. This is referred to in the President's Report, which Dr. Hoxie distributed to each of you. This Group functions in a situation like this. We have in the Department in a time of crisis a special arrangement for a 24 hour a day watch duty by a special task force. There are also telephones which are very handy in a crisis situation.

ANNA CHENNAULT: Your machinery works very effectively. This reminds me of an amusing incident. The other day my secretary called Dr. Kissinger's office for an appointment. His secretary (I don't know which secretary since he changes secretaries quite frequently) inquired of my secretary: "Is this call a social call or on official business?" My secretary is pretty smart, too; and she said, "I didn't realize that Dr. Kissinger takes social calls in his office."

GEORGE REEDY: I was a little startled a few minutes ago when I heard the statement that in the totalitarian countries they can take the long view and that they can make these decisions dispassionately without being worried by all those people crowding in on them who might have different ideas.

I am not familiar with the Soviet Union. But I have been in some totalitarian countries. The impression I have is that they are not likely to take the long view simply because they don't have to worry about people with different ideas crowding on them. I have in mind Peru, for example, with General Juan Velasco Alvarado taking "a long view," when he handled some of the fishing problems the way he handled them; when he handled the IPC [International Petroleum Co., Ltd.] controversy the way he handled it; or internally when he started promulgating an urban reform law earlier this year. Or was he merely reacting rather arbitrarily and capriciously, which he could now do considering his circumstances?

I have a very serious question about this long view thing in a totalitarian state. If there is a dictator with a long head, he may get a long view, but if he is not long headed, he will get a short view. Isn't it quite possible that what you are going to get out of the totalitarian powers is a much shorter view than in our country where the President has to take many factors into account?

HELMUT SONNENFELDT: You have made a very cogent point about the totalitarian system. We know a good deal about the Nazi system because the documents are available. We find that that is precisely the sort of thing that happened. From the outside it *looked* as though it was all working with careful planning and long range strategy. It was *not*, although it happened to get us all to the brink of disaster which is bad enough. I think this short range view and style to which you have referred is a characteristic of the totalitarian system.

THOMAS CORCORAN: Do the totalitarians have a machinery analogous to what we are talking about? For example, who decided that the Russian troops should go to Czechoslovakia? Who decided to put Russian pilots in the planes in Egypt? How do they make that kind of decision?

HELMUT SONNENFELDT: I wish we knew precisely how they do it. They have a staff system in the political and the party side, and they have a government, of course. We know something about the papers that are prepared and the people who come before the Politburo to be asked for their advice and things of that sort. There is not a Senate Foreign Relations

Committee, however, that the Politburo has to consult. That much is clear. There are some reasonably powerful bodies in the Party machinery that presumably are heard in some fashion; particularly if a particular venture costs resources; this presumably has to be matched in some fashion against other economic priorities that they have.

There is undoubtedly a machinery. But, unfortunately, Mr. Leonid I. Brezhnev does not report to the Supreme Soviet in the way President Nixon reported to the Congress on February eighteenth. So we're far less well clued in to the precise machinery that they utilize. My hunch on Czechoslovakia is that while perhaps the ultimate decision was one that they took rather rapidly, it was a decision that they were probably ruminating about for the better part of seven or eight months before they finally made it. So that it was *not* just a decision where someone pushed a button and said: "March into Czechoslovakia." I think that there was a good deal more argument, procrastination, and waiting around to see what would turn up. It was more than just that last minute decision in August 1968 would suggest.

Specifically, with regard to putting Soviet pilots into Egyptian planes, there is some argument or question as to whether that is what has happened. However, the problem of how the Soviets help the Egyptians militarily is one that's been keeping the Soviets pretty busy for a fair number of years. They haven't yet found a very clear answer to it. They, too, have to balance risks and costs against some particular course of action. As to the precise machinery, I just don't think we know how these things are arrived at.

WILLIAM CASEY: In my reference to the long view, I did *not* specifically have in mind Peruvian fishing vessels. I was referring to something like the Soviet decision in 1962 that they were going to build the greatest navy in the world, or to their 1962 decision that they were going to achieve nuclear superiority. For eight years they have been marching towards it, and they are not subject to the annual re-evaluation of that decision in the same way that we are.

There is a real distinction here between their ability to make long term commitments and our not being sure that our commitments are going to stick. I don't have the answer as to what we're going to do about it. But it is a very real problem.

ANNA CHENNAULT: I have a concern about the leaking of security information to the press. Supposedly such matters, as for example with Senate Committees, are discussed in closed hearings. Then the next day you read about it in the papers. How do the papers get this kind of information?

PANELISTS: The Senators leaked it to them. If you have a solution let us know.

JOHN THEOBALD: Do I gather from the comments that in a situation like Cambodia we don't have advance information as to what is developing, and that we do not have some tentative solutions? Do we do this at the last minute?

THOMAS CORCORAN: May I answer that question. I read [William J.] Bill Donovan's book the other day. Bill, you will recall, was our Ambassador to Thailand. He advised in a memorandum to the State Department that the Communists looked at the whole of Indo-China and Thailand as all one. They didn't look at it as separately Laos, Cambodia, Vietnam, Thailand—but as one. If they regard it all as one picture, if we were considering it from their point of view, we also must have that larger view.

RICHARD PEDERSEN: If your question is as specific as to whether we knew or could have known in advance that Prince Norodom Sihanouk was going to be removed from office when he was out of the country, we did not.

JOHN THEOBALD: No. I'm not being as specific as that, but we knew that there was an attempt to infiltrate Cambodia; we must have known through intelligence that there were also counter movements within Cambodia. I would have thought that we would have considered the possibility of a turn over there, a turn over on the one hand that was favorable or on the other hand that wasn't, and have had some preliminary answers at least prepared.

WILLIAM CASEY: This isn't quite an answer to that question, but even if you had some answers prepared, you would have had the question of whether Senator Fulbright would let you do it!

RICHARD PEDERSEN: We have a great deal of contingency

plans for situations of that sort, of all kinds. Sometimes you may have advance information from overt State Department sources or intelligence sources that something is likely to happen. At other times you don't. Sometimes the people that do these things don't make up their minds until the last minute; for example, as Hal [Sonnenfeldt] noted regarding the Soviets, they discussed going into Czechoslovakia for six months and didn't make up their minds until the last minute. Sometimes they don't even know what's going to happen until the last minute.

You usually know that there is a potentiality in a particular situation. But the potentiality could happen now or ten years from now. If you had looked at the situation of King Hussein in Jordan ten years ago, you might have said that any day there could have been difficulties in Jordan, but they never materialized. So you are always dealing with contingencies.

ANNA CHENNAULT: But won't you say that the Cambodia situation, i.e. the change of government, is more or less unexpected?

RICHARD PEDERSEN: No, I wouldn't say that.

WILLIAM CASEY: Are the dominoes falling?

RICHARD PEDERSEN: The use of the word dominoes portrays a totally false impression. The use of the word dominoes implies that you push one point and everything else automatically changes; I think that creates a wrong impression.

WILLIAM CASEY: There is a push in Laos, then something happens in Cambodia, then the Thais are pretty quick to get their troops into Cambodia; there does seem to be an effect.

RICHARD PEDERSEN: I'm not saying that there isn't an effect. I am saying that it is not mechanical, as would be connoted by the comparison with dominoes.

GORDON GRAY: May I comment on Tommy Corcoran's remarks and also the so-called dominoes theory. I am not a policy maker. I no longer advise policy makers, but it is possible to conceive that those events in Cambodia could have a reverse effect. Because, if the reason that Sihanouk was deposed was the presence of Hanoi and Viet Cong troops in the country, and if this new government should rally a determination to eliminate sanctuaries and make it stick, this could have a profound implication for the situation in Vietnam.

CONFEREE: Does the making it stick in Cambodia depend on us?

GORDON GRAY: No, not necessarily; of course, here I am speaking as a private citizen.

WILLIAM CASEY: What effect will all of this have on the big domino to the North, Japan?

ROBERT MURPHY: I don't believe that is going to effect the Japanese very much, Bill. Let me give another instance related to Mr. Reedy's question. You all remember the Hungarian episode years ago. I had to appear before a Congressional Committee about that time and the question was asked: "Did the State Department know that this was going to happen in Budapest?" We said: "No." I remember one of the Congressmen said, "I am only a country boy, but I knew about it." It turns out that he had heard from a Hungarian refugee in his state of Ohio that there might be a revolution in Hungary some day! But later on I had some talks with the Yugoslav Ambassador in Washington, who was really a very well informed man and very close to Tito. He told me that their embassy in Moscow had learned that this subject had been debated in the Politburo for several weeks before it happened and that there was great dissension in the body because this was a very serious thing for them to do. They didn't want to do it. Nobody in the Politburo really wanted to do this. It provided great risk.

But whenever their security situation is in danger in that Eastern zone, whether they dislike it or not, they end up by taking action. Such was the case both in Hungary and in Czechoslovakia. As Mr. Casey was suggesting, once they have made that decision, they go through with it, 100 percent. In the Hungarian case, I think they put in seven armies. They were ready to throw every man into that issue. Whereas they only used 23 divisions in the Czechoslovak case, again it was all out.

If I am to talk about Indo-China, Cambodia, that area, I better come back to what General Eisenhower said, that you *don't* win wars by hesitation. You don't do it by nibbling or piecemeal. If you make a decision to go to war, and, God knows, we don't want to make that decision, then you either do it or you don't do it. And I think that is one of our failures in Cambodia. I think our intelligence is working there very well. We did have information, but that doesn't mean that we know the answer. Maybe Sihanouk didn't know the answer.

HELMUT SONNENFELDT: I think we must distinguish between the *kinds* of decisions. The decision to march into a country, like the Soviet decision on Czechoslovakia and Hungary, is one kind of decision. One either goes through with it or one doesn't. The latter was the case with the British in Suez where they botched the thing.

There is the distinction between *that* kind of tactical decision and, for example, a decision to reorganize or reshape your entire strategic posture; such a decision has to be implemented over a longer period of time; it also requires a great many subsidiary decisions, constant re-evaluation, and, in our case, it requires Congressional involvement as well.

In brief, we are dealing with different types of decisions. When we are comparing totalitarian with democratic systems, I believe we can say that by and large totalitarian systems manage better with the first type of decisions (tactical like Hungary). But they don't manage nearly as well on the second type of decisions.

In our case, sometimes we do reasonably well on these more tactical type of decisions. But Vietnam is a case where piece-meal decisions were made when perhaps more basic decisions should have been made in earlier years. Likewise in the longer range decisions, whether in the domestic or the national security area, sometimes we do amazingly well when we get sufficient national consensus behind us. The Marshall Plan was a long range ideal with a lot of subsequent subsidiary decisions on which there was a lot of follow-through. It was watched over extremely carefully by the Executive Branch. Congress also worked well on it. It was a good and well implemented decision. Others, we've had second thoughts about; other factors came into play, and we didn't do too well.

In terms of the *machinery* as well as the *nature* of de-

cision making, we ought to distinguish between these two types of decisions.

ANNA CHENNAULT: I have one more question that I would like to direct to Ambassador Murphy. What do you believe will be the outcome of our conference with Japan in regard to export and import quotas, particularly with regard to the textile programs? It's a very touchy question.

ROBERT MURPHY: Mr. Chairman, that reminds me of the observation, "I'm so glad you brought up that question." I think the Japanese have dug in on this textile question. I'm not here to discuss such negotiations, of course. Mr. Pedersen is much better qualified, if indeed, anyone should discuss those things publicly. I know it's a rather difficult situation.

I'd like just to tell a little story. I happened to play golf years ago with an official who was in the White House at the time. We were then having rather difficult negotiations with the Japanese about textiles—ginghams, velveteens, and two or three other things in which they were taking a larger percentage of our markets than we thought that they should. This man with whom I was playing golf, this particular official, was a very nice man, a very honest man. The Japanese Ambassador had made his acquaintance and started to talk about the textile situation in a parallel way. My friend said "The Ambassador was an awfully nice man, he gave me a rather beautiful Japanese screen; I think it might even be valuable, too, but I thought it was a delicate approach to negotiations."

THOMAS CORCORAN: Can you interpret the North Korean action with regard to the Japanese plane that was forced to land at Pongyang? I was wondering whether this was collateral pressure on the whole Cambodia-Vietnam situation and whether birds were working together and whether it was another Pueblo.

ROBERT MURPHY: The fifteen students are staying; the crew is returning. It could well be the type of action you suggest, although it had not occurred to me. These foreign agents are curious.

GORDON HOXIE: In this extraordinary panel we have persons who have been related to foreign policy matters as early as the FDR period. At least one member as a junior foreign service officer goes back to the Woodrow Wilson era.

Quite correctly the panel has focused on *machinery*, in that the defining words of this Symposium on the White House are *organization and operations*. However, several of the panel have wisely suggested that the machinery reflects the desires of the particular Presidents. This again gets us to the matter of personality and the question of style and of substance, just as it did on domestic policy.

Our present Commander-in-Chief has been in office about a year and a quarter. Ambassador Pedersen and Mr. Sonnenfeldt assure us that the machinery is working effectively. Can we carry this a step further to some comparative comment between style and, if you will, the substance of this Commander-in-Chief and some of his predecessors that you gentlemen have also served? What has been the relationship of these Presidents to their machinery and to their principal foreign policy advisors? Can you assess the relative personal leadership of the several Presidents in the foreign policy sector?

WILLIAM CASEY: Who wants to get first in line on that one?

GORDON GRAY: Is your focus of evaluation here on the National Security Council?

GORDON HOXIE: I am speaking of it as an instrumentality, just as I am the use of staff, and the use of personal leadership. For example, to take one President: Dwight Eisenhower, it would appear, was the master of the use of staff. Secretary Dulles in large measure was the leader of foreign policy under that staff type of concept, with the limitations Bob Murphy wisely pointed out. Do we have with President Nixon a similar approach, a similar delegation, recognizing, of course, the role played by the machinery we have discussed here this evening? Or do we have in this instance perhaps from a Constitutional view a differing interpretation of Presidential role? Do we have from a personal view individual leadership of a differing tone? In brief, this is an historical, comparative question; in part it is stylistic and in part it is a substantive comparison of leadership.

GORDON GRAY: Mr. Truman had a very strong Secretary of State with a close effective relationship. Mr. Truman used the machinery of the National Security Council more as a forum for announcing decisions which he had arrived at, usually more or less privately with the Secretary of State.

General Eisenhower, as Dr. Hoxie points out, being a man who believed deeply in staff work and whose life work had been related to staff functions, made considerable use of the machinery. He did enjoy a very close rapport with Mr. Dulles, who was a strong Secretary of State. (I believe Bob, [Ambassador Murphy] will agree he had a less strong rapport with Chris Herter who succeeded Dulles.) General Eisenhower believed in what some people call the *codified* approach to the formulation and, in some respects, the implementation of foreign policy.

When you get to the next two Presidents, Kennedy and Johnson, they believed more in what has been characterized by some as an *ad hoc* approach to the formulation of the foreign policy: less use of machinery; more personal involvement; less reliance upon the Secretary of State.

In the present Administration there has been more of a return to the codification approach, but with innovations and adjustments as compared to what we might call the Eisenhower approach. I don't believe, looking at this as an outsider, that the Secretary of State comes through as strong a figure in this Administration as he did in the Truman and in parts of the Eisenhower Administration. This is an assessment of a private citizen.

WILLIAM CASEY: Ambassador Murphy, do you have anything you would like to add to this historical and comparative question?

ROBERT MURPHY: Just a footnote. I was sitting here listening to the two Gordons, Gray and Hoxie, on the formulation and operation of policy and also the suggestion of a possible constitutional issue. In my earlier remarks, I made reference to Woodrow Wilson's illness and the difficulties this created in matters of foreign policy. One thing we've never settled, constitutionally or otherwise, is what happens in the case of the illness of the President.

During the last months of Franklin Roosevelt's final Administration, the President was a very sick man. He was incapable of doing a full day's work. The burden of many decisions fell upon General George C. Marshall, the Chief of Staff, and on Harry L. Hopkins, Special Assistant to the President. They did the very best they could, but there was no mechanism, no organization which took care of that particular situation. Thus, no matter what your blueprint of foreign policy might be, in that kind of a situation, it would be subject to pretty severe shock and probably, under those circumstances, to very critical and dangerous failure.

ANNA CHANNAULT: I suppose at that time the Vice-President's position was not as strong as now.

ROBERT MURPHY: Well, I guess that's true; it certainly was not. The Vice-President today is kept far better informed. Shortly after Mr. Roosevelt's death, I happened to be at the Potsdam Conference with Mr. Truman. I discovered that he actually hadn't been informed of the vast bulk of the foreign policy decisions that were in progress. Nor did he really know the President's planning for the future. Thus, when Mr. Roosevelt died on the eve of the conference, it was extremely difficult for the new President who had nothing to do with it before.

I still remember at Potsdam one day that I was sitting behind President Truman who turned to Mr. [James F.] Byrnes, who was then Secretary of State. The President said, "Jimmy, do you realize we've been here ten whole days?" Answering his own question, Truman said, "God, you can settle anything in ten days!" Stalin was planning on six months as a minimum; he wasn't in any hurry at all, while Truman felt he himself had a great many things at home he ought to be doing.

WILLIAM CASEY: Thank you, Mr. Ambassador. If there are no other questions of burning urgency, from our symposium participants, I am going to thank all of the members of this unique panel for their far ranging and searching discussion and thank all of you other participants for your penetrating questions. Jointly you have made a contribution to the challenging subject of the how and why of the formulation and implementation of foreign policy. As a result of all of this, perhaps everyone can sleep just a little bit better tonight.

Dr. Hoxie reminds us that we shall gather tomorrow morning for the final session on White House Organization. The meeting is adjourned.

CHAPTER V

White House Organization

GORDON HOXIE: What a beautiful Sunday morning! I even saw Ambassador Pedersen stretching his legs walking the beach and gazing out over the ocean earlier this morning. This, I am sure, is good augury for the affairs of State!

Welcome to this fourth and final roundtable in our symposium on White House operations and organization. All good things, in a sense, come to a close; however, we really believe that this is an on-going pursuit that we have here initiated in the study of the Presidency. It is our hope to make this only the first of our annual symposiums for business and professional and labor leaders. It is our further hope that this annual spring event may be matched by an annual fall symposium for college students. We do believe that much good can come from the study of and an interchange with the most powerful lay office in the world.

From the penetrating insights that have been presented two suggestive titles are emerging:
(1) *The Institutional vs. The Political White House;* and
(2) *The Presidency: Sunset or Sunrise?*
Perhaps one of these will emerge as the title of our published proceedings. The eloquent remarks of several, especially Tommy Corcoran and George Reedy, have already been suggestive of such titles, and I am confident that such themes will emerge from this morning's roundtable.

In advance of the conference you were sent a series of background papers. One of these focused on the pending reorganization of the White House. There are certain landmarks in the creation of the modern Presidency; several of these are related to budgeting purposes and fiscal organization. President Taft's Commission on Economy and Efficiency in 1912 had pointed the way for the creation of the Bureau of the Budget in the Treasury Department as an antidote for Congressional "logrolling" and "pork barrel" activities. In President Harding's administration, this reform was accomplished by the Budget and Accounting Act of 1921.

The Presidential White House aides, however, remained very

few in number until well into the administration of Franklin
D. Roosevelt. In 1937, the President's Committee on Administrative Management, under the chairmanship of the public administration specialist, Louis Brownlow, recommended ex-
pansion and modernization of the White House staff. As a result,
the Reorganization Act of 1939 authorized an increase in the
staff and also the transfer of the Bureau of the Budget to the
Executive Office of the President.

As noted last evening, the next landmark of change in
White House organization came in 1947, with the creation of the
National Security Council. This was accepted by President
Truman on the insistence of Senator Robert A. Taft. In the same
year, President Truman named the elder statesman, Herbert
Hoover, as chairman of a Commission on the Reorganization
of the Executive Branch of Government, which among other
proposals in 1949 recommended the appointment of a Presidential staff secretary to coordinate the other aides and the
Cabinet committees. In other words, Herbert Hoover proposed
to "coordinate the coordinators." Organizational studies subsequent to the second Hoover Commission (1953-1956) were
led in the 1950's and 1960's successively by Nelson A.
Rockefeller, Ben W. Heineman, and Franklin A. Lindsay.
They did not result in major organizational changes
though the Heineman Commission recommended significant
functional consolidations of Executive departments.

Now, however, today as Herb Klein so well put it in his
keynote remarks, we are "gearing" up for the seventies. In
doing so, it is appropriate that we build upon these landmarks of the past. Thus, the proposed Domestic Council is
in a sense the counterpart of the National Security Council,
while the proposed Office of Management and Budget builds
upon its antecedents extending all the way back to the 1912
Taft Commission. Consideration may further be given beyond
the Office of the President itself to possible functional considerations of the Executive department. Guidance in this
most recent and perhaps revolutionary series of recommendations on Executive Branch organizational changes is coming
from the Ash Council, represented here this morning. The
Council gets its informal name, as in the case of the others,
from its Chairman; in this instance, Roy L. Ash, President of

Litton Industries. Its official name is the President's Advisory Council on Executive Organization.

Those of us who were engaged in planning this conference considered whether today's roundtable subject should be first or last. We believe we were correct in the order of choice. One can only understand the proposed White House reorganization by understanding program requirements and services, policy formulation and implementation. An organization must be built in terms of needs. We have then in our discussions been building towards this concluding session on future White House organization.

We have a splendid panel here this morning, students and practioners of government, participants in the planning for White House reorganization. Again I will only introduce the moderator. My good friend, Mr. Thomas W. Evans, is a partner in the law firm of Mudge, Rose, Guthrie, and Alexander. I'm sure you all recognize that two names have been removed from the name of the law firm. It used to be called Nixon, Mudge, Rose, Guthrie, Alexander, and Mitchell. The last mentioned became and is the Attorney General of the United States and the first mentioned became and is the President of the United States!

Mr. Evans helped in this process of changing the law firm's names through his service as National Director of Citizens for Nixon and General Counsel of the Nixon Campaign. Mr. Evans served for two years as Special Deputy Assistant Attorney General of the State of New York, 1964-1965. He's also served as chairman of the Young Lawyer's Committee and chairman of the Committee on Admissions of the Association of the Bar of the City of New York. A Korean War veteran, he was awarded the silver star and two purple hearts during his combat service as a Marine Corps platoon leader. A concerned student of political affairs, he was recently elected President of The Robert A. Taft Institute of Government, an organization akin to our own, devoted to better understanding of the political processes. It gives me a great deal of pleasure to introduce my good friend, our moderator, Mr. Thomas W. Evans, Esq.

THOMAS W. EVANS: Gordon, thank you very much. We've had three excellent roundtables over the last couple of days: we've had a discussion of the media and the Presidency, followed by domestic policy and the Presidency, and foreign policy and the Presidency. Today we're going to come to grips with something that has been discussed throughout all of these panels, that is the question of *organization*. Is there a way to do it better?

We have on our panel three men whom you have already heard; we have Dick Pedersen, the distinguished Counselor of the State Department who constantly works with the White House; the secretary of that Department, of course, sits on the National Security Council. We have George Reedy, who, prior to his work on the White House staff, served as an outstanding staff aide at the United States Senate. Lest we forget, prior to his becoming Presidential Press Secretary to President Johnson, he served as Special Assistant to Vice President Johnson. Indeed his service through the Senate, the Vice Presidency, and the Presidency with Lyndon Johnson extended over 14 years.

In again introducing Thomas Corcoran, a distinguished Washington attorney, one may, by example, point up the evolution of White House staffing. Mr. Corcoran has been a premier White House aide. In the context of our discussions this morning, related to the recommendations of the Ash Council, we may well ask whether they would eliminate the kind of generalist that Tommy Corcoran is and was. Remember, he came into White House service under President Herbert Hoover. Both for Mr. Hoover and subsequently for FDR he served as counsel for the Reconstruction Finance Corporation while performing additional significant service.

When we are thinking today of such special titles as Special Counsels, Special Assistants, and Administrative Assistants to the President, we may well recall that in the early 1930's, some of the key members of the White House team were actually assigned to other departments. For example, Rexford Guy Tugwell was Assistant Secretary of Agriculture and Raymond Moley was Assistant Secretary of State. These were men, who, like Tommy Corcoran, were plucked out of other departments and agencies under a scheme that did not depend on rigid formalism, did not depend upon a highly structured government.

To put us in perspective, when Tommy Corcoran was appointed counsel of the RFC in the latter days of the Hoover Administration, President Hoover had two White House aides, called White House secretaries. Realizing this was not enough, he drastically increased this number so that when he left office in 1933 there were four White House aides—there were three White House secretaries and one administrative assistant! When Roosevelt came into office, with his political sagacity, he avoided the decision of who was the top aide; that is, the one "Administrative Assistant." He avoided the decision as to whether it should be Tugwell, Moley, or whoever at that point in time was in top favor. Nominally, he had only three assistants in his first days in office, but he was able to call upon bright young men like Corcoran who ostensibly occupied other positions.

May I suggest that all of us here this morning assume the position of members of an advisory council that is going to try to propose to the President and to the Congress a plan whereby the Presidency may be made more effective. Possibly we can focus on what we have heard over the last couple of days and, in the light of history, attempt to make a recommendation *not* to *any* President, not to *past* Presidents, but to the incumbent in the White House, keeping in mind his own habits, his personality, his demands, his way of working.

To my right, we have three distinguished representatives of the positions espoused by the Ash Council. First of all, there is the Executive Director of the Ash Council, Mr. Murray Comarow, whom you have already met. Mr. Comarow has an outstanding record related to executive management. He served as Executive Director of the Federal Power Commission and more recently as Executive Director of the Kappel Commission, which proposed a significant postal reorganization, recently embraced by the President.

To Mr. Comarow's right is Mr. Dwight Ink, Assistant Director of the Bureau of the Budget and Director of the Office of Executive Management. Mr. Ink has been Assistant Secretary of HUD; he has served as Chairman of the President's Commission on Education. As we shall see, if the recommendations of the Ash Council are embraced by the Congress, in the form of a statute or as a temporary expedient by an executive order, the Bureau of the Budget will have a very significant role under a new guise in the new scheme of things.

Finally, we are fortunate to have on our panel, Mr. Walter Thayer, a distinguished advisor to the President, who has taken an active role in governmental affairs and political campaigns over the years. An eminent attorney and investment banker, the head of Whitney Communications, he formerly headed one of America's great and lamented newspapers, *The New York Herald Tribune*. A special counsel to the President, he is also a member of the Ash Council.

As Dr. Hoxie has noted, this is not the first council to propose White House reorganization. There have been two Hoover Commission studies; there was the Rockefeller Council report, and the Heineman and Lindsay studies. The Ash Council acknowledged all of those and most particularly the Brownlow Report as helpful in planning their methods of operation and establishing a point of departure. This report by Louis Brownlow had its origins back in those early FDR days when Roosevelt had nominally had only a handful of assistants and saw the need of more.

Thus, with this brief historical survey and introduction of the panelists, three from the earlier panels and three new, we are inviting all of you to consider the recommendations of the Ash Council. On March 12th of this year, the Council's recommendations were put before the Congress. They will now be put before you, ladies and gentlemen, for your decision. Should we go this route? Will the President be helped by the adoption of the Ash Council reports? The report presentation will be made initially by Walter Thayer, a member of the Council, followed by the Council's Executive Director, Murray Comarow, followed by the panel and then by all of you for questions and comments.

WALTER N. THAYER: After the lectures I received from Murray Comarow and Tom Evans as to why I should be brief in my opening remarks, in conclusion I should like to say. . .

The Ash Council, as it has come to be known, was appointed by the President about a year ago. It consisted then of Roy Ash as chairman, Dean George P. Baker of the Harvard Business School, former Governor John B. Connally of Texas,

Frederick R. Kappel, former chairman of American Telephone and Telegraph, and Richard M. Paget, President of Cresap, McCormick and Paget, management consultants. I was an added starter about a month afterwards, as the sixth member of the Council. I took on the chore, full time in Washington for three or four months, to help in the organization of the work of the Council and to help in getting a staff together. To the good fortune of the Council, and this has been borne out many times, we were lucky enough to get Murray Comarow as the Executive Director. He had had a distinguished career in government. Everything he has done all his life has qualified him for this job; everything he's done in this job demonstrates the fact that he brought great experience and a wealth of background to our work.

At the outset, the President made clear to us his ideas as to areas which he believed should be studied. The mission of the Council was to study the Executive Branch of the Government and make recommendations with respect to organizational and structural changes that might bring about more effective government. It wasn't our job to concern ourselves about efficiency. It wasn't our job to concern ourselves about policy. The question before the Council was, given the programs of the Government as they are, and as this Administration wants them, is the Executive Branch organized in the most effective way to carry them out?

There were certain areas that the President mentioned to the Council very early in the game. These included social programs, environmental problems, organized crime, as it related particularly to law enforcement activities in connection with narcotics, regulating agencies, and international trade. As we talked with people in government and as we accumulated a list of so-called "organizational" problems, we very quickly put on a piece of paper some 180 areas in which, for one reason or another, we would be justified in taking a look at the organizational structure of the Government as it deals with particular problems. Of course, we had to take into consideration our own limitations on time and our limitations on staff.

In trying to sort out the priorities to which we felt this Council should direct its attention, we quickly came to the conclusion that the number one problem in the Executive Branch, so far as organizational structure was concerned, was the Executive Office of the President. We took a look at the studies which had been carried on in government by inside and outside people over the past thirty-five years, in fact going back as far as the Brownlow Commission in 1936, through the two Hoover Commissions; Governor Rockefeller and his study for President Eisenhower in the early 1950's; and there had been two studies in the 1960's; one by Ben W. Heineman at the request of President Johnson and the other at the request of President Nixon prior to his inauguration, by a committee headed by Franklin A. Lindsay.

Throughout all of those studies, we found one common strain, that emphasis and stress had been directed to the organization of the Executive Office of the President. We concluded that if the Executive Office were structured as it could be, if Congress and the President were willing, many of the problems would not have risen in the form that they did; many of the organizational difficulties might have been avoided before they occurred; and many of the problems that existed today could be resolved.

After our early deliberations, we had a meeting with the President at San Clemente. We reported to him the conclusion we had reached with regard to the Executive Office. The President, after hearing us, readily agreed that the Executive Office of the President should be our first order of business and the first priority. As we looked at it, we recognized that since 1939 there had been no real change in the structure of the Executive Office of the President. This was despite the fact that the budget had grown from 10 billion to 200 billion; employees had increased from one million to two and one-half million; there were four new cabinet offices; twenty-some new independent agencies. As a matter of fact, we prepared a list of those who report to the President of the United States. There are 163 department and agency heads who, by legislative mandate or executive order, report directly to the President of the United States. These include, of course, some of the people in Washington who by legislative mandate should report to the President, but who would be lucky to see him at all in the four or eight years that he may be in office.

We all recognized that there are some basic functions which had to be carried on in the Office of the President. We believed that the Office should be structured more effectively to carry out these functions. First, there should be a more institutionalized and basic organizational structure to cope with the development of policies and programs on the domestic side. Much as the National Security Council handles problems of this kind on the foreign side, we concluded that there should be some type of similar structure to cope with the problems of this type on the domestic side.

We felt that in addition to the basic functions carried on by the Bureau of the Budget in connection with the development of the budget and review of expenditures, there should be a more specific responsibility fixed for the coordination of programs carried on in the Executive Branch. For the evaluation of programs in the Executive Branch of the Government, we felt that the President was at a disadvantage and that his office was at a disadvanatage because it did not have an adequate *information system* to keep him advised about the progress and development of programs, to provide him with the kind of information executives need to have in order to carry out and be alert to the responsibilities that arise, and to provide a warning of difficulties before those difficulties hit his desk.

We believed also there should be an *on-going* kind of responsibility placed in a division in the Executive Office of the President of the kind this Council took on and has carried out with respect to study of organizational problems within the Executive Branch.

The Council has spent hundreds of hours in discussion of these questions. The staff spent thousands of hours in studying the means of assuming and carrying out these basic responsibilities in the Executive Office of the President. We talked with over 150 people at considerable length; people who had been in the Executive Office of the President, scholars, executives, cabinet officers, and former cabinet officers. We tried to reach everyone whom we felt could make a contribution to the thinking of these problems.

It is a subject on which a great deal of study has been carried on in the past; a subject on which, when you get through with the conclusions reached by various committees and councils that have studied this matter, there is really no significant or basic difference. Some people, perhaps, would approach it a little differently. But everyone recognized that the President, in order to do his job, needs tools, equipment, and machinery which he doesn't have today. This doesn't for a second mean that the people around this President and former Presidents aren't capable, hard working people. They are.

I suppose each President in the past twenty years has felt that he had the best structured organization in the Executive Office of the President. Perhaps each of them was right. The fact remains that, when one looks at this organization objectively, there are many deficiencies which we felt could be cured if it could be structured along the lines that have been recommended.

Basically, we have recommended that there be two added organizational structures in the Executive Office of the President: one, a *Domestic Council,* which would cope with the policy matters and the other, an *Office of Management and Budget,* which would cope with the present problems handled by the Bureau of the Budget and the added responsibilities which I have outlined.

Now with this introduction, I am sure that Murray Comarow will cover in more detail these matters which I have gone over with a big brush. Murray, thank you for your indulgence, and, Dr. Hoxie, thank you for inviting me.

MURRAY COMAROW: You all have every reason to be optimistic with the work of the Council, what with men like Roy Ash, President of Litton Industries, which, according to the financial pages, has been having a few problems! But then if you're basking in optimism, don't forget that Walter Thayer used to run the late *New York Herald Tribune!* Yet it has been and is a pleasure to work with them and their colleagues on the Council.

Let me comment on the accumulated conventional wisdom that we have gained in our studies and in interviews with persons who have served in the White House, or in cabinet posts or independent agencies, or from scholars with "the detached outside view" like Louis Koenig. Such people tell us that the Cabinet and the agency heads have been losing prestige, that their authority has been eroding over the years, and that more and more decisions are being made in the White House by the White House staff.

The Council listened carefully and looked closely into these allegations and came to the conclusion that they were right. It is not a black and white matter, but there is little doubt in the minds of anyone on the Council that more and more decisions are being made by the White House staff. We confronted the White House Staff with this brilliant insight, and they said, "Of course." John Ehrlichman ticked off at 11:30 A. M. half a dozen decisions that he had made that morning; he said, "At least four or five of these things, in an ideal world, should not have come to the White House. But tell me, where should the decisions have been made, where *could* they have been made?"

That, of course, is the problem; there is no decision point for many problems, some so trivial that they should not demand White House attention. And so, the White House Staff, in a world whose complexities are growing exponentially, is trying to cope with the flood of policy and operational decisions. Some of the decisions, as I said, are astonishingly trivial. But they have to cope with them, because there ain't nobody else to do it.

We examined the reasons for this. By and large it is *not* because of too many second rate people in government struggling for power. Of course, there are some such persons and struggles, but this is not the underlying reason. We think that the real lack is a way, a tool, a technique, a device for getting decisions made at the appropriate level. The White House staff has been accused for many Administrations of grabbing for every bit of power it can get—and now and then the charge is true. But most of them would just as soon NOT make many of the decisions forced upon them. Of course, there will always be decisions that the President will personally make or the President's personal advisors will make. The question is one of degree.

Today, we have over 1,500 social programs alone, separate categorical programs, split among sixteen agencies. Sometimes those agencies, at the field level, conduct their affairs as if the town of Yellow Springs or Bedford-Stuyvesant is a kind of turf on which war is waged. There is no effective mechanism for guiding that kind of operation.

As Walter Thayer has said, the Council came to the conclusion that the President does not have the kind of information he needs. True, the paradox is that he is overwhelmed with information; yet, he doesn't have the *kind* of information that he needs and can rely upon. An information system needs to be developed.

The President doesn't have some other management tools which Walter didn't mention. He doesn't have an evaluation system; he doesn't know how his programs are doing in the field except in crude and sometimes frenzied ways. He doesn't know what is NOT being done. How can he know? Can an agency head, no matter how objective he may be, report accurately on programs which cut across the lines of four or six agencies? Who can give the President a report on how the manpower program of government is going? (There are at least six agencies in it.) Who can give the President a report on how the fight against pollution is going? (There are several dozen involved here.) Who can give the President accurate information on overall trends in the regulatory agencies?

The President doesn't have a group of people who understand and who focus all of the time on organizational questions. Every ten years the Office of the President of the United States reacts convulsively and along comes Brownlow, or Hoover, or Rockefeller, or Lindsay, or Heineman, or Ash, and tries to straighten things out. Dwight Ink has a few people who try their best. They are inundated by the flood. Dwight Ink, incidentally, is primarily responsible for the no-dollar functions of the Bureau of the Budget. He knows as well as any man in Washington the needs of which I speak.

The President does not have a coordination mechanism, the counterpart of the industry expediter, the man who, not of great rank or prestige, can go out in the field and work many things out. The new Office of Management and Budget will have such men. They will not be able to solve everything; they won't be able to bring the parties together in every case. But suppose they are able to bring the agencies together in one-half of the cases, or in a third, or in a fourth. The gains will be enormous.

Finally, a word on the Domestic Council. Last night we heard some interesting things about the National Security Council. The learned people on the dais told us that before the Council was established, decisions tended to be made on an *ad hoc* basis. Gordon Gray made a point which I would like to underline. He touched on it lightly not because it was unimportant, but because he is used to the idea.

The President in the case of the National Security Council acts on the basis of rational information. An objective, institutional staff prepares papers with the help of the agencies involved. On the domestic side what the President gets is more often like a multi-layer cake. He will get a proposal from an agency and comments on it from others and comments on the comments *ad infinitum, ad nauseum*. Very often the facts will be in dispute. The White House simply isn't staffed to sort those things out. It is most difficult for decisions to be made in that context.

The proposal here is for a Domestic Council of nine men, consisting of the Cabinet members primarily concerned with the domestic affairs, plus others the President may wish to name, but excluding Defense, State and the Postmaster General. (I might say parenthetically that the President has decided to include the Postmaster General and the Director of the Office of Economic Opportunity so long as they retain cabinet rank.) These men would not sit as a body by and large. The mode is not hierachical. These men would form and reform into groups or committees, as necessary to develop a position for the President on specific tasks. For example, a group might be put together on prison reform, and then dissolved. This is the way in which many progressive modern corporations, management consultant firms, have learned to operate rather than standard, hierachical, organizational chart methods.

The design would be to group and regroup the cabinet officers on the Domestic Council, supplemented by outside people and by an institutional staff along the model of the National Security Council. The purpose would be to give the President a reasoned position, including alternatives, on which to act.

The President is extremely interested in this. He has met

with the Council five times; on one occasion in San Clemente he was with the Council about two and one-half hours. He understands this problem. He is approaching it in a most objective, non-partisan way, and we are gratified by his view that this will help, not only his own office and his own decision making process, but the rest of the Executive Branch.

What this may do is reverse this trend where the Cabinet people have been losing authority and prestige. They have been losing, because for several decades Presidents have been nervous about not getting the right information, not having an evaluation system, not having a proper organizational system. Under such circumstances, a President then tends to get more and more personal advisers immediately around him to do things that the institutions ought to be doing. Those personal advisers, I might add, will always be needed for many problems. I take a solemn pledge here now, Mr. Chairman, that I will NOT eliminate Tommy Corcoran and the likes of him.

THOMAS EVANS: Thank you very much, Murray, for that enlightening discourse; also for the pledge. I think we all abide by that.

We began with the premise that we want a more effective Presidency. We have seen now a mechanism which has been suggested for that purpose. May I ask you once again in your role as a Council to advise the President to determine whether this mechanism is going to be effective. In doing so we can look at testimony now from history, from people who have lived through these processes. Just to recount very briefly some of the comments which have been made from earlier panels, we have seen that the Eisenhower Presidency was one that was highly structured, where you did have a good deal of staff work. We have our own assessment of the Presidency.

By contrast, the Franklin Roosevelt Presidency was unstructured, yet extremely effective. Indeed, the initial Roosevelt staff, we have seen, was an increase in an informal staff, rather than what Edwin Corwin called and has been referred to here, as an institutionalized Presidency. And so, the question arises in viewing the Roosevelt and Eisenhower experiences, in trying to assess this proposal, are we making the Presidency more effective or are we simply engrafting on the Presidency still another bureaucratic mechanism?

I am going to call as our first witness on this a man who worked closely with President Roosevelt in that unstructured, highly competitive atmosphere, to see whether this new mechanism, this Domestic Council, would, in his estimation, be more or less effective.

THOMAS CORCORAN: I am an exhibit out of a neolithic era. I have been very impressed these last couple of days with these proceedings. You have started something in your Center for the Study of the Presidency which I hope you will continue. It needs being done. Yours is a unique Center.

With regard to all the talk about management and budget, I am reminded of a story. It concerns the first day Mr. Roosevelt faced up to the fact that he was going to have to greatly enlarge the budget, after having campaigned for a balanced budget. I was an editor of speeches, participating in the discussion. The President said, "I made a speech in Pittsburgh criticising the Hoover spending and promising to balance the budget with total expenditure of 3 billion dollars. How am I going to reconcile that speech with this enormous increase in government expenditures?" Sam Rosenman replied, "Mr. President, there is only one answer. You must loudly declare that the speech you made in Pittsburgh was not your speech; it was made by an imposter pretending to be you."

With regard to management, I have long been obsessed with the idea that in the public sector the problems in this country are fundamentally political and not managerial. I said yesterday, and I reiterate, this government has to be conceived on a realistic basis as an honest broker weighing and balancing conflicting forces. I have never conceived of the Cabinet as fundamentally managers of their departments. I have conceived them always as political officers, specializing in regional or interest group relationships. They were put in charge of that portion of administration of the Government about which they had the most political sensitivity.

For example, I've always understood that the Secretary of the Interior should come from the West and be a politician. If he must steal from the public domain for the Western people what they want, he must be one of them. I've, likewise, believed that the Secretary of the Treasury should come from New York or Chicago and have a political sense, because fundamentally he was dealing with the money lobby. Likewise, the Secretary of Labor must be someone who understood the political implications of the decisions you make in labor.

All of the technology and all the efficiency should never make us lose sight of the ultimate problem of government; keeping the political processes of brokerage going so that we do not have civil war.

Specifically, with regard to the Domestic Council idea, I like it. Cabinet meetings have become very formal things in which they really don't talk about their own problems. It is outside of the Cabinet that every man in the Cabinet goes to the President with his own problems. By this Domestic Council we create an instrument in which these Cabinet members can gather to decide specific problems which don't have to be taken over by the mere technicians in the White House. If we thus create a situation in which technical problems are discussed in this Council by the master politicians, each a master in a particular political segment of the country, much can be accomplished.

Make no mistake, each would be carrying a torch for his own political interest. But there is nothing wrong in that. From the highest to the lowest interest in local problems, all this motivates government service. You wouldn't be in government service if you didn't carry a torch, because you can make a lot more money outside. It's a good thing to have an instrument which can funnel up specific problems to a formalized business in which the Cabinet officers sit down and know that they are all talking politics together. But don't forget the fact that technical problems have to be resolved in that ultimate political brokerage by which a democracy is kept together.

About politics and Cabinet officers, I'll tell you another story. Once in the '36 campaign, I was riding on the train from Cairo, Illinois to Chicago. Mr. Roosevelt was whistle-stopping through the Illinois country which, of course, was interested in agriculture. To the political leaders of that region the Secretary of Agriculture was, aside from the Presidency, the most significant of all posts. Mr. Roosevelt let me sit in the drawing room on the train. He would stand on the platform at the end of the last car of the train and talk to the people at each whistle-stop. Then as a mark of special political favor he would let the political leader of the area ride with him to the next whistle-stop. There the guest would get off, and Mr. Roosevelt would take another boss on.

Finally, at the end of the day, having overheard the conversations, I opened, "Mr. President, I believe I learned something today about politics." He said, "I hope you have." I went on, "I believe I'm a good enough lawyer to understand that you did NOT specifically promise the Under Secretary or the Secretary of Agriculture to any one of those bosses who rode a whistle-stop with you." His reply, "You are exactly right." I went on, "But if I understand the impact of the English language on the untutored mind, any one of those guests of yours would believe that you did promise it to him." His reply, "You are absolutely right." Then I pressed, "May I ask one more question? By what test do you ultimately give it to one of these?" He said, "I give it to that son-of-a-bitch who, if he didn't get it, would make me the most trouble!"

THOMAS EVANS: George Reedy, you also worked for a President who was viewed as a master politician. Do you think that the Domestic Council as proposed is going to be totally frustrated by political considerations that stand in the way of this rather structured decision-making?

GEORGE REEDY: It may well be. I hope it is at least governed by political considerations. At this point I really could not pass judgment upon the plan as presented. I have not studied it carefully enough to determine whether it meets what I regard as the basic tests as to what should be done at the White House. If it succeeds, not so much in *institutionalizing* the White House as *in putting the institution somewhere else*, then I am strongly in favor of it. I am not quite ready to go as far as Tommy in endorsing it.

But I start from the same premise Tommy has. And that is that the business of the White House is basically politics; the problems of this country today, to a tremendous extent, rest upon the fact that too many institutional decisions have been made and too many institutions have been crowded into a mansion which, *if* it is not fundamentally political, is not fulfilling its purpose.

I start with a feeling of somewhat less than enthusiasm for any type of governmental reorganization. I've been through too many of them. I've observed too many of them, both as a newspaper man, and as a government official in both the Legislative and Executive Branches of the Government. I think that they frequently have very good effects. For example, they were responsible for pay raises for me, and that's a contribution to the general welfare in my judgment! I'm not certain that they really simplify and streamline the Government.

I have very vivid memories of the Legislative Reorganization Act of 1947 which took approximately 30 Senate committees and 40-45 House committees and reorganized and simplified them into about 385 standing sub-committees, each complete with chairman, staff, stationery and budget! I think it was very good that Congress got this extra staff, because in Congress the fundamental business of the body is so political and there are so many political men that the institutional aspects cannot overshadow the basic political outlook of the Congressman. He knows that as a member of the House he faces his constituency every two years and as a Senator every six years.

Many extremely fine and able men have worked on these reorganization studies. But what I am concerned about is that when they become a reality, what they amount to is adding more people and building in what is known as an "institutional memory." In politics one of the worst things you can possibly have is an institutional memory. Indeed, quite frequently in life one of the worst things you can have is a memory! The best thing you can have is a human memory with some idea as to how things react in people.

Some of my caution may be formed by the fact that I had a very close look at the White House in the process of its institutionalization. This is one of the reasons for the title of my book, *Twilight of the Presidency;* I had seen the institutionalization of the White House. I had seen too many decisions that seemed to make sense from the elementary standpoint of someone saying, "Here's the problem; what is the solution to the problem?" But the solutions had left out of account the political facts.

Let me take, by way of example, a very minor decision that Lyndon Johnson made to amalgamate the Commerce and the Labor Departments. From an organizational standpoint this made a tremendous amount of sense. They are now both weak agencies. Commerce has practically lost everything except the Environmental Services Administration; (there's something else in there; I've forgotten what now.) The Labor Department, to a large extent, has become an agency for gathering statistics and supervising a few social service programs.

In this instance, the institutional air of the White House for political caution was forgotten; the program was advanced and stated publically. Two weeks later, I heard the idea smashed to pieces in about three minutes flat when David Dubinsky of the Garment Workers looked poor Charlie [Charles Louis] Schultze (then Director of the Bureau of the Budget) in the eye. Charlie had never had to deal with the Garment Workers. In fact he's never had to deal with the AF of L-CIO. Dubinsky simply said: "Mr. Schultze, we fought for this agency. Mr. Schultze, we got our heads beaten in for this agency. Mr. Schultze, I started out my career in the labor movement fighting for the Labor Department and now you want to take it away from us, WHY?"

Now, I think, if the White House at that point had not been in the process of becoming so institutionalized and if there had been a few more people there with some political sensitivity, that proposal would never have been allowed to get out of the cubby hole in which it originated.

Parenthetically, may I add that political sensitivity is something you can't measure. This is one of the reasons that the institutionalized approach tends to drive out the political approach. The institutionalized approach can only bring in figures and statistics which seem terribly convincing in an age in which we worship mathematics more and more.

Beyond the Commerce-Labor proposal, I can see some far more serious proposals that floundered on the same rocks. I am becoming concerned increasingly with the fact that Presidents find that they are in almost inescapable hot water in about two years; that they have lost the confidence of the people. I can see the beginnings of some of this now. This I must admit I see purely from a political sense; of course, I could be wrong; I am partisan. But at the same time, I believe, I can be a partisan and somewhat objective, too.

What I'm looking for in this particular proposal for Executive reorganization is a very simple thing: Are we going to take the institutional atmosphere out of the White House and put the White House back into its basic business? That business is politics. I use the word in a very high and noble sense. We tend to derogate the word politics too much in this country; we tend to think of it as a brutal voice. But, basically, we're talking about *what moves people*, and statistics *don't*. Basically, we're talking about what moves people and what doesn't move people; what people will do, and what people will not do. Basically, we're getting back to that very eloquent discourse that Tommy Corcoran gave yesterday, the first talk on politics that I've heard in about 30 years on which I would place the label of true political science.

THOMAS EVANS: Thank you very much, George. In that political treatise of yesterday we really have the guidelines by which we should try to measure the comments that are made today. Indeed, Mr. Corcoran has given us an instrument for measuring whether the Domestic Council will be an effective mechanism or not. You will recall the standard is the thesis of a *balance of forces;* this is the determinant in this great country of ours of the effective carrying forward of programs on the one hand and preventing civil war or civil disorder on the other. As Tommy Corcoran pointed out yesterday, these are not just great broad principles; they can go down to such detail as the drafting of a piece of legislation. That can be a crucial art, and a number of other staff functions can drastically effect that precarious balance.

The last two speakers have talked about politics vs. institutionalization and the relationship of the two. They both focused on the Cabinet in the course of their remarks. Now, Dwight Ink, as I understand the proposed Domestic Council and the proposed reorganized Office of Management and Budget, the former is for policy formation and the latter for implementation. Can you tell us how these organizations in their roles of policy formulation and implementation are going to be able to evaluate political considerations? Can they? Should they?

DWIGHT A. INK, JR.: By way of answering your question, let me say that if the institutional machinery proposed by the Ash Council had been in existence and had given consideration of the matter that George [Reedy] gave as an example, viz, the problems growing out of the proposal for the possible merger of the Commerce and Labor Department, the problem might have been avoided or at least minimized.

As a matter of fact, the institutionalized part of the Executive Office of the President was not involved in that proposal. Parenthetically, I might add that such institutional machinery as does now exist for handling organizational matters has been often bypassed over the years. In George's example you have a reverse process of what should have happened and what is contemplated. The people who are concerned in political problems were trying their hand at the craftsmanship of management, not very successfully. Those who should have been weighing and balancing the political factors in the broad sense, were preoccupied in an effort in which they were *not* equipped to deal. Consequently, as I saw it, George, really neither the management talent nor the political capabilities of the Presidency were brought to bear on that proposal.

The Ash Council proposals endeavor to sort those things out, to the extent one can sort them out, and re-establish and advance the capabilities to conceive and develop the organization and management concept in support of political considerations, broad policy considerations, and broad policy objectives. So it seems to me, Tom [Corcoran], that the Office of Management and Budget should be in a position to provide a management foundation, which should lead to better decision making. It should help to support options which can be considered on a broad policy basis, options which are susceptible to implementation.

The *manner* of problem solving has become increasingly significant. It has increased in importance in recent years, in part, because of the complexities and the varieties with which we are dealing, and the tempo by which they came about.

The rapidity with which a President is faced with major crucial decision making has increased tremendously in recent years. This, in turn, has led to a sense of *urgency* regarding decision making. As a result, there is a greater and greater tendency to feel that one is in a position of having to make many crucial decisions without the impact of these decisions having really been staffed out, or thought out in terms of the ability of the Government to carry them out.

Lee White mentioned yesterday that he had been on one of the "inner rings" around the White House, in the Executive Office of the President. I am one of those who through four Administrations has been on the outside rings; in fact so far outside that I'm not always sure such a ring exists! But one of the things that has struck me through these four Administrations is the fact that in the national security area there is a much shorter shake down period which is required for a new President to get hold of the machinery and make it function. Presidents, I think, generally are not satisfied with the extent to which the machinery is responsive; but by comparison with the domestic area, it has permitted a much more rapid response to the limit of the machinery's capability. Of course, in the case of President Kennedy, the Bay of Pigs incident greatly accelerated the process of getting control of the machinery.

With this present Administration, I was much impressed with the relative speed by which the National Security Council's functions and operations were picked up and provided quite soon much of the kind of support and information which the President needed on which to base his decisions. We have gone through a much longer period to shake down on the domestic side. One of the reasons I welcome this proposal is I think it will help provide on the domestic scene some of this kind of capability which through an evolutionary process we have had now for a number of years in the national security area.

The problems today are such that we simply cannot afford to spend the first year of a new Administration, which is the year of opportunity, the year when things can best be done, can most easily be accomplished, in trying to sort ourselves out and organize ourselves to provide the President with what he needs on the domestic scene.

Political decision making and stronger, better, more effective management, are *not* in competition with each other. As a matter of fact, I feel that they are mutually re-enforcing. I think that political judgments are better made with this kind of management support.

The credibility of the Government is enhanced to the extent that political decisions turn into reality. I do not believe these problems can really be entirely overcome. Nonetheless, through a stronger and more effective management capability we can minimize the problems of overselling and underfunding, and we can thereby regain some degree of credibility and develop a governmental process which is somewhat more responsive to the problems of the country and the needs of the people.

THOMAS EVANS: Thank you, Dwight. The parallel of the National Security Council has been noted several times in this Symposium. As was pointed out, President Kennedy gained respect for the National Security Council *after* the Bay of Pigs. You may recall also that President Truman, who tended to view the NSC at the outset in 1947 as "Forrestal's Revenge," came, as a result of the experience of the Korean War, to use the NSC constantly as a distinct arm of his Presidency.

Just because these are foreign policy considerations before the NSC, does *not* mean that they do not have political implications at home; quite the contrary: many of these foreign policy decisions, as for example, those related to the Middle East mentioned here, have grave political impact at home. Dick Pedersen, I should like to ask you, based upon your own experience working with the NSC and also your study of it, how does that institutionalized aspect of the Presidency cope with political problems?

RICHARD PEDERSEN: That's an interesting question. The effort of the national security people, from the point of view of the Department, is an effort to minimize purely domestic political considerations in the formulation of policy.

For example, the whole effort in establishing a policy in

the Middle East is to try to establish a policy that we think best suits the interests of our country in our external relations *without* basing that decision upon domestic political considerations.

Now obviously an elected official of the country, the President, when he makes decisions, has to take other factors into account. But the structure of the National Security Council is designed to focus on the factual and the decisive elements of our interests abroad rather than on the domestic political considerations.

There has been a good deal of discussion here regarding the value of the National Security Council in providing the President with a common statement of facts and information and getting it to him so that he is assured that everyone is working on the same basis. Indeed, this is what we try to do.

However, I don't think we should overstate the success that we've had in the process. Whenever you go through an important issue, you always have these points of contention and difficulty. The first one is getting a common statement of what the *facts* are; this isn't as easy as you may think, because of different points of view and different responsibilities of different agencies; sometimes there is considerable dispute as to what the facts are. Although you make every effort, you don't always iron out those differences. Secondly, even if you do have common agreement as to what the facts are, there are still considerable differences of interpretation as to the *significance* of facts and different weighted evaluations of the relative significance of the parts. Then, if you can go with both of those two, you can still derive quite different conclusions with the same set of facts as to what your *policy response* should be.

The processes that have been set up force all of these things into the open. As a result, we produce in the national security field better results across the board in terms of providing a common data for the President and a close interpretation of the facts, but we shouldn't overemphasize our successes in securing agreement.

GEORGE REEDY: I'm not quite so impressed with the National Security Council and the National Security Council staff.

If I do wind up being sold on the Domestic Council with the domestic staff, it is going to be because it does NOT parallel the National Security Council staff. I agree with Ambassador Pedersen that this concept of producing a common statement of fact is somewhat overstated.

I have sat through enough National Security Council meetings to know that you sit there and wait for the conflicting reports to come in. It's always a chaotic situation. The world is not a neat, orderly, tidy place where a group of men who must answer some life and death questions in a hurry can depend upon a common statement of fact. They might depend upon a common statement of background, yes, but I think that could come out of the State Department just as well.

One thing the National Security Council has done is to bring more assistants into the White House, and I think that *per se* is bad. It increases the amount of jostling, the amount of elbowing; it places the "right of the long knives" on a continuous run basis, seven days a week. It is a large factor in the White House; one of the most powerful and one of the largest staff segments which is applying an institutionalized approach.

As Ambassador Pedersen pointed out, the NSC is trying to do this without reference to domestic considerations. I personally would rather have approaches and recommendations that leave out the so-called domestic political considerations emanate from an office located a few blocks away. I would rather have them come into the White House in such a manner that they can be properly weighed in the light of political considerations. I would prefer this over an aseptic, non-political approach coming from within the President's personal family, his personal staff, which I think should be just as highly political as it can be made.

We have all accepted a few assumptions a little too easily. We have assumed that because an approach is familiar to intellectuals and rather attractive to intellectuals, and familiar to management people and rather attractive to management people, it becomes a progressive institution *per se* and should find its parallel in other fields.

I believe we should take a look as to whether this has not already made a heavy contribution to the de-politicalization of a political institution and whether the new thing that is being proposed (the Domestic Council) is going to proceed along the same lines.

THOMAS EVANS: We have here Mr. Reedy's suggestion of "aseptic" of "antiseptic" decisions being made before they get to the White House and then being processed for political considerations. Mr. Reedy has also made the point in passing about the intellectuals who might staff this process and inferentially has suggested their non-political basis.

Assuming a decision is made antiseptically, what happens when it gets to the White House staff who, Tommy Corcoran says, have a torch to carry? If they get the President's ear on their favorite aspect of that position, doesn't this really negate staff work which has gone on some blocks away where there is no opportunity to rebut at that point?

THOMAS CORCORAN: That worries me. What I like about this proposed Domestic Council is that it will upgrade the Cabinet meeting by giving it specific matters to chew. Otherwise I think a Cabinet meeting has ceased to have meaning in a totality even under Mr. Nixon.

In Mr. Roosevelt's time Cabinet members were picked to be ambidextrous fellows who had both management ability and at the same time were versed in the political implications of a particular field and a particular region.

As a Democrat, I am not sure I don't believe in a government that functions in the heat and pressures of disorderly genius. I am not sorry that once in a while the Republicans come in to tidy the joint up. Because the joint has occasionally to be tidied up! Although every President uses his Cabinet in his own way, quite candidly I would have wished that Mr. Nixon's Cabinet had been even more politically oriented than it was. That is, because I believe so strongly that a problem far greater than the efficiency and technical proficiency of this Government is the problem which Mr. Nixon recognized so well in his Inaugural when he said "let us seek to go forward together...."

What frightens me is that a bureaucracy always tends to think in terms of a surface *efficient* way and misses the big problems of political balance. Mr. Roosevelt didn't have much in the way of a technical bureaucracy to bring decisions to him. I remember my partner James Henry Rowe, Jr., who was deeply involved in the Brownlow Report, arguing one day with Mr. Roosevelt about the "efficient" way to do something. Mr. Roosevelt said, "Well, I'm not going to do it that way." Mr. Rowe urged, "Well this is the right way to do it." Mr. Roosevelt responded, "What is the right way to do it depends on who is the President of the United States. I am the President of the United States."

The reason I am more for the Domestic Council than George is that I have a conception of the Cabinet as an ambidextrous cross between men who are administratively capable and at the same time have that instinctive understanding that a certain amount of maneuverable inefficiency may be necessary to meet Mr. Nixon's goal of bringing us together again.

I saw, in my service, denigration of the Cabinet meeting, as I believe George Reedy also saw it; men at the Cabinet table not showing their cards to their colleagues at all, and after the meeting going around to the back door to talk to the boss. I believe George would agree in favoring the Domestic Council on the following conditions: (1) if this will upgrade the Cabinet by technical knowledge and political instinct being brought together in a formal way; (2) if it helps assure that Cabinet members will discuss their problems in Cabinet; and (3) if this system will encourage each Cabinet member to refrain from going behind his colleague's back. Under these aforementioned conditions the Domestic Council would upgrade the Cabinet system, and I would be all for it. Such institutionalization, if you will, I favor.

GEORGE REEDY: I agree with you, only I'm not certain it will work out that way.

THOMAS CORCORAN: We raise many expectations in this country that are going to be very difficult to meet. Let me lay it on the line with reference to emerging expectations. For instance, political leaders single out the Negro and promise him much on the basis that the rest of the country owes him something just because he is a Negro. That bill of goods can't be sold for the reason Eric Hoffer gave that the country won't buy it. Wouldn't it be more prudent and wise and saleable if, instead, we would put the promises in this light—that genius and ability can and must be found in *every* level of the poor people in the country; the poor white, the poor Japanese, the poor submerged Chinese, the American Indian, the Mexican, as well as the Negro?

You have to begin selling the idea by saying this country doesn't owe anything to anybody. We are all lucky to be around including my Irish kin. But for the sake of the whole country, all of us should seek to upgrade every bit of genius in the United States, no matter what its origins. If you approach that way the people who have to pay for the promises, from the point of view of the total of *all* peoples, then instead of creating antagonism you can make all the people *want* to make this a better place for *everyone* for the security and glory of our nation and the well being of all of us.

For instance, if we're going to make the Negro a part of the main stream, in the light of our promises we are for a time going to have to place him in every business and profession regardless of his productivity "on an educational basis." The cost of that education may be so large as to require us to go into a kind of economic isolation for a generation until we have brought the Negro to the productive competitive level of the foreign work force. We've done something like that before. In days when we are talking free trade, let us not forget that by devaluing the dollar Mr. Roosevelt put on a protective tariff and placed us in a form of economic isolation while our wages and prices were being raised to get us out of the depression.

What I am saying in general is, in government we have to consider *human values* as well as *efficiency* values. Democracy does not necessarily find its virtue in maximum efficiency. Ours is the greatest human conglomerate on earth and not presently thereby necessarily the most efficient.

If this Domestic Council can combine political understanding and technocracy, if it can revitalize a Cabinet system that understands the relationship between efficiency and politics, then I am for it. I only hope that's what really happens. I want it to raise the Cabinet level by recreating the *concept* of the Cabinet as a political technocracy as well as an efficient business management device.

THOMAS EVANS: Thank you. That is brilliant and incisive

once again and a good note for our mid-morning coffee break.
GORDON HOXIE: Just a brief word before returning to our
moderator and panel for this final session. As I indicated at the
outset, something of the theme of this conference was inspired
by George Reedy's new book, *Twilight of the Presidency*.
I further indicated that the angle of the sun is the same at
sunrise as at sunset. I am reminded of an incident in the closing day of the Constitutional Convention in Philadelphia,
after the members had worked throughout the hot late
spring and summer of 1787. Finally, on September 17, the
members signed the completed document. As the chairman,
George Washington, rose from his arm chair, which was
inscribed with a gilded half-sun, the oldest member of the
convention, Benjamin Franklin, age 81, observed:

> I have often and often in the course of this session, and the vicissitudes
> of my hopes and fears as to its issue, looked at that . . . without being
> able to tell whether it was rising or setting; but now at length I have
> the happiness to know that it is a rising and not a setting sun.

In like spirit, all concerned constructive students of the
Presidency in our beloved land, including George Reedy,
hope they are, and I believe they are, contributing to "a ris-
ing and not a setting sun."
THOMAS EVANS: Dr. Hoxie, I have no particular station to
do this except that I have the microphone. But I would like to
take the occasion right now, personally, and I believe for all
of us, to thank Gordon Hoxie for providing this splendid
weekend in this beautiful setting, and giving us an opportunity to learn so much. Gordon, you have organized this Symposium so well.
EDWARD MILL: May I just add, based upon many years of
attending scholarly meetings, that this surpasses any and
all in its resources and vitality. In this I include even the
American Assembly Conferences, which I have generally considered tops.
KENNETH W. COLEGROVE: May I just say amen to that
comment based upon not 30 but 60 years of attending learned
conferences. It assuredly tops anything that has been presented
by even the American Historical Association or the American
Political Science Association on this subject.
THOMAS EVANS: Before throwing this open to questions

from the floor, may I direct a further question to the panel. Tommy Corcoran and Gordon Gray and others have made reference to the concept of the President-in-Council. Whether or not there will be a Domestic Council to be the running mate of the National Security Council and whether or not there will be an Office of Management and Budget, we see that there has been and is a tremendously important role for the personal assistant, for the staff. We have seen in Washington today, for the first time since the Eisenhower Administration, a Chief of Staff, H. R. Haldeman. We see great power residing in John Ehrlichman on the domestic side and in Henry Kissinger in foreign affairs.

The question arises, with or without the institutionalization we have been talking about, how much does decision-making in the White House depend on those very powerful men who are close to the President? For initial comments on that I would like to turn to a student of politics and an active participant member of the Ash Council and also a Special Consultant to the President, Walter Thayer.

WALTER THAYER: Perhaps one of the problems that we face, Tom, is the type of institution that has grown up around the Office of the Presidency. I don't think that there is a significant difference between the White House staff today and the responsibility carried by men like Bob Haldeman and John Ehrlichman compared, for example, to that carried by Sherman Adams under President Eisenhower. There were some people in the 1950's who thought too much authority and responsibility was concentrated there. There were some people who thought that President Eisenhower was very difficult to see.

I didn't have experience in dealing with Joe Caliafano, but here was an extraordinarily able man obviously who had great authority and responsibility in President Johnson's Administration. And Walt Rostow's role was quite comparable to that of Henry Kissinger. It is inevitable that a President will find and use men of this quality and character in trying to carry out his responsibilities. It is probably inevitable, the way the White House is structured at the present time, that too much authority and responsibility gets centered in too few people of this kind; however able they may be, their limitations are very great; they are concerned with the problems, and have to be, that are of the most concern to the President at the moment.

I don't find myself in disagreement with anything that Tom Corcoran or George Reedy said. I think I even share somewhat the apprehension that George Reedy has that this may be too much institutionalization when it's finally organized. I certainly agree with Tommy Corcoran that it is a great thing to have the Republicans come in once and a while to tidy things up. I might add, that if, for no other reason, so we can have people like Tom Corcoran come in and mess them up! He made a great contribution to this country in which we live. I should think he could take great satisfaction in the contribution he has made.

It seems to me that a basic problem we face in this country today is the lack of confidence in government to deliver what it says it will deliver. I don't question the fact that political decisions must be overriding and that the President in the last analysis is a political animal; he has to be; he wouldn't be there if he weren't; and perhaps decisions on a policy level are made more often on a political basis than not. This won't change.

The question is, however, how you carry out those decisions, how you implement them. The question is whether or not the Government is going to be able to deliver its programs in a manner that will gain the respect and the credibility of the people in this country. And I think over the past many years there's been a gradual diminution of confidence in government's ability to deliver. This is no one's fault, really. I think this is a real question as to whether the Government can, in fact, deliver on the programs it undertakes.

Although the President may be and is deeply concerned and preoccupied with the political decisions, nevertheless, like it or not, he is the manager of the biggest enterprise in the world. He is the manager of a budget of 200 billion dollars; he is the manager of 163 departments and agencies, and he is the court of last resort. There is no where to go except to the

President of the United States to resolve differences of opinion and differences of policy that creep into the administrative end of government.

I had an experience with some of the present Cabinet in connection with trying to relate to them the program that the Council has undertaken. Others on the Council went different ways to talk to different Cabinet officers to try and have them understand what we were trying to achieve.

I talked to one Cabinet officer, who shall be nameless, who was a governor of a state; he is involved in some problems involving transportation. He is a very volatile man! I wouldn't want to identify him because it wouldn't be fair! But for the first hour and ten minutes that I spent with this gentleman, he told me about the problems *he has* in trying to get policy decisions related to his department cleared in the White House. Tommy Corcoran talked about Cabinet officers who lacked political sensitivity. This guy has got to have some political sensitivity, because he's been a governor, and he stumped the country for this President when this President was a candidate, before as well as after the nomination. He has to have had administrative experience and responsibility.

Let me tell you, it must be a tremendously frustrating experience for people who have this kind of background! (There are three governors down there now heading Departments.) Such persons come into government with a high sense of purpose. This, certainly is the only reason they are there. They develop programs they believe essential to the economy and to the urban problems of the nation. For one reason or another these people do not have the access they think they need to the President; they are not able to get programs cleared; they don't even know on whose desk those programs sit and why they aren't cleared!

As I say, I don't want to tell you who this fellow is. But that's what he said to me in an hour and ten minutes. If you could have a recording of that conversation you could have a good understanding of the frustrations that do exist. Why? Because the Bob Haldemans, the John Ehrlichmans, the Sherman Adams, the Joe Caliafanos, of all the Administrations are just simply swamped and overwhelmed by the priority problems of the moment. They are addressing themselves to the

1 or 2 percent of the problems that take 99 percent of the President's time, of their time, because those are the key issues today, be it Vietnam, Middle East, or Washington.

But all these other affairs *do* go on. What we have tried to create here is the machinery by which political decisions can better be made and administrative programs, whether Democratic or Republican, have a better chance to be carried out.

I want to say that these three Cabinet officers, who have been governors and did have broad administrative responsibilities in their respective states, were among the first to say that they think the Domestic Council will bring about a great improvement in the manner in which this government functions. They believe it will bring great improvements both in deciding on domestic issues and in seeing that those issues are carried out programatically.

I don't believe that anyone could have sat through the hundreds of hours that have gone into the discussion on this and come out with any conclusion other than the following: that this decision making and administrative machinery that has been suggested *can be* a potentially tremendous asset to the effective Administration of the Executive Branch of this Government. I believe that. I don't think we're going to see it tomorrow or next week or next month. But I believe over a period of time this machinery will serve this President and Presidents in the future very well, indeed. And I think that perhaps this may be the most significant administrative reorganization within government in a long, long time.

After years of experience in trying to listen to, sit through, and participate in looking at these problems, you realize how little time and how little possibility there is for a person on the active firing line in government—whether it's the President, whether it's Dwight Ink, whether it's John Ehrlichman or Bob Haldeman—to sit down and look objectively at the organizational problems of government and come up with solutions. They simply don't have the time to do this. This is a great lack and deficiency in this government today. That is one of the reasons why we want to see a well-trained and experienced staff take this on as an on-going responsibility.

Perhaps the greatest lesson I brought away from this is that unless you have this kind of capability, this kind of objective look at the Government from time to time, you just simply can't hope to cope with the organizational problems as they arise.

THOMAS EVANS: George Reedy, I would like to ask you this question before throwing the questions open to the floor. You have written, and I'm going to quote it verbatim, if I may, "It is certain that whatever neurotic drives a President takes with him into the White House will be fostered and enhanced during his tenancy. He lives in a world that is the delight of the immature personality—a universe in which every temper tantrum is met by instant gratification of the desire which caused the tantrum."

Now is it possible that this staffing, this possibly making somewhat more remote some of the decision making processes and presenting options, might remove that palace guardsmanship which could lead to that effect?

GEORGE REEDY: If he gets the staff out of the White House, yes. I personally think that one of Mr. Nixon's biggest mistakes was enlarging the White House staff. Believe me, any White House assistant with any sensitivity could get out and write a novel about the court of Paleologus in Byzantium; all he would have to do would be to get out and look up a few Greek names. Now you can take it as virtually certain that the more dedicated, progressive, creative, innovative men you crowd into the place, the more jockeying you are going to have, and there will be more people trying to envelope the central man in the kind of blanket that he doesn't need.

Let me take this one step further. I believe that Tommy Corcoran and I have some differences simply because I'm a little more steeped in the Legislative Branch of the Government than I am in the Executive Branch. I have been in both, and I've observed both as a newspaperman. And I have a feeling that the man I worked for was essentially one of the great men of our history. I'm quite a student of Senate history, and I'm convinced that he was the greatest leader the Senate ever had. I can only think of two others who even came close to him, and I doubt whether very many people in this room know whom I'm referring to. I'm talking about John Worth Kern of Indiana and Joseph Taylor Robinson of Arkansas.

The thing that really made Lyndon Johnson a great leader, and also probably Robinson and Kern, was that every morning he would have to confer with some rambunctious personality like Allen Ellender, who was a very forceful man and who minced no words; then about fifteen minutes later he would have to encounter, with all storm signals flying, Wayne Morse, who is no shrinking violet either; then he'd have to face Dick [Richard B.] Russell, with an immensely subtle mind; and then he'd have to meet Mr. [Everett McKinley] Dirksen, who was quite a character.

Out of all of this, I think, a certain type of humility evolved and a certain type of awareness arose that there are other strong minded people in the world. You know that nobody is strong minded around a President; let's get that thing established right now. It just doesn't exist. As far as the President is concerned, it is always: "Yes sir," "No sir" (the "no sir" comes when he asks whether you're dissatisfied); and "Thank you, sir."

I really don't think that there's anything within your reorganization plans that would effect this particular problem. I think that there's a far deeper thing at stake. I do think, however, that if you can get some staff out of the White House, reduce the number of knives, I think you might be able to ameliorate the problem. In such case the twilight might last a little longer than I personally think it's going to, though I do join in Gordon Hoxie's fervent hope.

THOMAS EVANS: Thank you, George. Let's have some questions from the floor.

JOHN MARTIN: I was going to introduce my question by saying to Mr. Thayer, be good to me; I work full time for Roy Ash and would not like to get fired for the question I was about to ask. However, from your last comment I find us in closer agreement.

I would like to question two premises. The first may sound cynical, but I don't mean it as such. We started, Mr. Thayer, on the first premise that we wanted a more effective Presidency. I'm honestly not certain this is a sound premise with the already imbalance between the Congress and the Presidency. It would appear by your further strengthening of the Presidency you would aggravate the imbalance already existing between the Legislative and the Executive

Branches. It seems to me that the job needed is to make more effective our Congress.

Secondly, we see more eye to eye in your second presentation, because we were talking more in terms of decision making and only incidentally in terms of getting the facts. Moreover, we seem to equate decision making with follow through. In my brief government experience it seems to me that the big problem is the follow through. And here the analogy of the Domestic Council with the National Security Council breaks down. In the first place, the NSC has a much, much simpler problem. (I'm sure nobody involved thinks it is.) It is not unlike business in terms of having a common denominator, against which we can make organizational decisions. In business, the common denominator is cents. In NSC, the common denominator is the defense of the whole country. Also in NSC there are really only two agencies involved, albeit two very strong agencies, and one is the leader of the other. The State Department leads and the follow through is by a strong Defense Department.

On the other hand, in the domestic field, when you try, for example, to equate surplus agricultural products with the civil rights problem, there is no correlation. You have, then, in the proposed Domestic Council a quite different thing than the NSC. How is the information gathering and particularly the follow through made more effective? For example, if the follow through is up to the Secretary of the Interior in carrying out a compromise program of the Domestic Council, might the Secretary of Interior not have had more enthusiasm for implementation if he had sold the program to the President?

THOMAS EVANS: I'm going to ask Mr. Thayer to comment as you suggest, and then I'm going to ask Dwight Ink to speak particularly to this matter of the follow-up through the Office of Management and Budget.

WALTER THAYER: I think Dwight is much better qualified for the second part of your question. Let me address myself to the first part quite quickly. There may be an imbalance between the Legislative and the Executive Branch of the Government. I agree that it would be a good thing to have an organizational study of the Congress, particularly with regard to the committee structure.

However, our job is *not* just how the President can be more effective, but how the Executive Branch can better carry out the responsibilities which it has as a result of the legislation which has been passed: how you deliver the merchandise; how you deliver the goods; and whether you do it effectively and in a way that gains credibility and is done in some measure of effectiveness in relation to the cost of doing it. This is the *only* area to which we have directed our attention. Really the question is conflict or confusion between agencies and the capability of the Office of the President to follow through and do the administrative job which is necessary to see that programs are carried out.

We are going to make recommendations in six other areas. We happened to have concluded this one on the Executive Office of the President, first, because we thought it was most important and should receive a priority. We are going to make recommendations that deal with: (1) social programs; (2) natural resources and environment; (3) regulatory agencies; and three others. These have been studied by part of our staff over the past several months. We hope to have all of them completed by June 30th. In that sense we are dealing on a much broader basis; i.e. with the Executive Branch problems and not simply the Executive Office of the President. We hope that this will make a contribution in these areas as well as the one related to the Office of the President.

DWIGHT INK: It seems to me that the ineffectiveness of the Office of the President does not help Congress. It certainly does not help the people. I think that the Congress can deal better, can respond more effectively, and make its decisions more effectively, and make its decisions more intelligently when it is dealing with an Executive Branch which can demonstrate more clearly the basis for its decisions and can hopefully demonstrate the resources that are required to carry out its decisions, and hopefully can better demonstrate that the enactment of legislation will result in something tangible happening. There are times when some Congressmen, because they are so wrapped up in the tremendously important legislative process, tend to think that legislation is the culminating process, whereas in reality, it is only the enabling. I believe George [Reedy] with his years on the Hill, tends to feel with these Congressmen. Congress provides the opportunity. It provides no action in itself. There are times when I have felt that Presidents and the White House staff (and here I do *not* include George Reedy) have looked upon press releases as self-implementing. In point of fact, press releases never created action in themselves, but have often created the illusion of action.

It is out of these kinds of things which I think we have another kind of imbalance—a focus on the legislation, a focus on the press release and an over shadowing of the hard nitty-gritty nuts and bolts business of making the legislation work, of carrying out what the press release promises. I don't think we're providing a service to anybody, certainly not to the Congress, or the people, when we promise a neighborhood center for every ghetto in the country and then only through the most laborious of processes we manage to start the implementation process in a total of 14 ghetto areas in the country.

It is out of this sort of thing that citizen disillusion is born. We're not serving anybody when we appropriate and authorize billions of dollars for urban renewal programs which displace thousands of low income people for four or five years, or for programs which take ten years to put into effect. By the time an urban renewal project is completed, the original objectives are generally out-dated. This is a fast moving environment with which we are dealing; communities are dynamic, more dynamic with the passage of every year. Most of our machinery on the domestic scene simply isn't up to the task which is assigned to it by Congress or the President. This is one of the reasons that credibility in government is suffering.

Now, with regard to comparison of the National Security Council with the proposed Domestic Council, I agree with the gentleman from California, [John Martin] as I am sure the Ash Council members do, that they cannot be compared. I think there are some parallels, some similarities, some lessons that we have learned from the National Security Council, and some worthwhile products that have come out of the NSC that have applications here. But as you point out, Mr. Martin, the two areas are very much different; there are some basic differences; and the one is *not* intended to be a carbon copy of the other.

With respect to implementation, the Office of Management and Budget is to provide the kind of institutional arm which actually was contemplated in many respects by the Budget and Accounting Act many years ago [1921] to which Dr. Hoxie referred. As he indicated, much of this management concept had been in the original act of 1921 and the executive order of 1939. But as a practical matter, it hasn't amounted to much, because it has been over-shadowed again by the budget process. When you think of the Bureau of the Budget, what do you think about? You think about cutting the budget.

Several weeks ago, I was meeting with the National League of Cities. I was tremendously interested in talking to a group of mayors and city councilmen and a few city managers about the red tape problem which has so hampered our grant-in-aid process; Murray [Comarow] mentioned this earlier. I was from the Bureau of the Budget. All they were interested in talking about was why this Administration hadn't put more money in the budget for programs in which they were interested. I *never* was able to get to the business of cutting red tape. I was never able to get to the business which *they*, several of the mayors in that group, had written letters to the White House complaining bitterly about. They didn't think that anyone from the Bureau of the Budget would be concerned with anything other than the Budget.

So the new plan provides, you see, a much better balance in the management arm of the President, for being concerned not just with budget cutting, but also for moving forward those programs and projects (which are funded). You do this in many ways: through seeing that the agencies strengthen their management capabilities; seeing that they set schedules; seeing that they set targets; you do it through the Program Coordination Group recommended by the Ash Council. The Group will spend much of its time out in the field studying what is holding up the projects, expediting in some ways similar to what was done in World War II in much of the defense industries; similar to what we did in the Savannah River "H" Bomb projects.

You have here something which really not only helps the President, but in helping the President, making the President over a period of time more effective, it indirectly will also help the Congress.

THOMAS EVANS: Thank you, Dwight.

ROBERT H. SHARBAUGH: Would any of the members of the panel comment on whether the Ash Council did include or should have included the potential redefining of the political and managerial role of the vice-presidency in making these recommendations to revise the Executive Branch organization?

MURRAY COMAROW: The Council looks upon a Vice President, any Vice President, not just Spiro Agnew, as the man who should want to do exactly what the President wants him to do; no more and no less. It would be a mistake to institutionalize that position.

GEORGE REEDY: Not only a mistake, but not possible. I cannot picture any President, even if he is Casper Milquetoast, institutionalizing a Vice President.

MURRAY COMAROW: I believe this comes more directly to answer your question: You are, I understand, the president of a large corporation [Sun Oil Company]. You and Mr. McFarland [Chairman of General Mills] and some of the other leaders here of billion dollar plus corporations will be interested in the fact that among the proposals presented to our Council was one for two or three super vice presidents presiding over super cabinet posts like "Human Resources," "Natural Resources" and the like. These proposals were rejected.

FRANCIS H. HORN: I'm one of the educators in this crowd. My question is only indirectly related to the Council. My question is not only with regard to how decisions are made, but the caliber of the people making them. My question is primarily this: If we accept Mr. Corcoran's and Mr. Reedy's assumption that government is *political* and that decisions are best made by men who are political to their fingertips, what is the implication with regard to bringing people into the

Executive Branch of the Government, into positions of responsibility, who are *not* political?

As an example, take the Office of Education, with one of the biggest budgets in the Government today. Nobody lasts very long in this particular role. Now, are we going to discount and leave out the talents of business and industry and education? (Lawyers are political to their finger tips, I assume, in any case). Are these business and professional leaders to be excluded for consideration for important positions in the Executive Branch?

GEORGE REEDY: I think I can answer for both myself and Tommy [Corcoran] in that. I assume the question is addressed to us basically. The answer: of course, not.

The point is that I feel about technicians and experts in government the same way I feel about the military. I want the military under firm civilian control, and I want the technicians and the experts and the men of very high caliber under firm political control.

I am very, very sympathetic with what the Ash Council is seeking to do. Let me give you an example. I can see right now one very big problem Mr. Nixon's going to have. It's going to explode along about July of this year, because someone got awfully careless when he tinkered around with the draft act; this is a purely technical thing; I'm absolutely amazed that the problem wasn't called to somebody's attention in time! I think everyone was in a hurry. But sooner or later they are going to have to start drafting a bunch of kids that thought they weren't going to be drafted. In fact, they have been told they weren't going to be drafted. I think that this was due, not to the lack of human caliber, but to the fact that somewhere along the line there was some inefficiency in the organization which did *not* bring the problems to the point where the decision was being made. Some of the consequences and some of the nuts and bolts of the selective service system were not carefully handled. As a result, there will be a pretty big blow up.

This, to my mind, could have been avoided with a more efficient type of organization. I am *not* opposed to efficient organization. However, if I have to make a choice between inefficient or *ineffective* organization and *good political control* I'll take the political control, although I'd rather have both.

MURRAY COMAROW: I don't really think that there's an argument here. George [Reedy] just has a way of looking at things. The Council to a man rejected the notion that everything must be sacrificed on the altar of efficiency. The Council would *not* defend the proposition that statistics are more important than human judgment. The Council considered a great many alternatives including, as I indicated in answer to Mr. Sharbough's question, some suggestions about two or three super vice presidents. It rejected them.

It came to the conclusion, to a man, that the problem was one of reducing the difficulties to human scale, so that fallible human beings could cope with them. We are in no way interested in the far out management technocrats to displace democratically oriented men. I agree that the military should be under civilian control.

I want to make it quite clear that we were *not* terribly impressed with the argument which some had made to us that you solve the problems of government by applying business principles. I don't think that government is the world's biggest corporation, and I don't think that anyone on the Council does either. Government operates on the basis of political consensus: Political survival is the *sine qua non* of a government agency; Economic survival is the *sine qua non* of a business.

What government agency can you think of that went bankrupt because of poor leadership? Our society knows how to get rid of businesses that don't make out. They go broke, although some are lucky and ride the waves of the economy and overcome their own inefficiencies. On the whole, and in the long run, most badly run businesses go down the drain. Badly managed agencies get more money!

ROBERT E. SIMON JR.: I think that, perhaps, the credibility gap that we have been talking about this weekend is the hallmark of our society today. I am not sure that there is not a correlation between political control of technicians and the credibility gap. The politician tends to tell people what he thinks they want to hear. The technician tends to look at what is possible.

There is a government analogy to business bankruptcy in housing and urban development. Think of the promises of the previous Administration and the present Administration— 600,000 low cost housing units a year, 600,000 starts a year. In 1968, the government had only 200,000 low cost housing units, a fraction of the low cost housing projected. This is bankruptcy in government form.

True, political animals get political offices. But I have been concerned at the unanimity at the head table of the value of having politicians really in control telling people who are much better able to understand realities than some of us recognize, things they want to hear but are not delivered.

GEORGE REEDY: We could have quite an argument over who looks at reality, and what's feasible. Almost every un-feasible proposal has come from the technicians; this does not mean that they are bad technicians; it does mean that they are absorbed in a subject, necessarily so; it takes time to become technicians; they have been so absorbed in their subjects that they have *not* had the time to master a totally different subject, the political art.

Now, of course, there are good and bad politicians, and I think you can get yourself locked in semantics. There is a tendency in this country to think of a politician as the old-fashioned Tammany guy hanging around city hall looking for somebody to give him a few bucks for approving a paving contract. There is a tendency to decide that politics and statesmanship are not compatible—which, again, is not true.

I'm thinking of the politician solely and simply in terms of the man who has some concept of what moves people, what they will and what they will *not* do. This is where so many proposals that are submitted in government become extremely unfeasible. It is *not* because inherently they may be incorrect, not because they may be wrong organizationally, but simply because while they take into account physical and natural resources, they do *not* take into account *human resources*, what people are conditioned to and what they are not conditioned to.

Like anything else, there are good politicians, and there

are poor politicians, and there are politicians that are "middlin' fair." That's true of any corporation; it's true in the law or in engineering; most people are "middlin' fair." You have to assume that in this political art there is a greater likelihood that men who will get up to the top will be better than middlin' fair. That's true of almost any other profession; I don't know why it shouldn't be true of that one.

But most of the unfeasibility in recent years, it seems to me, is something that has been stopped in Congress before it gets too far. Oh yes, I've seen an awful lot of proposals that came out every year that are like the laundry list that simply won't be bought by the man in main street.

We tend to forget that government is basically a question of politics. We've operated under an American myth that there's a group of bad guys called the politicians. This goes back a long, long ways. We've always assumed that a man who is a failure and can't do anything else goes into politics.

The basic point I'd like to make, is that while the failure of government to carry through programs has had something to do with the credibility gap, I think the deeper feeling is that *government is no longer responsive to the people*. Almost everywhere I go I find this; that the Government is a huge monolith, obsessed with polls, that it really doesn't take into account people's feelings, the fact that they've lived a lifetime in a certain way and all of a sudden that way is interrupted. That can be a very dangerous thing.

Last night, for example, I heard a reference to a poll being taken which indicated that Mr. Nixon's speech on Vietnam was accepted by 77% of the people. I don't know why anybody would need a poll to prove that; it is very obvious. What did concern me, however, was the relationship of the speech and the poll to the big mobilization meeting in Washington. The kids that were there, ranging from very radical to extreme right wing, all left Washington with a feeling that the Government wasn't listening to them.

This same feeling is true to some extent in almost every element of the population—the middle class white suddenly finds bussing closing in on top of him; the black, who has seen the big headlines through the years about all the programs training him to do this and training him to do that, still can't find a job; both feel that nobody listens to them. There is no line these days from the ghetto into city hall. The old-fashioned working politician had one virtue; he made the guy in the ghetto feel that he had a voice. That is now gone. It is in this sense of detachment, impersonalization, that I believe you will find more of the causes of the credibility gap than in the failure to deliver.

THOMAS EVANS: I have a man to my right who is a career government official, a technician, if you will, who wants one minute in rebuttal.

DWIGHT INK: George [Reedy], up to this point I think I've been in full agreement with you, but I have to say that in my judgment the credibility problem, which is not limited to any one individual or any one Administration, has grown at least as much out of political considerations as it has the other.

GEORGE REEDY: Yes, but out of poor politics!

DWIGHT INK: I would agree with that, George!

THOMAS EVANS: Gentlemen, thank you, distinguished members of the panel. I would like to exercise the chair's prerogative, if I may, and add a conclusional comment or two. One thing that hasn't been mentioned in the course of our discussion, aside from Walter Thayer's touching on it at the outset, is the *single merit* of this suggested reorganization which may override all other considerations.

As has been mentioned over the last three days, Presidents have different personalities; many have strong, great personalities, but they differ from man to man. Each man has his own way of doing things. And I would add a personal note, having worked with this President in politics and in law, I think *this* is the way *he* wants to do it. I think he likes a sense of organization. I think he likes a structural staff. Some of this comes from his work in the law and from his vast experience in government but more particularly from his days in the Eisenhower Administration. And I *think* that factor *alone* should be a compelling reason to adopt the Ash Council report to enable this President to become more effective, because this is the way he believes that he can be more effective.

By way of a final remark: we are concerned about staffing; we are concerned about machinery; but I recall a comment that John F. Kennedy made at a press conference. A reporter asked him whether McGeorge Bundy and the National Security Council were not getting a little too powerful, were not getting too important in the scheme of things, were not carrying the ball, where it should be carried elsewhere. President Kennedy thought for just a moment and said, "I shall continue to exercise *some* residual functions."

On that note, and again with congratulations and thanks to our host and our host's organization, this now historic symposium stands adjourned.

CHAPTER VI

Summing Up: A Resume
by R. Gordon Hoxie

THE KEYNOTE

The Keynoter, Herbert G. Klein, on Friday evening posed the haunting "question as to whether or not modern government . . . finds us almost ungovernable." The other thirty-four contributors joined Mr. Klein in facing this central dilemma of our time. The Director of Communications of the Executive Branch points out that "the complexity and enormity of our problems are in many ways unprecedented."

In seeking to find the answer, Mr. Klein from his unique vantage point, proposes a dual program: (1) adhering to basic principles; (2) gearing up for the 70's. He reaffirms James Madison's observation that "a popular government without popular information or the means of acquiring it, is but a prologue to a farce or a tragedy or perhaps both."

Recognizing the urgency of population, minority, and environmental problems, Mr. Klein asks in candor: "What should be the role of the Federal Government. . .?"

In suggesting principles for the answers, Mr. Klein points up a further concern of the Symposium, the awesome decisions the President must make, the machinery for decision making, and the "distinction [that] must be made between policy formulation and policy execution." He recognizes "that in trying to make changes in government today there is considerable resistance." And he asserts that if the critical problems of the 70's are to be resolved, "the qualities of leadership, organization, and esprit must be such that when the President has finally decided that this is the direction he will take, he may be confident that his policies are being executed." He concludes that the strong President "must carry the thing all the way through."

Mr. Klein, a close and unique advisor to the President, assesses President Nixon as "a man who knows the direction he wants to take and is attempting to lead the nation in that particular direction." He notes the critical concerns pointed up by George E. Reedy, Jr., whose new book, *The Twilight of the Presidency,* by its very title set the stage for the Symposium.

As Mr. Klein expresses it, it is the thesis of Reedy's book that the President "lives in really a very unreal world, one which is not conducive to making the proper decisions based on all the facts that are available." Mr. Klein's very position in the Nixon Administration was, in part, inspired to answer this concern and "to find a better way of establishing a two way communication between government and its people. . . ." He notes the imperative of an effective leader, maintaining "the confidence of the people. . . ." And he notes the tragic examples of loss of confidence suffered by Presidents Hoover and Lyndon Johnson.

In an administration which has already surfaced deep rooted differences between the Executive and the Legislative, Mr. Klein acknowledges that "to lead effectively, the President must work with the Congress." But he admonishes that "to legislate well the Congress must be fully conscious of the power of the Presidency and the power of the Executive Branch of the Government as it seeks to execute the policies and programs that the President deems vital for the country." To formulate and execute policies and programs, the Executive Branch needs an organization looking to the future. The so-called modern Presidency dating from the New Deal is outmoded, as are the national, state and local relationships.

Delivering this keynote on the eve of the most thorough-going reorganization in the history of the Office of the Presidency, he viewed the proposed organizational changes as gearing up to "meet the challenges of the 70's." In particular, he noted this then proposed, now established, new Domestic Affairs Council and the Office of Management and Budget. Among specific legislative proposals, he underscored the importance of "the new welfare program" as well as the ongoing challenge of school desegregation.

Returning to principles in seeking to answer in his concluding remarks whether "government is governable," he answered in part, by the example of "great deeds in science, in medicine, and in technology." He concluded that "if man can perform such miracles, surely government is governable, and this instrument of the people can enrich our lives as it improves our environment." He asserted that "the Presidency can take the lead not only in solving problems of government, but it can also take the lead in setting the goals and priorities." Among such goals he noted, "peace for all mankind . . . understanding of all mankind . . . better education . . . better job opportunities . . . more thorough integration, . . . a more true look at what is really a sound economy."

Government alone will not accomplish these goals. "It requires a people of compassion and courage who . . . will do their part. . . ." It requires a proper participating by their criticism as well as their support. It requires a people not only with high goals but also determined, as Neil Armstrong expressed it, "to watch the trail."

Emphasizing the importance of the programs of this Center, particularly its Symposia, Mr. Klein concludes "that if we look at the over-all problems of the Presidency itself in this and in future symposiums these are aspects we should be examining as we go along."

THE MEDIA

The following morning Herbert Klein joined Peter I. Lisagor, Washington Bureau Chief of the *Chicago Daily News*, Robert B. Semple, Jr., White House Correspondent of the *New York Times*, George E. Reedy, Jr., Press Secretary to President Johnson, and James C. Hagerty, Press Secretary to President Eisenhower, in a lively discussion on the Media and the White House.

As moderator, Mr. Hagerty emphasized the role of the Media as "a hairshirt of the Government. It is up to the news media to ask why and how. As long as those reports are honest and fair, and," Mr. Hagerty concludes, "the great, great majority of the American press and their reports are honest and fair, they are providing an indispensible service."

In similar theme, particularly because of the isolation of the President, as described in Reedy's *Twilight of the Presidency*, Mr. Lisagor emphasized that the press is kind of an open conduit to what the country is all about. . . ." Inevitably, the Vice President's criticisms of the media, entered the round-table discussions. Mr. Hagerty believed, "we overreacted like hell!" Mr. Lisagor charged the Vice President with having questioned "the *right* of the TV networks or analysts to offer a contrary or dissenting opinion of the administration," concluding "that can be dangerous." Attorney William J. Casey arose to disagree, stating: "What the Vice President did was to question whether the networks performed a fair and proper function by giving only a critical" view of the President on Vietnam.

Mr. Hagerty, Mr. Klein, and Mr. Semple all agreed that particularly with the electronics media, i.e. radio and television, it is difficult to discern news from commentary and that commentary should be so labeled. "What I believe the Vice President was saying," Mr. Hagerty stated, "is that communications is a two way street, and that he and other public officials have the right to respond to these commentaries." Mr. Semple pointed out that by contrast to the electronics media, "In a newspaper it is very easy to see that distinction between interpretation and straight news."

Mr. Lisagor "cannot see the reason for all this concern about what a commentator says." He believes "one underestimates the minds of the American people. . . . The text is there; the newspapers are there; people of this country are literate."

New Deal architect, Thomas G. Corcoran, now distinguished Washington attorney, joined the panel; like Mr. Reedy, he believes that Mr. Agnew not just on Vietnam but also in problems at home joined in the sense of "frustration" at the plethora of bad news. "I wonder if . . . our free press with its detailed sensationalism, its detailed evil, isn't breaking up the spiritual cohesion of society?" Mr. Corcoran inquires. In like spirit, Mr. Semple asks, "Why don't we talk about some of the good things that President Nixon is doing? Or that President Johnson did? Why don't we talk about some of men's good works in the world rather than just the trouble of our time?"

This inspired the commentary of Mr. Lisagor that if you review history, including the whiskey rebellion of the 18th century, and the Molly Maguires of the coal mines of the 19th, "and remember that lynchings were commonplace in the south just two generations ago in this country; if you remember the labor . . . violence . . ., then you'll see . . . it's been far worse than it is today." Lisagor concludes that "the television makes it seem worse today."

Mr. Hagerty suggests that the Nixon Administration is trying to move the country "from the left to the moderate center" and that this, in turn, inspires "this dialogue and this discussion within our country." He concludes that "historically, it has always been the kind of debate and dialogue that you get in these circumstances."

Mr. Reedy believes that especially the President, any President, does not have press problems, but rather political problems. All agree that each President has his own style, his own approach. Mr. Johnson perhaps did a disservice to himself by removing all distance between the press and himself. Mr. Lisagor, President of the White House Correspondents Association, to the surprise of many, stated that it was best for both the President and the Press that the President maintain an arm's length relationship with them. Nevertheless, he concluded that "the vigorously self-enforced privacy of President Nixon is going to hurt him."

The implications of technology were discussed. No previous war has been brought so vividly into the home as that in Vietnam. While the electronic media may have brought more bad news into the home, it has also helped bring, as with the case of the drug problem, a constructive reaction. Moreover, with communications satellites the day may be near when the largest audience in human history will view a conversation between the President of the United States and the Prime Minister of the Soviet Union.

Several spoke on increasingly insistent problems of the cost of television time in political, and particularly presidential, campaigns. Mr. Hagerty believes "that for a Presidential election, once every four years, we can forget public entertainment for part of the night and put candidates for the President of the United States on for free. But I also urge," Hagerty underlined " . . . that Congress gets enough guts to pass appropriate legislation to allow us to do it."

Mr. Klein emphasized that "analytical interpretative journalism is essential in all that is now taking place. It would be a mistake if in any way this resulted in less interpretation either on the air, or less interpretation in terms of printed media."

He believes good had come from the so-called Agnew controversy "both from the public standpoint and the press standpoint." He believes "it best serves the relationship of all parties; government, press and public, now that the questions have been raised and looked at carefully, if all of us go to work and see if we can do a better job. It is," he concludes, "my observation that this process is taking place."

In response to the question as to why the new post of Director of Communications for the Executive Branch was established, Mr. Klein emphasized "the goal of doing a better job as related to our Federal Government of providing the American public with information regarding the Executive Branch." Moreover, there is an effort to serve those beyond the nation's capitol, "to provide the background information in other parts of the country."

Mr. Klein concluded that "today, with the high cost of newsprint and media production the fact remains very fugitive. . . . The key to the positions of press secretaries for all of the executive agencies and departments, and the key to my own job, is to constantly be on guard that you are providing the facts. If you are providing the facts, whether or not the people like those facts, you are fulfilling a basic responsibility in our Republic."

Given the facts, all of the panelists expressed with Mr. Hagerty an "abiding faith in the common judgment of the American people."

DOMESTIC POLICY

The second roundtable (Saturday afternoon) concerned itself with the formulation and implementation of domestic policy. Its moderator was United States Court of Appeals Judge Leonard P. Moore. Its members were former Counsel to Presidents Kennedy and Johnson, Lee C. White; Presidential Assistant Charles L. Clapp; Presidential scholar, Louis W. Koenig; Executive Director of the President's Council on Executive Organization, Murray Comarow; and Thomas G. Corcoran, friend of every President since Herbert Hoover. The focus was on the definition and accomplishment of objectives in the domestic sphere.

Mr. White analyzed these processes for the Kennedy-Johnson period. Much of the high legislative productivity of the early Johnson period he credits to the harvesting of programs sown in the seemingly less productive Kennedy period. Theodore C. Sorensen, domestic programs coordinator under Kennedy, had been followed successively by Bill D. Moyers and Joseph A. Califano, Jr. under Johnson. Such lesser structural programming as they represented, Mr. White favored over the Nixon proposed, more formalized Domestic Council.

As instruments for program proposals, Mr. White noted the State of the Union message, the annual Economic Reports, and the Budget. *Vis. a vis.* the Cabinet, Mr. White viewed the Presidential White House staff as increasing in importance. On the staff, he concluded, "not only should you have skillful and experienced people, but also people whose personalities and capacity to work with others will permit them to work with the Cabinet and not ruffle their feathers and not get them going cross-wise, and not having them feel that they're left out. That staff man, then, better serves his President."

Dr. Clapp described the role of the Presidential task forces. "They may be used to provide visibility to the President's interest in a subject or problem, to elicit some new ideas, to evaluate on-going programs, to provide a view independent of that of a department or departments concerned with the subject matter, to provide support for a program important to an Administration, and," Dr. Clapp further explained, "to encourage citizen participation in the problems of the day in a direct and meaningful way."

The increasing importance of the task force represents a shift "in recent years in the policy-making process at the Executive Branch level." Formerly most legislative proposals had emanated from the departments and agencies. Commencing with President Kennedy, who developed the task force concept, "the people around the President, as well as the Bureau of the Budget, began taking a more active role in new proposals and activities." President Johnson increased this activity, having 50 such groups in 1967. He not only regarded their reports as personal and confidential but even declined to disclose task force membership. By contrast President Nixon has publicly announced the task force memberships. He has also made the membership by-partisan.

Despite the present importance of the task forces for both domestic and foreign policy problems, one should not lose sight of the fact that there are 850 agency committees and 1,400 public advisory committees; many of these are working on problems similar to the task forces. Although it is not expected that "every recommendation will be implemented or should be implemented," Dr. Clapp concludes "that task forces are valuable assets to any Administration and that they should be continued by whatever name one wants to apply to them."

Dr. Koenig, Professor of Government at New York University, turned from the matter of "apparatus and technique" to the matter of "relevance and genuineness." These, he indicated, are the concerns of youth, as is the matter of access—"access to groups in our society that by traditional standards have inadequate access to public policy in governmental affairs." He includes such groups as the aged, the ill, the poor, and the consumer. Whether the new Nixon "structure . . . may be relevant, not only to the groups which have had particularly good access to governmental policy, but also to that portion of our society that has had much less access remains to be proven." Dr. Koenig does see an advance in social concerns. "Certainly when we compare . . . the days of the late William Howard Taft or Calvin Coolidge with those of Dwight Eisenhower or Richard Nixon, and the agendas of these Presidents, we have a sense of progress in social concerns."

Dr. Koenig pointed up the perennial problem of the relationship of the career civil servant with the President and his staff. He noted that "organization or reorganization is not a substitute for a policy. . . ." He applauded President Nixon "moving us away from some of the cliches of the New Deal era, 1930's, which are so much outworn. It's high time," he concluded, "that we had some of the extensive re-evaluation of programs which we are in. There's a suggestion of new approaches and fresh approaches; all of this, indeed, is very much in order, and the administration is performing a great service in taking these approaches." Further, Dr. Koenig believes the past decade has brought in too many "false promises." He approves "the present administration ... making a very valuable curb on political rhetoric." He hopes where recent administrations have *not* been effectively organized "at the implementation level," this one may be.

Murray Comarow reminded the Symposium participants that "policy making is an enormously complex thing involving the interaction among three parts: White House, the cabinet agencies, and the independent departments." He further drew a distinction between "the *institutional* staff of the President and the *personal* staff of the President." He posed the question: "How do you improve the making of policy? How can institutions [such as the Bureau of the Budget, the National Security Council and the proposed Domestic Council] help?"

Thomas G. Corcoran delivered a remarkable essay on "the nature of this Government." He would in no way discount any "institutional device," that would help. Yet, short of a dictatorship, there is only one means to "insure domestic tranquility," and that is by a *"balance of forces."* Mr. Corcoran recalled how he had first gone to Washington in 1926, as Secretary to Supreme Court Justice, Oliver Wendell Holmes. Mr. Holmes, who had served as a Captain in the American Civil War, had often told Corcoran that "the prime purpose of government in this kind of a democracy is to avert civil war." Corcoran warned that the Supreme Court by proposing social change before the people are prepared to accept it may "precipitate an issue." Because they were mindful of this "in Holmes' court and Brandeis' court, and Cardozo's court, the Supreme Court very carefully never put itself in the situation where Justice Taney helped bring on the Civil War in the Dred Scott decision."

Corcoran traced the historic efforts not alone to balance forces among the people but also with the Executive, Legislative, and Judicial Branches. For example, he inquires, "What is Fulbright doing? Basically, Fulbright is trying to re-establish that relationship between the Foreign Relations Committee of the Senate of the United States and the Presidency that Borah achieved when he took on Wilson . . . which Roosevelt reversed." Only the President, according to Corcoran, can achieve balance among those forces within and without the Government.

Mr. Corcoran warned of past over-promising both at home and abroad. He further warned that "the President has to maintain a relationship to Congress so that it will try for him." He perceived of the Cabinet members as particularly important in strengthening the Congressional relationship. In this connection he expressed the wish that Mr. Nixon would "have the kind of a fire-power Cabinet Roosevelt had." Mr. Corcoran concludes that "ideological right or wrong is not determinative in the political process. What is determinative is the skill to work among conflicting forces; as Holmes expressed it, a bartered price of not having civil war. . . . If a President makes a decision that shocks the life out of Congressional apparatus, as FDR did with the Court Plan, he will not get the results he is seeking."

Mr. Corcoran believes that Mr. Nixon must learn from these lessons of history if he is to achieve his admirable goal "to bring us together." It is such learning that will tell "to what degree all of the apparatus in the White House will help him. . . ." Mr. Roosevelt, who flew in the face of his own wisdom in his fights with the Supreme Court, might better have remembered his own statement: "I am the captain of the ship, but the seas control the captain."

In response to a question, Mr. Corcoran indicated that *vis a vis.* the legislative, "the balance of power" as compared to the F. D. Roosevelt period, "has shifted way over to the Executive. . . ." In so answering, he views the Executive as "continuous" and the Legislative as "fragmented among the committees in Congress." He believes the "institutional *continuity* of expertise that has been built up in the Executive has way over-matched that available in the operation of individual Senatorial and House Committees." The Congress, he regretfully reports, is needful of "some sense of institutional unity. . . ." He further advised of Lord Mansfield's 18th century dictum which remains true today: a law that 10% of the people choose not to obey is not a law. Moreover, the delays in application of justice compound the problem. Corcoran concluded with Holmes that "Any man can have anything in this world he wants, provided he wants it hard enough. But the trick the good Lord played on the universe was that he made few man who could want what they wanted hard enough."

Judge Moore, almost Mr. Corcoran's contemporary, concluded with a footnote to history that "we have seen the division of powers undergo many changes for the many years that you and I have been around. It reached its heyday, from a legislator's point of view any way, probably in 1932. We saw a very strong man, hated to be sure, make changes by the temper of the times and the social conditions; for some 12 years, he was very responsive to those needs." More recently, Judge Moore, believes, "we have gone through a period where the Judiciary has taken over. . . ." Deploring recent rule by 5 to 4 decisions, deploring the earlier decline of the legislative authority, reasserting the efficacy of the doctrine of the division of powers, nonetheless Judge Moore would agree with Mr. Corcoran's view that the President has a unique vantage point from which to consider "the proper division of powers within the Government . . . the comparative effectiveness of forces outside the Government, and the equilibrium of the total demands of all the people in the country."

FOREIGN POLICY, FORMULATION AND IMPLEMENTATION.

A talented roundtable consisting of William J. Casey, Esq., member of the General Advisory Committee of the U.S. Arms Control and Disarmament Agency, as moderator; and as members, Ambassador Richard F. Pedersen, Counselor, Department of State; Ambassador Robert D. Murphy, former Under Secretary of State for Political Affairs; Professor Louis Koenig, of New York University; Hon, Gordon Gray, of the President's Foreign Intelligence Advisory Board; and Mr. Helmut Sonnenfeldt, senior staff member of the National Security Council, on Saturday evening discussed both the formulation and implementation of foreign policy.

Mr. Casey traced the historic development of instruments of foreign policy, noting, that the role of the President has become "increasingly complicated by the expanding range of our global interests, rapid communications, instant news, multiple levels of conflicts, psychological, unconventional, conventional, and strategic."

In particular, Mr. Casey emphasized "the role and the need for the National Security staff. . . ." This includes, he enumerated: "The awareness and anticipation of problems, the identification of issues, providing full information, a full range of options, evaluating alternatives, getting a full reflection of the view of the various agencies, forcing decisions, following the full implementation, and finally coordinating the agencies." The use of the NSC by each President, Mr. Casey further noted, has been "according to his style and background."

Secretary Gray, in turn, traced the evolution from the World War II State—War—Navy Coordinating Committee to the National Security Act of 1947 which "established the beginnings of the modern machinery." It not only unified the armed services in the newly created Department of Defense and established the NSC, "but also very importantly, it established for the first time, a statutory based intelligence agency (CIA) recognizing intelligence as a necessary ingredient in the formulation of foreign policy. As the fourth of seven who have served as Special Assistant to the President for National Security Affairs, Secretary Gray noted the more recent importance of that post, under McGeorge Bundy, Rostow, and now Kissinger. He also emphasized the importance not just of policy formulation but also of implementation "in accordance with the wishes of the President." Observing that the "National Security Council has *no* power but to advise the President, he stressed that the NSC is in reality the "President in Council." According to Secretary Gray the Council has eliminated "the yo-yo form of arriving at policy decisions," whereby with presidential advisors each separately presenting their views, policy seemed to depend on who saw the President most recently.

Ambassador Murphy traced the development of national security policy to an earlier period. By examples of President Wilson's and President Roosevelt's illnesses and the resulting severity of the problems in foreign policy, he pointed up the need to resolve the problem of succession in the event of the incapacity of the President. Fortunately, he noted, the

Vice President today, is much better briefed on foreign policy matters than had been the case of Mr. Truman, who had to go to Potsdam following Mr. Roosevelt's death with but little background knowledge.

Stressing the importance of the NSC, Ambassador Murphy viewed as a grave error the virtual suspension of the NSC by President Kennedy. Following the Bay of Pigs fiasco, Mr. Kennedy revived reliance on the NSC for high policy recommendations.

Mr. Sonnenfeldt, noting that the President of the United States has "a greater accumulation of power and authority in his hands than in any comparable hand today," stated, as a result in the foreign policy and security field, he is "able to shape and mold his machinery very closely to what his own wishes and desires are." This further denotes that "our system is sufficiently flexible and sufficiently capable of being tailored to the man." He also observed that "a crucial function of the White House operations in all its facets is to make the President as comfortable a chief magistrate, a chief executive, as possible—" this, the contrary view of much of the press notwithstanding.

As did Secretary Gray, Mr. Sonnenfeldt emphasized the distinction between decision making and implementation. The latter is far more difficult. Mr. Sonnenfeldt does not believe "that a President is a great President only if he makes wise decisions. He becomes truly a great President only after he has succeeded in enforcing those decisions. . . . And machinery itself is not the answer for this very crucial problem; the implementation of the presidential will."

Ambassador Pedersen, noting that "one of the favorite parlor games in Washington . . . is to talk about the demise of the State Department," observed that "it hasn't happened yet." He sees no conflict between the Department and the security apparatus at the White House—it must be there, and the Department works with it. He believes the Secretary "will continue to be the principal advisor to the President in the area of foreign policy. So also will there continue to be a National Security advisor at the White House." Moreover, he favors the range of alternatives put forward by the NSC as better serving the decision making process "than in a case where a single recommendation is put forward, where critical elements may be obscured by departmental compromises."

Dr. Koenig emphasized the political risks in security matters. In the 1952 Presidential election the Korean War was costly to the Democratic Party as was the Vietnam War in 1968. How, he asks, will the "current swift developments in Southeast Asia" effect the future of the Nixon Administration two years hence?

Dr. Koenig suggests that in 1965 President Johnson was so "preoccupied with his great legislation program" in the domestic field that "there was an atmosphere there of second class citizenship so to speak for the decisions related to Vietnam." As a result the increasing U.S. involvement became "a kind of sliding operation being developed rather incrementally."

Dr. Koenig expressed a concern for "an atmosphere of unpredictability among the staff" regarding such matters as a major foreign policy address by the President. A related concern is "the adequacy of access" of presidential staff. He voiced another concern as to whether innovative qualities in foreign policy suffer from "elaborate machinery."

Mr. Casey observed that "there's a point at which the machinery has done its job," where, so to speak, "the buck stops." In response to Mr. Casey's question regarding asymmetry between the methodologies of dictatorship and our own, Mr. Sonnenfeldt noted that "the Soviet Government . . . is not without its peculiar pressures and countervailing arguments and pullings and haulings." Mr. Sonnenfeldt perceives "Significant advantages that accrue to us in functioning in our system. . . . The vigor of the press, the vigor of Congressional involvements, all of these things go into the system of checks and balances . . . that can frequently prevent grave error. . . ." Moreover, the Soviets have their own problems of decision implementation; such, for example, contributed to Khruschev's downfall.

Secretary Gray spoke of the important role of the Secretary of Defense in NSC policy recommendations. Mr. Reedy challenged long range totalitarian planning. Mr. Sonnenfeldt concurred, giving as an example the predominance of short-range planning in Nazi Germany. Mr. Casey countered that so far as strategic planning is concerned the Soviets do march relatively unimpeded towards their goals. For example, in 1962, they made decisions to achieve both naval and nuclear superiority Subsequent political changes have not impeded their march towards fulfilling these goals.

Secretary Gray presented a hopeful view of events in Cambodia and their effect in Vietnam: ". . . if the reason that Sihanouk was deposed was the presence of Hanoi and Viet Cong troops in the country, and if this new government should rally a determination to eliminate sanctuaries and make it stick, this could have a profound implication for the situation in Vietnam." Ambassador Murphy added: "If I am to talk about Indo-China, Cambodia, that area, I better come back to what General Eisenhower said, that you don't win wars by hesitation. You don't do it by nibbling or piecemeal. If you make a decision to go to war, and, God knows, we don't want to make that decision, then you either do it or you don't do it. And I think that is one of our failures in Cambodia. I think our intelligence is working there very well. We did have information, but that doesn't mean that we know the answer. Maybe Sihanouk didn't know the answer."

Mr. Sonnefeldt agreed that "Vietnam is a case where piecemeal decisions were made when perhaps more basic decisions should have been made in earlier years." He added that "when we get sufficient national consensus behind us," as with the Marshall Plan, then in the area of long range decisions, both domestic and in the national security area, "sometimes we do amazingly well. . . ."

ORGANIZATION

In his own introductory remarks, in this concluding Sunday morning session, the President of the Center, this editor, noted "certain significant landmarks in the creation of the modern Presidency." These included, going back as early as 1912, President Taft's Commission on Economy and Efficiency, which heralded the establishment 9 years later of the Bureau of the Budget in the Treasury Department. In 1939 this Bureau was transferred to the Office of the President. If this marked the beginning of the modern Presidency on the domestic side, so likewise the creation of the National Security Council in 1947 signalized the modern Presidency on the foreign policy side. The proposed Domestic Council in the Spring of 1970 became the NSC counterpart on the domestic side, while the Office of Management and Budget was founded "upon its antecedents extending all the way back to the 1912 Taft Commission." The Councils and Commissions on Executive organization from 1936 to the present, from Brownlow to Ash were noted. It was suggested that in the light of history Ash may prove most revolutionary and might even encompass consolidation within the Cabinet posts, i.e. the Executive departments.

Following this historical introduction, Mr. Thomas W. Evans, Esq., of the law firm of Mudge, Rose, Guthrie, and Alexander, skillfully moderated a panel including previously introduced Ambassador Pedersen, George Reedy, Thomas Corcoran, and Murray Comarow, and newly introduced Dwight A. Ink, Jr., Assistant Director of the Bureau of the Budget and Director of the Office of Executive Management, and Walter N. Thayer, Special Counsel to the President, member of the President's Advisory Council on Executive Organization (i.e. the Ash Council).

In turn, in his own introductory remarks, Mr. Evans proposed that the Symposium participants for this final session be constituted as a body considering the recommendations of the Ash Council. Mr. Thayer traced the background and the work of the Ash Council (named for the President of Litton Industries), consisting of six members plus a small supporting staff headed by Murray Comarow as Executive Director. The overall mission of the Council, which has not yet completed its work, is "to study the Executive Branch of the Government and make recommendations with reports for organizational and structural changes that might bring about more effective government." Focusing first on the Executive Office of the President, the Council reviewed earlier studies including the Brownlow Commission of the late 1930's, the two Hoover Commissions of the late 1940's and the early 1950's, the Nelson Rockefeller study of the 1950's, and the two studies in the 1960's, that by Ben W. Heineman and the most recent headed by Franklin A. Lindsay.

Mr. Thayer reported that the Ash Council recommended: "there should be a more institutionalized and basic organizational structure to cope with the development of policies and programs on the domestic side. Much as the National Security Council handles problems of this kind on the foreign side, we concluded that there should be some similar structure to cope with the problems of this type on the domestic side." (the proposed Domestic Council). Further, they proposed the revision of the Bureau of the Budget into the Office of Management and Budget. In both of these recommendations President Nixon had manifested great interest, and he had in the continuing work of the Council.

Mr. Comarow emphasized the need for a means "for getting decisions made at the appropriate level." In the absence of such a device too many decisions are being made by the White House staff, and there has been an erosion of authority of the Cabinet and agency heads. The new Office of Management and Budget will have men out in the field working with the agencies to get the job done at that level. Even if they are able to do so in only 25% of the cases, "the gains will be enormous." Mr. Comarow further envisioned that with Cabinet members sitting functionally on the Council, it would mean a restoration of the authority and prestige of the Cabinet.

In introducing Mr. Corcoran, Mr. Evans contrasted the structured, institutional Presidency of Eisenhower and Nixon with the unstructured F. D. Roosevelt Presidency. Mr. Corcoran viewed the problems as "fundamentally political and not managerial." In like manner he had "never conceived of the Cabinet as fundamentally managers of their Departments." Rather, Mr. Corcoran, has viewed them "as political officers, specializing in regional or interest group relationships." By Mr. Corcoran's conception their area of administration should be that in which "they had the most political sensitivity." Such had been the inspiration for Franklin Roosevelt's appointments; Mr. Corcoran wishes that more of Mr. Nixon's Cabinet appointments had been so politically motivated.

Mr. Corcoran liked the Domestic Council idea, with its potential for upgrading the importance of the Cabinet. Mr.

Reedy was skeptical that this would be accomplished. He believes the White House is already over-institutionalized. It is this institutionalization which prompted the title of his book, *Twilight of the Presidency*. He asserted that "the business of the White House is basically politics; the problems of this country today to a tremendous extent rest upon the fact that too many institutional decisions have been made and too many institutions have been crowded into a mansion which, if it is not fundamentally political, is not fulfilling its purpose." As an example of an institutional rather than a political decision, he noted the unsuccessful attempt in the Johnson Administration to combine the Commerce and Labor departments. Carrying this further, Mr. Reedy advances his reservations on Governmental reorganization.

Challenged by Mr. Reedy's remarks, Mr. Evans inquired of Mr. Ink how the proposed Domestic Council, in policy formation, and the proposed Office of Management and Budget in policy implementation, will "be able to evaluate political considerations." In responding, Mr. Ink used the same example as Mr. Reedy, the proposed Commerce-Labor merger, stating that it was the politicians trying their hand at institutional matters that had botched the business. Mr. Ink focused on the importance of the decision making process. He noted that "the manner of problem solving has become increasingly significant. It has increased in importance in recent years, in part, because of the complexities and the varieties with which we are dealing, and the tempo by which they come about. The rapidity with which a President is faced with major crucial decision making has increased tremendously in recent years."

In the national security area, the President, through the NSC, has had the supporting machinery for his decision making. It was readily adapted to President Nixon's requirements. By contrast, Mr. Ink noted "we have gone through a much longer period of shake down on the domestic side." He further observed that "the problems today are such that we simply cannot afford to spend the first year of a new administration, which is the year of opportunity, the year when things can best be done, can most easily be accomplished, in trying to sort ourselves out and organize ourselves to provide the President with what he needs on the domestic scene."

"Political decision making," Mr. Ink continued, "and stronger, better, more effective management, are *not* in competition with each other." He contended "that political judgments are better made with this kind of management support."

As with several other of the Symposium participants, Mr. Ink turned to the matter of credibility. As he put it, "The credibility of the Government is enhanced to the extent that political decisions turn into reality"—this through the then proposed management instruments of the Domestic Council and the Office of Management and Budget. Mr. Ink perceived a minimizing of "the problems of overselling and underfunding. . . ." By such means, Ink concluded, "we can regain some degree of credibility and develop a governmental process which is somewhat more responsive to the problems of the country and the needs of the people."

By contrast with the Domestic Council, the National Security Council, Ambassador Pedersen pointed out, is not designed to include domestic political interests in its concerns. The Ambassador cautioned against overstating the success of the NSC in the decision making process. There are many areas of disagreement. There is not only the matter of the facts but also their significance and the policy of response.

The very fact that the NSC is a non-political institution prompts George Reedy to propose that it should *not* be in the White House, which with its staff, he believes "should be just as heavily political as it can be made." Similarly, Reedy views at arm's length the Domestic Council as posing additional "de-politicalization of a political institution. . . ."

What continues to concern Mr. Corcoran "is that a bureaucracy always tends to think in terms of a sure fire efficient way and misses the big problems of political balance." He believes that "a certain amount of maneuverable inefficiency may be necessary to meet Mr. Nixon's goal of bringing us together again." He further believes that in the past we have raised too many false expectations, especially with certain minority groups; such false hopes have only done them a disservice and created antagonism. Nonetheless, he believes that "in government we have to consider *human values* as well as *efficiency values*. Democracy," he concludes, "does not necessarily find its virtue in maximum efficiency. Ours is the greatest human conglomerate on earth and not presently thereby necessarily the most efficient."

Mr. Evans raised the question whether, even with this increased institutionalization at the White House, there will not remain a significant role for the Presidential assistant. In answering affirmatively, Mr. Thayer nonetheless envisions the elimination of much of the frustration of the Cabinet members who have had problems of access and senior White House staff who have been "swamped and overwhelmed by the priority problems of the moment." In his own concluding remarks, Mr. Thayer also emphasized the matter of credibility, of "diminution of confidence in government's·ability to deliver." In the long range views he believes these organizational changes will help to restore a sense of confidence, and he believes that history may record this as "the most significant administrative reorganization within government in a long, long time."

In response to the question whether this further strengthening of the Office of the President will increase the imbalance with the Congress, Mr. Ink reminded the conferees that an ineffective White House will not help the Congress. He further reminded them that the enactment of legislation is only a stage in an accomplishment. There remains the "nitty-gritty . . . of making the legislation work, of carrying out what the press release promises." He concludes that in the reorganization, "You have here something which really not only helps the President, but in . . . making the President over a period of time more effective, it indirectly will also help the Congress."

Mr. Reedy concluded "that while the failure of government to carry through programs has had something to do with the credibility gap . . . the deeper feeling is that *government is no longer responsive to the people.*" On this Mr. Ink rejoined that "the credibility problem, which is *not* limited to any one individual or anyone administration, has grown at least as much out of political considerations. . . ." To this Mr.

Reedy added: "Yes, but out of poor politics." He sees a major challenge for the nation in building a sense of respect for the profession of politics.

Finally, the moderator, Mr. Evans, a friend and former law partner of the President, pointed to "the single merit of this suggested reorganization which may override all other considerations." Lest we forget he suggests that he believes this reorganized, this structured staff is the way President Nixon believes he can best serve. Mr. Evans believes the President "likes a sense of organization. . . . Some of this comes from his work in the law and from his vast experience in government but more particularly from his days in the Eisenhower Administration. . . . That factor *alone*," Mr. Evans concludes, "should be a compelling reason to adopt the Ash Council report" because the President thereby "believes that he can be more effective."

And so this unique Symposium on the Presidency adjourned. By way of epilogue we may note not only that the Ash Council report was adopted but also that by late summer 1970, the new institutional features, the Domestic Council and the Office of Management and Budget, were in operation. In a very real sense these discussions on administrative changes were a precursor of point six of President Nixon's State of the Union Address of January 22, 1971. By that time, the Ash Council's further studies on functional consolidations were to lead to the President's recommendations for consolidating several of the Cabinet posts and Executive departments.

So far as restoration of credibility in Government, elevation of the status of a political career, and, indeed, answering Mr. Klein's question whether "Government is governable," and Mr. Reedy's proposition whether we are witnessing the twilight of the Presidency, a longer period of time, faith and work will be required. The President's recognition of these basic problems in this same recent State of the Union Address is a forward step towards their resolution. Taken together, all these elements may bring dawn rather than twilight.

Index